D1213832

An Improvised War

ALSO BY MICHAEL GLOVER

Wellington's Peninsular Victories
Batsford, 1963

Wellington as Military Commander
Batsford, 1968

Britannia Sickens
Leo Cooper, 1970

Legacy of Glory
Charles Scribner & Leo Cooper, 1972

1815: The Armies at Waterloo
Leo Cooper, 1973

An Assemblage of Indian Army
Soldiers and Uniforms
Perpetua Press, 1973

The Peninsular War: A Concise History
David & Charles, 1974

Rorke's Drift
Leo Cooper, 1975

General Burgoyne in Canada and America
Gordon & Cremonesi, 1976

Wellington's Army
David & Charles, 1977

A Very Slippery Fellow
O.U.P., 1978

The Napoleonic Wars
Batsford, 1979

A Gentleman Volunteer
Heinemann, 1979

Warfare from Waterloo to Mons
B.C.A., 1980

Warfare in the Age of Bonaparte
B.C.A., 1980

The Velvet Glove
Hodder & Stoughton, 1982

The Fight for the Channel Ports
Leo Cooper, 1985

An Improvised War

THE ETHIOPIAN CAMPAIGN
1940–1941

Michael Glover

'It was an improvisation after the British fashion of war.'

Wavell

'A general commanding . . . should possess a talent for sudden and appropriate improvisation.'

De Saxe.
Réveries

Leo Cooper : London

Hippocrene Books : New York

First published 1987 by Leo Cooper

Leo Cooper is an independent imprint of
the Heinemann Group of Publishers,
10 Upper Grosvenor Street, London W1X 9PA.
LONDON   MELBOURNE   JOHANNESBURG   AUCKLAND

Copyright © Michael Glover 1987

ISBN: 0-85052-2412

Hippocrene Books, Inc.,
171 Madison Avenue,
New York, NY 10016

ISBN: 0-87052-456-9

Printed in Great Britain by
Redwood Burn Ltd Trowbridge,
and bound by WBC Ltd Maesteg

Ft Leavenworth / KS
26 June 92

CONTENTS

Acknowledgements   ix
Abbreviations   xi
Foreword   xxi

1. Theatre of War   1
2. Summer of Discontent   18
3. Interregnum   37
4. Limited Offensive   61
5. The Gate   74
6. The Backdoors   89
7. Decision   106
8. Pursuit   126
9. Strongholds   143
10. Mopping Up   166

Appendix
  Orders of Battle   183
Bibliography   189
Index   193

Ft Leavenworth | KS
26 June. 92.

LIST OF ILLUSTRATIONS

1. General Sir Archibald Wavell.
2. Lieutenant-General Sir William Platt.
3. Lieutenant-General Alan Cunningham.
4. Brigadier Frank Messervy.
5. Agordat.
6. Keren.
7. A Wellesley en route to Keren.
8. Haile Selassie and Orde Wingate.
9. Hoisting the Ethiopian flag, 20 January, 1941.
10. Consultation in Gideon Force.
11. Pontoon bridge at Yonte.
12. The Marda position.
13. The Marda Pass.
14. Emissaries arrive at Diredawa.
15. Hartbeest dropping message to Brigadier Fowkes.
16. The Duke of Aosta's cave.
17. March Past at Amba Alagi.
18. The Duke of Aosta surrenders.
19. The Wolchefit Pass.

Nos. 2, 3, 8, 9, 10, 12, 13, 14, 16 and 17 are reproduced by kind permission of the Imperial War Museum.

For
J.C.B.S.
Son-in-Law and Son

ACKNOWLEDGEMENTS

Among the many people who have helped with this book, I would like particularly to thank Mr and Mrs Stephen Alexander, Colonel Kenneth Allen, Colonel T. J. Bowen, Brigadier Shelford Bidwell, Mrs Judith Blacklaw, Professor David Curnow, Miss Carolyn Davage, Major Dereck Davin, Mrs Douglas Fabin, Brigadier P. H. Graves-Morris, Mr and Mrs Richard Hann, the late General Sir James Marshall-Cornwall, Professor J. E. Morpurgo, Col. M. A. C. Osborn, Dr Richard Pankhurst, Mrs Eric Palmer and Lt. Col. J. C. B. Sutherell. I am also grateful to Chester Read for the care and patience with which he drew the maps.

However much they all helped (and it was a lot), the whole thing would never have got written without the help and care of my wife.

ABBREVIATIONS

A.A.	Anti-Aircraft
A.O.C.	Air Officer Commanding
A/T	Anti-Tank
C.I.G.S.	Chief of Imperial General Staff
C.I.H.	Central India Horse
C-in-C	Commander-in-Chief
D.M.O.	Director of Military Operations (a senior staff officer)
E.A.	East Africa
F.A.A.	Fleet Air Arm
F.E.A.	French Equatorial Africa
F.O.O.	Forward Observation Officer
G.C.	Gold Coast
G.O.C.	General Officer Commanding
G.S.O.	General (i.e. Operational) Staff Officer
H.L.I.	Highland Light Infantry
I.E.A.	Italian East Africa (i.e. Ethiopia, Eritrea and Italian Somaliland)
K.A.R.	King's African Rifles
l.m.g.	Light Machine Gun
M.T.	Motor Transport
M.T.B.	Motor Torpedo Boat
N.R.R.	Northern Rhodesian Regiment
O.P.	Observation Post
R.F.F.R	Royal Frontier Force Regiment (12th) or Rifles (13th)
S.A.	South Africa
S.A.A.	South African Artillery
S.A.A.F.	South African Air Force
S.A.E.C.	South African Engineer Corps
S.A.T.C.	South African Tank Corps
S.D.F.	Sudan Defence Corps
S.N.C.	Special Night Squad
T.H.A.	Transvaal Horse Artillery

MAPS

___

1. The Mediterranean and Northern Africa   xiv
2. The Horn of Africa   xv
3. Sudan and Eritrea   xvi
4. The Kenya Frontier   xvii
5. French and British Somaliland   xviii
6. Western Ethiopia   xix
7. Mogadishu to Addis Ababa   xx
8. The Battle of Keren   75
9. The Battle of Amba Alagi   153

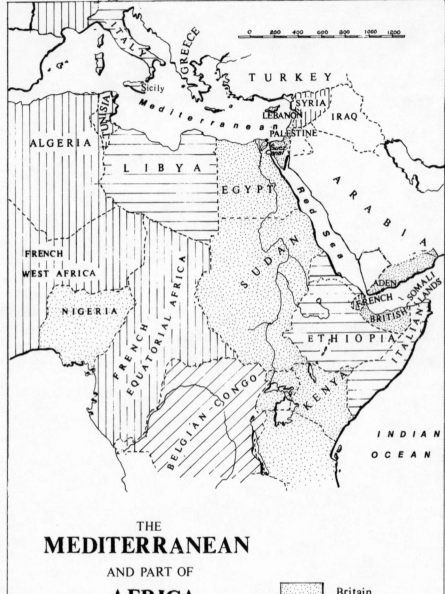

THE
MEDITERRANEAN
AND PART OF
AFRICA

Showing territories occupied by :-
JUNE, 1940

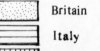

	Britain
	Italy
	Vichy France
	Belgium

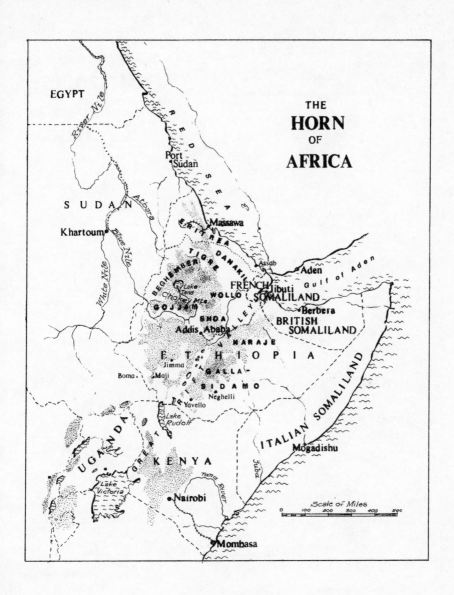

THE
HORN
OF
AFRICA

EGYPT

SUDAN

Khartoum

Port Sudan

RED SEA

River Nile

Atbara

Blue Nile

White Nile

Massawa

ERITREA

DANAKIL

Assab

Aden

Gulf of Aden

TIGRE

BEGHEMDER

Lake Tana

Choke Mts.

FRENCH

Jibuti

SOMALILAND

WOLLO

GOJJAM

Berbera

BRITISH SOMALILAND

SHOA

Addis Ababa

HARAJE

ETHIOPIA

GALLA

Jimma

Maji

SIDAMO

Boma

Neghelli

Yavello

Lake Rudolf

ITALIAN SOMALILAND

Mogadishu

UGANDA

KENYA

GREAT RIFT VALLEY

Lake Victoria

Tana River

Juba

Nairobi

Scale of Miles

0   100   200   300   400   500

Mombasa

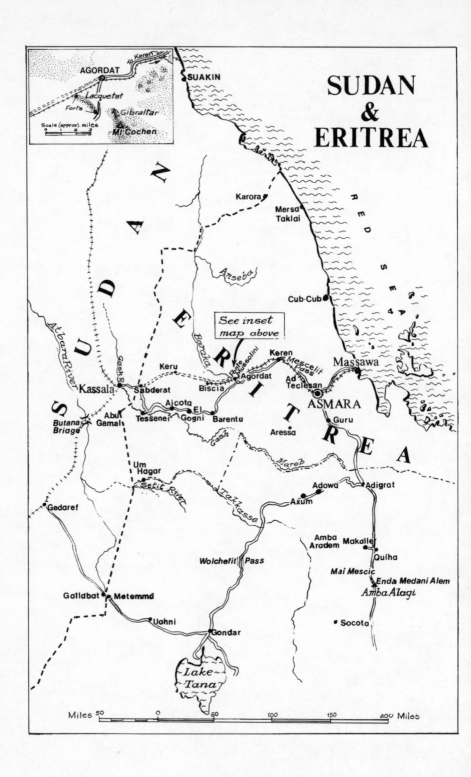

SUDAN
&
ERITREA

AGORDAT

SUAKIN

Kerert

Lacquetat

Forts

Gibralter

Mt Cochen

Scale (approx). miles

Karora

Mersa
Taklai

RED SEA

Anseba

Cub-Cub

See inset
map above

Keru

Baraka

Ponte Mussolini

Keren

Mescelit
Pass

Massawa

Kassala

Sabderat

Gash R.

Biscia

Agordat

Ad
Teclesan

ASMARA

Atbara River

Abu
Gamal

Ajcota

Tessenei

El
Gogni

Barentu

Guru

Butana
Briage

Aressa

Um
Hagar

Gash

Mareb

Sefit River

Takkasse

Adowa

Adigrat

Gedaref

Axum

Amba
Aradem

Makalle

Quiha

Wolchefit Pass

Mai Mescic

Enda Medani Alem

Amba Alagi

Galldbat

Metemma

Socota

Uahni

Gondar

Lake
Tana

Miles 50   0   50   100   150   200 Miles

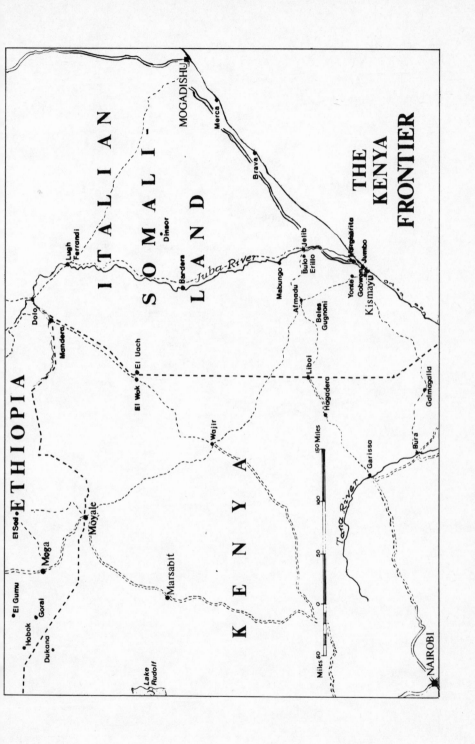

THE KENYA FRONTIER

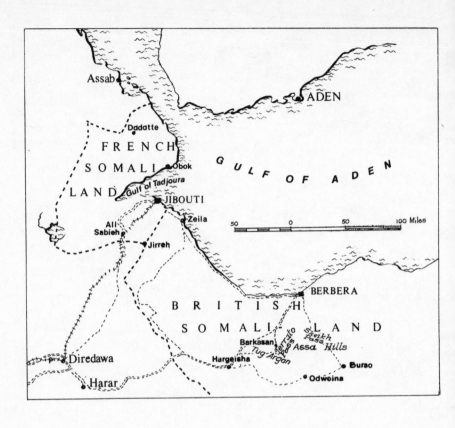

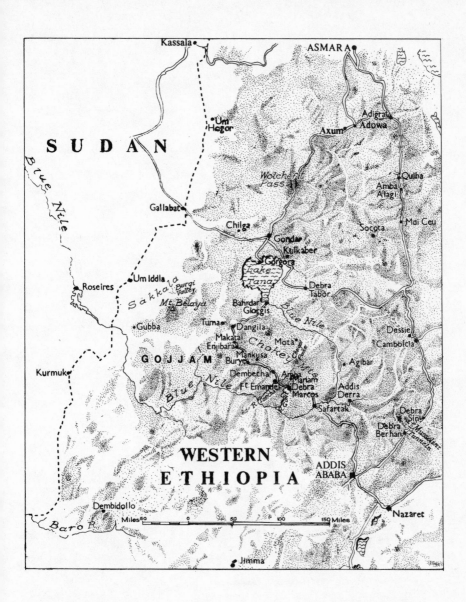

SUDAN

Blue Nile

Kassala

ASMARA

Um Hogor

Adigrat
Adowa

Axum

Quiba

Wolcheft
Pass

Amba
Alagi

Gallabat

Chilga

Socota

Mai Ceu

Gondar
Kulkaber

Roseires

Um Iddla

Sakkala

Burgi
Valley

Gorgora

Lake
Tana

Debra
Tabor

Mt Belaya

Bahrdar
Giorgis

Blue Nile

Dessie

Gubba

Tuma

Dangila

Chokey Mts

Makatal
Enjibara
Mankusa
Burye

Mota

Camboicia

GOJJAM

Agibar

Blue Nile

Dembecha
Ft Emanuel

Amba
Mariam
Debra
Marcos

Addis
Derra

Debra
Sina

R Tammi

Safartak

Debra
Berhan

Massalini
Tunnels

Kurmuk

WESTERN
ETHIOPIA

ADDIS
ABABA

Dembidollo

Baro R.

Miles 50

0

50

100

150 Miles

Nazaret

Jimma

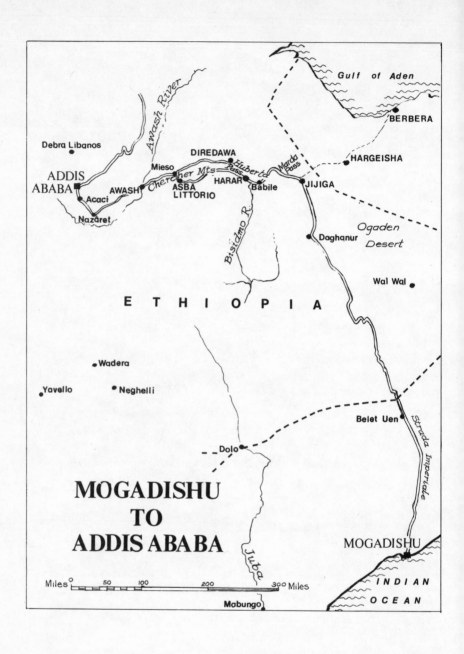

Gulf of Aden

BERBERA

Debra Libanos

DIREDAWA

HARGEISHA

Awash River

ADDIS
ABABA

Mieso
Chercher Mts
AWASH
ASBA
LITTORIO

Huberta
Pass

Marda
Pass

HARAR
Babile

JIJIGA

Acaci

Nazaret

Bisidmo R.

Daghanur

Ogaden
Desert

ETHIOPIA

Wal Wal

Wadera

Yavello
Neghelli

Belet Uen

Strada Imperiale

Dolo

MOGADISHU
TO
ADDIS ABABA

MOGADISHU

INDIAN

Miles 0   50   100   200   300 Miles

Mabungo

Juba

OCEAN

FOREWORD

Any campaign in which 700,000 square miles defended by more that a quarter of a million soldiers were conquered, apart from outlying centres of resistance, in five months must be of interest and yet, even at the time, it was overshadowed by other events. In the month that the capitals of Eritrea and Ethiopia were captured by Commonwealth troops, the Germans invaded and took Greece, Rommel made his first advance in the Western Desert and laid siege to Tobruk and, importantly at the time, there was a pro-German *coup d'état* in Iraq which threatened Britain's supply of oil. In the following month, when the main Italian army in Ethiopia surrendered, the newspapers were more interested in the German airborne invasion of Crete. In Churchill's majestic account of the Second World War Italian East Africa gets little mention and most of the great man's comments are carping. From the diaries of Count Ciano one gets the impression that the Italian Government lost interest in East Africa almost as soon as they declared war.

Nevertheless the campaign in the Horn of Africa is of interest as one of the most spectacular advances in all military history, conducted, as it was, with a minimum of resources against not only a hostile climate and terrain but against an enemy who was capable of fighting very hard and courageously indeed. The Battle of Keren, narrowly won after fifty-three days, was a great battle by any standards, except perhaps in the numbers involved, and does great honour to both the armies. Moreover the campaign saw the emergence of several characters who were to leave their mark on British military history, notably Orde Wingate, who was to die, full of fame and controversy, leading the Chindits, and his great chief, Field-Marshal Sir William

Slim who, as a brigadier, sustained a sharp defeat and was later wounded in the bottom.

One or two points may need some explanation. Since the inhabitants appear to prefer it, I have referred to the country as Ethiopia but at the time it was always called Abyssinia in England so that where I have used contemporary quotations that form of the name persists. While on the subject of Ethiopia, it must be made clear that, to this day, the country is imperfectly mapped and all the distances mentioned are approximate. Similarly no two sources agree on the spelling of most place names, partly as a result of transliteration from the Amharic and partly because British, French and Italian works all tend to use their own version of proper names. The most I can hope for is consistency in the versions I have used.

Leaving out the small Free French and Belgian contingents in the invading armies, soldiers and airmen from Britain, India, South Africa, all the British colonies in East and West Africa and the Sudan took part in the campaign, to say nothing of nine real and a large number of imaginary Australians. There is no generic term to cover this multi-racial assembly. 'Commonwealth' will not do because the colonies were not members of the British Commonwealth (as it was then called) and nor was the Indian Empire. Nor is the term 'imperial troops' permissible since the Sudan did not belong to the British Empire. More from desperation than for any logical reason, I have used the term 'British' to cover them all and I can only apologise if, inadvertently, I have caused any offence.

There is no doubt that the fractional designations of Indian battalions (e.g. 4/11 Sikhs or 2/5 Mahratta Light Infantry) is confusing to all but specialists in Indian military history. It can only be said that the creation in 1922 of large regiments with a substantial number of battalions in each made the nomenclature of Indian army units slightly less confusing than it was before. The Rajputana Rifles (vulgarly known as the Large Banana Trifles) are referred to as 'Rajrifs' to distinguish them from the Rajputana Regiment, who are known as 'Rajputs'.

CHAPTER 1 Theatre of War

IN THE YEARS before the Second World War Britain had a guilty conscience about Ethiopia, stemming from her shabby behaviour when Mussolini's armies invaded the country in 1935. There were, of course, *raisons d'état* for her craven conduct. With Japan threatening the Far East by open aggression, Britain, and even more her ally France, saw fascist Italy as the only effective partner in restraining a Hitlerite Germany which was beginning to show herself as a menace to Europe. As the Secretary to the Cabinet put it:

> We have our [German] danger in the west, and our [Japanese] danger in the east, and we simply cannot afford to be on bad terms with a nation which has a stranglehold on our shortest line of communication between the two possible theatres of war.

Worse than that, any wholehearted attempt to stop the Italian invasion risked war and, given the state of Britain's armed services, it was far from certain that she could defeat Italy in the Middle East. Malta, main base for the Mediterranean Fleet, was totally devoid of air defence. Alexandria, its unprepared alternative, had no fighter protection and, while there were a few Egyptian anti-aircraft guns which might be prepared to assist, there was very little ammunition for them. The British garrison in Egypt was too small and ill-equipped to be relied upon to resist an invasion from Libya even supposing that much of the British strength would not have to be devoted to maintaining quiet among the Egyptians. Neither the British dominions nor any other considerable nation seemed disposed to assist her in a war with Italy, least of all France where Laval was foreign minister and took a strongly pro-Italian stance. In Britain

1

itself, still digesting the ambiguous message of the so-called 'Peace Ballot', there was no wish to risk war but there was a widespread belief that Italian aggression might be halted if comprehensive economic sanctions were imposed by the League of Nations. Since Germany, Japan and the United States were not members of the League and were most unlikely to implement such measures, this belief was somewhat naive. Britain was faced with what Churchill, on another occasion, described as 'a choice between war and shame' and, probably rightly, chose shame. There was a long charade when partial sanctions were imposed in the full knowledge that they would be ineffective and would result in driving Italy into the arms of Germany. Not the least sickening part of this display of hypocrisy was the sight of Britain, with the largest colonial empire in history, preaching anti-colonialism to the Italians.

A by-product of this shoddy episode was the acceptance, particularly in Britain, of a highly misleading picture of Ethiopia as an African 'Brave Little Belgium'. It was forgotten that when, with Italian sponsorship, Ethiopia applied to join the League of Nations, Britain had opposed it on the grounds that the country was too backward and unsettled. In 1935 it was noticeable that, among the chorus of 'progressive' demands for effective action against Italy, the voice of the Anti-Slavery Society was conspicuously absent since slavery was rife in Ethiopia. No one doubted that the Emperor Haile Selassie wished to abolish it and had pronounced laws against it but, as with most of his projected reforms, there was no reasonable prospect that the practice would not continue. The Emperor's title was itself revealing. He was *Negus Negusti*, King of Kings, meaning that he was the overlord of all the other kings and rases* within his empire but at no stage during his reign could he count on the loyalty of all these powerful underlings. Enlightened himself, he had to be more than cautious in attempting to implement any reform, most of all the abolition of the lucrative slave trade, against the wishes of the Rases, a highly reactionary group. Far from being dragged by its Emperor into

---

* During the reign of Haile Selassie there were no subordinate Neguses (although the Italians created one during their occupation). A Ras was, however, supreme in his own province, except in name. Strictly a Ras was the commander of an army but, as under the feudal system, a provincial governor had the duty, not always fulfilled, of leading his army to the support of the Emperor when called upon. Technically the appointment was not hereditary but each governorship tended to be handed down within one family.

the twentieth century, Ethiopia was advancing from barbarism by slow and reluctant steps – a state of affairs less apparent to those, the usual visitors, who saw only Addis Ababa and its only approach, the railway from Jibuti.

Ethiopia was the last part of Africa, with the dubious exception of Liberia, to escape the grasping hands of imperialists. She was, indeed, a notably grasping imperial power herself. Her continued independence she owed to her unattractiveness as a colonial possession. Ethiopia consisted of an inhospitable tract of mountain and desert and was barely, and discontinuously, able to feed herself. She commanded no sea routes, hid no discernible mineral wealth and exported nothing, apart from numbers of nubile young women, except small quantities of coffee, hides and beeswax. Had they thought the prize worth the effort, the British could have annexed the country in 1867. In that year Sir Robert Napier, leading a force of British and Indian troops, had advanced deep into Ethiopia to release a number of European prisoners, including the British Consul, who had been seized by the demented Emperor Theodore II, whose pretext had been that Queen Victoria had failed to answer one of his letters. It seems that this letter had been diplomatically 'lost' by the Foreign Office since it proposed that, without more ado, the British and Ethiopian empires should embark on a crusade against Turkey. Throughout his notably successful expedition Napier received great help from the Rases through whose territory he passed. Theodore killed himself rather than surrender.

Much of the fissiparous nature of the Ethiopian empire was due to its situation in the greatest mountain *massif* in Africa where the terrain made communication almost impossible. This encouraged the independence of the Rases whom the *Negus Negusti* could only control by difficult and expensive military operations. Another factor was that the whole concept of the empire was based on a myth, the belief that the Emperor, whose throne was by no means hereditary, was the descendant of King Solomon and the Queen of Sheba (whose kingdom may have been in southern Arabia) through their son Menelik I. The real origins are obscure. At some distant time, probably a century or two before the birth of Christ, the ancestors of the Amharas, a Semitic people who spoke a language bearing some relation to ancient Armenian, crossed the Red Sea and established themselves in roughly the area of what is now Eritrea. From there they expanded north, south and west, appropriating the Ethiopian

3

highlands and, according to some accounts, ruling over everything between Omdurman and Lake Nyasa. In the fourth century they were converted to Christianity through the agency of two shipwrecked boys and became a branch of the Coptic Church of Egypt, the Primate of Ethiopia, the *Abuna*, being appointed from Alexandria. From the seventh century onwards the spread of Islam started to sweep down the Red Sea coast and eventually the Amharas, now with a substantial infusion of Hamitic blood, were driven out of Eritrea (which they did not reoccupy until 1962) and into the great mountain fastness. There for hundreds of years they defended themselves with more or less success until, in the sixteenth century, they were rescued by Portuguese mercenaries who tried unsuccessfully to convert them to the Church of Rome.

For the following three centuries Ethiopia secluded herself from the world, protected by inaccessability and visited only by rare and intrepid European explorers or adventurers. Not that it was a time of peace, for the Amharas were a quarrelsome lot and eventually divided themselves, apart from minor principalities, into four kingdoms. Closest to Eritrea was Tigre, culturally the most separate of the four, with its capital at the religious centre of Axum, and later at Adowa. To the west of it was Beghember, centring on Gondar and divided by Lake Tana from Gojjam, which is partially encircled by the great bend in the Blue Nile and had its capital at Debra Marcos. To the south and east of Gojjam was Shoa which, until the late nineteenth century, had no fixed capital. There was almost always at least one *Negus Negusti* but his powers were usually minimal and the four kingdoms passed the centuries in warring with and within each other in constantly shifting alliances, and in resisting external invasions from the heathen (though increasingly Muslim) Gallas from the south, the ferocious Somalis from the east and the bellicose tribes of the Sudan from the west. Such cohesion as there was came from the Coptic Church which preserved the cultural heritage of the Amharas but was unflinchingly preservative in its political and social attitudes. Reform was little in the air during those lost centuries, but any that was mooted came to nothing when faced by the resistance of the church, based not only on religious grounds but on the fact that it was the greatest landowner in the empire.

Not until the middle of the nineteenth century did an effective emperor arise and start to achieve a measure of unity. He was not one of the four kings but the son of a minor nobleman from Gondar who graduated through brigandage to the control of Beghember and, after defeating the Negus of Tigre in 1855, had himself crowned *Negus Negusti* under the title of Theodore II. For a time it seemed that he might succeed in forging a real empire in the Amhara lands, but absolute power, and alcohol, corrupted absolutely and he managed to unite most of his subjects against him even before his excesses brought down on him a European nemesis in the form of Sir Robert Napier. With his suicide, competition for the imperial throne became open and two year later Ethiopia crept nearer to the centre of the world stage when, in 1869, the Suez Canal was opened.

Inevitably this new sea route drew the attention of the European powers to the Horn of Africa. Even before de Lesseps had started work some travellers to India and the Far East had found it advantageous to cross the ninety-mile stretch of desert which separated the Mediterranean from the Gulf of Suez in a mule-drawn vehicle 'closely resembling a bathing machine' and thus reducing the six-month journey from London to Bombay to forty-one days. The enterprising Mr Shepheard, who opened his Cairo hotel in 1841, found it worth his while to secure the contract for victualling British troops on their way to and from India. To secure this route the East India Company had arranged to lease a coaling station at Aden as early as 1839, while in 1843 the French secured rights over Obok, across the Gulf of Tadjoura from Jibuti. This they had negotiated with the Negus of Shoa, whose title to the area was, to say the least, nebulous. However, they did little or nothing about the concession until 1859 when a naval force visited the area to avenge a consular official who had been murdered on a nearby island. At this stage they arranged the cession of all what later became French Somaliland, making a treaty with the Sultan of Donakil who, as much as anyone did, controlled that stretch of the coast. Two hundred miles to the north the Italians bought the cession of Assab, a small port isolated by salt marshes and desert, for 6,000 thalers (1870).

Suzerainty over the whole coast belonged, in name, to the Sultan of Turkey although coming more realistically under his nominal subordinate, the Khedive of Egypt. By 1885 the Khedive was finding it difficult to administer anything and was glad, with British encouragement, to hand over the excellent port of Massawa to Italy while making over his Somali territory to the British who declined, however, to burden themselves with another of his nominal possessions, the Sultanate of Harar. To the south the Italians accepted

5

Somaliland from the Sultan of Zanzibar who was very ready to unburden himself of it. Even the Russians tried their hands at the game and founded New Moscow at the small port of Sagalle. Carelessly they made their settlement within the French colony and, refusing to move, were evicted, not without bloodshed, by a warship. The Czar disavowed their activitiès.

While the Europeans were consolidating the coastline, the Amharas in their highlands had returned to their traditional activities. Three aspirants proclaimed themselves *Negus Negusti* on the news of Theodore's death. At Gondar, traditional site of coronations, Wagsum Gobaze, Negus of Beghember, had himself crowned as Tekla Georgius, while away to the south, Sahle Maryam, Negus of Shoa, announced that he was the Emperor Menelik II. Both these kings had promised Napier their aid against Theodore but the man who had produced actual help was Ras Kassa Sabagades of Tigre and, as a reward, he had been given 800 percussion muskets, a supply of ammunition and a quantity of commissariat stores which the British had found too difficult to remove. On top of this Napier arranged for six mortars and six field howitzers to be sent to Tigre from India. This armament made Ras Kassa the most powerful man in Ethiopia and, after a pause while an Englishman, John Kirkham, trained his army, he attacked and defeated Tekle Georgius (1871) and proclaimed himself as Emperor John IV.

While this had been going on Menelik had been making a spirited but unsuccessful attempt to conquer the Muslim enclave of Wollo and, realizing that John was too strong for him, acknowledged him as Emperor in return for the confirmation of his own kingship. Recognizing the Emperor had the disadvantage that tribute had to be paid and, rather than burden his Shoans with heavy taxes, he sent his armies south to colonize the areas occupied by the Gallas and Sidamos and east to the Sultanate of Harar, a noted centre of the slave trade which he was able to keep supplied with Gallas and Sidamos. As governor of the Haraje he installed his cousin, Ras Makonnen, whose eldest son was born there in 1892. This son, Ras Tafari, was to succeed to the throne of Ethiopia thirty years later as Haile Selassie. In all the regions he conquered Menelik sent, beside administrators, Coptic priests to convert the indigenous population. He also sent time-expired soldiers who were given grants of land which they farmed in return for an undertaking to supply rations for a given number of soldiers. Menelik was, in fact, a considerable imperialist and pursued a

6

system not dissimilar from that employed by the Normans after their conquest of England and Ireland.

Although John IV was uncomfortably aware of Menelik's growing power, he felt unable to check him in view of his other commitments. He had constant trouble on his Sudanese frontier, trouble that became worse when the Khedive's government was overthrown by Mohammed Ahmed, a civil servant turned slavetrader, who proclaimed himself Mahdi, the Islamic Messiah, and led the Sudanese, desperate with Egyptian misrule, to revolt. He died in 1885, soon after seizing Khartoum, but his successor, the Khalifa, led his fanatical army eastward, defeating John's army and burning Gondar (1888). At this Menelik, remembering his allegiance to the Emperor, started to march his army into Beghember but, before it came into action, the Sudanese, riddled with disease, fell back across the border. Not that this was John's only problem. The Italians found Massawa unhealthy and began to edge up into the more salubrious highlands. At Dongali in 1886, John attacked one of their columns, masquerading as a scientific expedition, and left 450 dead on the field. His Indian artillery was insufficient to subdue European fortifications and he was unable to drive them into the Red Sea.

Menelik saw the Italians as his natural allies against John and he had encouraged them to occupy both Asmara and Keren on the Eritrean high ground, hoping that this would keep the Emperor's armies tied to the north. In return the Italians supplied him with arms originally for cash, later on credit. A secret agreement was reached whereby the Italians would attack from the north while Menelik advanced from the south but nothing came of it since the difficulties of co-ordination were great and neither side trusted the other to any extent. As it happened, the lack of a combined attack was unimportant since John was killed on 9 March, 1889, in a fight against a Sudanese army near Metemma. Menelik succeeded to the imperial throne with, by Amhara standards, very little trouble save in Tigre where resistance to the Shoan was intensified when the Italians, availing themselves of Menelik's advice, occupied Asmara and established themselves behind the natural frontier represented by the dry bed of the Mareb River. To the Tigreans this represented alienation by the Shoan Emperor of land which was rightly Tigrean.

On coming to the throne Menelik found himself embarrassed not only by a Tigrean rebellion but by a debt of two million *lire* to Italy for his arms purchases. He could have repaid this debt had it not been for a disastrous drought and the resulting famine which afflicted the empire for the first three years of his reign and it was against this background that a treaty of understanding was hammered out between Ethiopia and Italy. Unfortunately the document was bedevilled by the petty dishonesty of the Italian delegate, Count Pietro Antonelli, the only man in the negotiations with an adequate knowledge of both Italian and Amharic. According to the Italian version of the document, Menelik would conduct all his relations with foreign powers through the Italian foreign ministry; in the Amharic version he was at liberty to do so if he wished. Thus Italy believed she had established a protectorate over Ethiopia while Menelik considered himself the head of a fully independent state. To make matters worse, the Emperor discovered the discrepancy in a most humiliating way. When he addressed himself to the heads of other states, his advances were rebuffed. For example, the British Foreign Office replied,

> The Italian Government have informed Us that, by a Treaty, the King of Ethiopia consents to avail himself of the Government of the King of Italy for the conduct of all matters which he may have with other Powers or Governments. We shall communicate to the Government of Our Friend the King of Italy copies of Your Majesty's letter and Our reply.

The result of Antonelli's stupid piece of chicanery was that Menelik lost confidence in Italy's good intentions, a situation made no better when the Bank of Italy, apparently in honest error, grossly over-calculated the interest due on the two million *lire* debt. The Emperor turned to France, importing arms through Jibuti, a *volte-face* which induced the Italians to foster actively the revolt in Tigre.

It was unfortunate that at this stage Italian policy was directed by Francesco Crispi, a Sicilian of Albanian descent, whose government, reeling under a bank scandal, was badly in need of a success. He ordered the occupation of the whole of Tigre, regardless of the fact that there were insufficient troops in Eritrea to carry out such an advance. The commander on the spot, General Baratieri, was a notably brave man who had won a considerable victory over the Mahdist Sudanese at Kassala but he refused to embark on such a foolhardy adventure and contented himself with occupying Adowa and Adigrat where he fortified himself. Crispi was dissatisfied and sent mandatory orders for a force to be sent to the great watershed position of Amba Alagi, an advance which moved Menelik to declare war. In December, 1895, the Emperor, at the head of 30,000 men, attacked the unfortunate Major Pietro Toselli at the Amba Alagi pass. Toselli had been sent discretionary orders to retire but they had become mangled in transmission and he felt himself obliged to make a do-or-die stand which resulted in his force being annihilated. Another failure in staff work resulted in the loss of an isolated Italian battalion at Makalle.

Reinforcements, many of them of poor quality, were immediately sent from Italy and Baratieri entrenched himself at Adowa with 17,700 men, 10,500 of them Italian, and fifty-six guns. There seems no doubt that he could have sustained himself there at least until Menelik's army, now swollen to 100,000 and quite without a supply system, was forced by hunger to disband itself. Crispi, safe in Rome and desperate for a victory, thought otherwise. Openly accusing the General of cowardice, he appointed a successor. This was too much for Baratieri's patience, but his military skill did not match his courage. Attempting to repeat his victory at Kassala over the spear-armed Sudanese, he ordered that his army should advance shoulder to shoulder and enjoined that 'the bayonet should be used on every occasion'. This was a suicidal tactic when employed against a superior army which included some 80,000 men with rifles as good as his own and with forty-two modern artillery pieces. To make matters worse he called for an attack by four disconnected columns over ground that was neither mapped nor reconnoitred. On 1 March, 1896, 7,500 of his men were left dead on the battlefield; the fact that 5,000 men and some wounded were extracted from the slaughter was entirely due to Baratieri's skill and persistence in organizing a series of rearguards.

Menelik made no attempt to drive the Italians out of Eritrea, being content to leave them behind the Mareb River, thus allowing them to occupy what might be considered part of Tigre. He eventually repatriated 1,759 Italian prisoners whom he had treated as well as his circumstances permitted. His Eritrean prisoners he punished as traitors. Regardless of the fact that their homeland had not been under Ethiopian rule for many centuries, each askari had one hand and one foot amputated.

The victory at Adowa established Menelik II as the ruler of all Ethiopia in a way that none of his predecessors had achieved and for almost a decade the empire was safe from external threat and, apart from a revolt in Tigre (1898–99), there was a wide measure of internal peace. The armies pushed further south and established a new frontier on the latitude of Lake Rudolf and treaties with France and Britain trimmed areas of desert off their Somali possessions, the British ceding 13,500 square miles. Even with Italy relations became almost cordial but it was to France that Menelik looked for help, especially in arms, and France contributed the only improvement in the country's communications. Although he seems not to have been interested in road-building, the Emperor gave a French company a concession to construct a railway from Jibuti into the interior.* The contract was ratified in 1897 and seven years later the line reached Diredawa. It was not until 1917 that it was extended to Addis Ababa which, after a number of previous choices, was chosen as the imperial capital.

The eight years that followed Adowa were the highpoint of the Ethiopian empire. There was some brigandage and it is significant that until 1936 the French had the right to station a garrison at Diredawa to protect the railway, but, on the whole, the country was quiet. This stability rested on the dominant power and personality of Menelik, assisted by a small *élite* of Shoans. As his War Minister commented:

> The Gojjamis, the men of Kafa, the Tigreans, the inhabitants of Jimma, the Arussi, the people of Sidamo, Borena, Harar and Gondar [are] the people of conquered regions.

This state of affairs was unlikely to outlast the Emperor and in 1906, when his health began to deteriorate, he made dispositions for a peaceful transfer of the throne to Lij [Prince] Isayu (or Yasu), his grandson by a daughter of his first marriage and a Ras, formerly a Muslim, from Wollo. Isayu was to be provided with a council of Regency but Ethiopian politics were too Byzantine for such a council to operate successfully and the Empress Taitu, Menelik's last wife and a Tigrean, was anxious to put forward the claim of another of her step-daughters, Zaudita. When Menelik was wholly incapacitated, she achieved some success in her schemes until she was removed from power by a palace coup, an event which brought on yet another revolt in Tigre. At this stage the President of the Council, Menelik's nominee, died and the fifteen-year-old Isayu insisted on taking the chair himself. As a national leader he was an unsatisfactory figure, leading a notably dissolute life, imprisoning ministers at his whim and, occasionally, strangling a palace servant. Nor was he attentive to government business, apart from pressing to be declared *Negus Negusti*,

* In 1904 the British were granted permission to build a railway from British Somaliland to the Sudan. They never appear to have had any serious intention of doing so.

10

although his grandfather was still alive, an ambition he realized by seizing the palace at the head of 20,000 men in February, 1913.

At the end of that year Menelik finally died. The Shoan establishment was determined to dispose of Isayu and he played into their hands. When war broke out in Europe in August, 1914, Ethiopia was neutral, though marginally pro-French, except for Isayu who advocated joining the Central Powers as the ally of Turkey and re-establishing the old, imaginary empire by seizing the three Somalilands and Eritrea. When he got no support from his ministers for this scheme he went in 1916 to Harar and began recruiting Muslim troops, letting it be known there that he had embraced Islam. This instantly rallied all the Amharas to unaccustomed unity. Isayu's Muslim troops were easily dispersed while he himself fled and was at liberty until 1921 when he was captured and imprisoned.

Zaudita was then proclaimed Empress with Ras Tafari Makonnen as regent and heir apparent. Zaudita was expected to be little more than a figurehead although her husband, Ras Gugsa Wule of Beghember, was both powerful and ambitious, but for ten years he was quiescent and the restraints on Ras Tafari were exercised by two other men, the *Abuna* Matteos and Habta Georgius, Menelik's most successful General and his Minister for War. Both men were determined to reduce the imperial power and, especially in the case of the General, a man of great wealth and wide estates, to increase the independence of the provincial Rases. For a decade, during which Ethiopia was admitted to the League of Nations, the government was little more than a facade and exercised little or no influence over the outlying governors. Both these reactionaries died in 1926 and, while the Abuna was replaced, after an interregnum, by a somewhat less conservative prelate, Ras Tafari acquired from the inheritance of the General not only the bulk of his estates but control of the central army, 60,000 strong. Though he was no soldier, he was now the most powerful man in the empire and was able in 1928 to resist an attempt to remove him from power organized by the Empress. Having failed, she was persuaded to name him *Negus*, but, in the following year, her husband raised a formidable rebellion which was only quelled when (March, 1930) he was killed in action. The Empress died, of natural causes, a few days later and, in October, 1930, before a crowd of international notabilities, Ras Tafari was crowned as *Negus Negusti* with the title Haile Selassie (Power of the Trinity).

The new Emperor may have had little formal education, though he spoke French and understood English, and had none of the military skills of his more successful predecessors, but he had great advantages. He had matchless ability at managing people, especially his turbulent subjects, a nicely calculated combination of ambition and caution, a genius for intrigue, a real desire to improve the condition of his Amhara people, the capacity for ruthlessness, boundless self-confidence and a great gift for public relations. Given time he might have dragged his empire from the Middle Ages but, from his coronation, he had only five years and those were not marked by internal tranquillity. Apart from the endemic brigandage in outlying regions, Lij Isayu escaped from captivity in 1932 and, although, thanks largely to the operations of the French mercenaries who flew in the embryo air force, he was quickly recaptured, it became clear that he was in league with the powerful Ras Hailu of Gojjam, who was betrothed to one of the Emperor's daughters. Hailu was imprisoned and heavily fined, whereupon one of his sons broke into rebellion. These and other disturbances meant that much of Haile Selassie's time and resources had to be devoted to building up his army and that army, trained by Belgian and Swedish missions, was designed not against external enemies but against over-powerful Rases. He was acute enough to appreciate that breaking the power of these governors, however much many of them abused and exploited their subjects, must be a long business and, in the meanwhile, concentrated his energies on building up a strong central government, complete with constitution, and on creating a facade which would impress such foreigners as might be useful in procuring financial assistance. Addis Ababa was largely paved; government offices were built and staffed by the few Amharas who were literate; a more or less free press was established which greatly impressed visitors who failed to realize how few Ethiopians could read; a motor road was built from the capital to Dessie and, conveniently sited beside the Jibuti railway, so that it could be inspected, was developed the model district of Asbe Tafari, a prototype of what the empire would be like one day. Haile Selassie was wholly sincere in his wish to bring the benefits of good government and technological advance to his people and can scarcely be blamed for showing the country's best face to the world while concealing that, in less accessible parts of his empire, things went on much as before with oppression, grinding taxation, a judicial system which included mutilation among its punishments and, despite its abolition, large-scale slavery.

12

No amount of misgovernment, or absence of government, could justify the Italian invasion of Ethiopia, far less the use of mustard gas as a means to victory. In his younger days, before the First World War, Mussolini had opposed his country's colonial war in Libya and had described the Government's efforts to extend their foothold on the Horn of Africa as 'the dream of a jingoist minister'. Once he had attained power for himself, he found himself faced with Italy's two inherent curses – rural poverty and over-population. It was certain that the existing colonies, particularly Libya (where there was then no sign of oil), could not solve these problems. The fertile tracts of the Ethiopian highlands, on the other hand, could provide land for many thousands of Italy's surplus peasants. Moreover few Italians could forget the shame of Adowa and to avenge it would greatly strengthen the prestige of the fascist régime. There seemed a fair chance that Ethiopia might be conquered in an almost bloodless war. The internal divisions of the country were obvious and not a few of the Rases were in touch with the Italians, some in receipt of bribes and retainers. What was needed was an 'Ethiopian provocation' which would justify an invasion.

Mussolini, whatever his home policy, had a remarkable ineptness in his dealings with the outside world and the peak of his ineptness was reached in his arrangements for a provocation. He contrived a skirmish at the wells of Wal Wal in the Ogaden desert, claiming that the Ethiopians had infringed the frontier with Italian Somaliland. Such an incident might have served his purpose except that, even on Italian maps, Wal Wal was sixty miles on the Ethiopian side of the frontier. Ironically this ridiculous miscalculation made it more difficult to draw back. For a dictator who relied for his effect largely on his own style of bombast, Mussolini could not, by admitting an error in map-reading, reveal himself as an incompetent buffoon. Rather than jeopardize his position, he was ready to risk a full-scale war for which his army was ill-equipped and even the slight risk that France and England might stand by the Ethiopians.

Considered as a military operation, the Italian invasion of Ethiopia was no mean achievement. Any army can be proud of an advance of 400 miles, most of it against opposition, through roadless mountains rising to more than 11,000 feet. Like any campaign in Ethiopia, it was primarily a quartermaster's war. The basic problem was to keep the troops at the front supplied and this entailed building roads on a massive scale, an activity at which the Italians are masters. Their enemy was brave but inclined to the belief that wars were better settled in one day's glorious action than by patience and art. Their generals tended to disregard the plans of their high command and fought the decisive battle of the campaign at a spot some sixty miles forward of the much stronger position on which they had been ordered to make their stand. On 5 May, 1936, Italian troops marched into Addis Ababa, the Emperor having left the city for Jibuti three days earlier.

The Italians managed to pacify their newly acquired empire with remarkable speed, particularly in view of the scope much of the country offered for guerrilla activities. In July, 1936, the last organized remnants of the Ethiopian army made a concentric attack on the capital against a much reduced and criminally negligent garrison. One column succeeded in reaching the city but, once the defence was alerted, they were driven off without difficulty. Many of the Rases and other notables made their peace with the conquerors and, apart from routine banditry, Ethiopia was fairly quiet. That it did not remain so was the fault of the Viceroy, Marshal Graziani, a man who, encouraged by Mussolini, believed in a policy of unrelenting severity towards the slightest sign of dissent. Unsurprisingly, an attempt was made to assassinate him with hand grenades at a public ceremony on 17 February, 1937. He was only wounded and his response was massacre or, in practice, two massacres. In the first three days after the incident the Blackshirts and even less desirable elements were given *carte blanche* to murder any Ethiopians they met by whatever means occurred to them. It was noted that the regular army and, in particular, the *carabinieri*, greatly outnumbered as they were, did their best to check this bloodbath in which they took no part. In the weeks that followed Graziani did his best to eliminate all those educated Ethiopians and such figures of influence as might be suspected of wishing that the Italians had not conquered the country, not excluding many who had genuinely made their submission. This second purge reached its climax with the murder of the entire adult community of the monastery of Debra Libanos, the main theological centre of the Ethiopian church.

As always a policy of mindless retribution brought its own reward and resistance, which had been reduced to a few enthusiastic but mutually antagonistic groups in the less accessible mountains, flared up throughout the Amhara heartlands. Large scale operations, vastly expensive and far from wholly successful, had to be undertaken and

14

induced Mussolini to make one of his few thoroughly sensible decisions. He removed Graziani, recommending him to devote himself to growing bananas – 'our market always needs them' – and replaced him with the thirty-nine-year-old Duke of Aosta, cousin to the King of Italy. The Duke's father, one of the few senior officers to emerge with credit from the disaster at Caporetto in 1917, had supported the fascists in their early days, but the son, a professional soldier and later airman, had kept clear of politics. He had been an artillery officer in 1915–18 and had later commanded the Camel Corps in Libya. He was popular with the regular armed forces, no recommendation with Mussolini, but, as with the rest of his family, disliked by the King, and it was an excellent if unexpected decision to promote him in November, 1937, from the command of an air division in Italy to be Viceroy of Italian East Africa. He was a success from the start: immensely tall, 6 feet 6½ inches, charming, athletic and determined to do his best for the people, Italian and Ethiopian, placed under his care. He released thousands of detainees, insisted on judicial processes being used against suspected rebels. He tried to improve the standard of the fascist functionaries who had installed themselves in the administration and of whom, as he reported, half were incompetent and a quarter corrupt. Naturally this process was much hampered by obstructionism from those concerned and by intervention, either interested or ignorant, from Rome. Reversing the policy laid down since the conquest by Mussolini, he employed the Ethiopian notables who were prepared to cooperate as adjuncts to his government. By using negotiation rather than repression he had, by 1939, greatly reduced the need for active military operations within the empire.

He was helped in his task by the fact that Italy, even under Mussolini, was prepared to spend money on her colonies rather than regard them as merely sources of strategic advantage or potential trade. The Italian empire had been created as a settlement for surplus population and the home country invested money in Ethiopia in a way which far surpassed anything contemplated by Britain, France, Belgium, Portugal or the United States in their own colonies. Hospitals and schools were built, agricultural schemes were launched and teams were set to exploring for minerals. The great estates of the Rases were dismembered and, while some of the expropriated land was given to Italian settlers, more went to Ethiopian peasants. Moreover, these settlers, many of them peasants themselves from the rugged south of Italy, were, despite fascist exhortations, the least racist colonists in history and were perfectly prepared to work in the fields alongside the Ethiopians in a way which would be unthinkable in Kenya or Senegal. Above all, the Italians built roads, the vital first step towards developing the country. In their five years of occupation they built 3,000 miles of motorable roads, half of them metalled, and, given a few more years, would have connected all the main centres. Many of these roads are masterpieces of engineering, frequently following the crestline of a mountain range. Here again these splendid achievements were created by Italian and Ethiopian labourers toiling side by side.

By 1939 most of Italian East Africa was quiet. The south of the country, united by the occupiers into the single huge province of Galla-Sidamo, was better off than ever before and made it clear that the inhabitants preferred their new overlords to the ruthlessly exploiting Amharas who had preceded them. Much the same was true of the predominantly Muslim Haraje and even the traditionally turbulent Tigre was, for Tigre, notably quiet. Only a minority of Shoans and Gojjamis continued, in mountain fastnesses, to disrupt the peace, though they might have had more impact had their leaders been capable of working together. Ethiopia was as quiet as it could have been expected to be under the Solomonic emperors and it was being modernized far faster than ever before in its long history. Nothing can excuse the immorality of the Italian aggression and their early repression but it is fair to say that no colonial power ever did so much for their conquest so quickly.

When war broke out in Europe in 1939 the Duke of Aosta was even more anxious than most Italians that his country should not be dragged into the fighting at the heels of Germany. Both his mother and his wife were French and he had many friends in both France and Britain, but, despite his low opinion of the Blackshirts, he was a loyal Italian and realized that, if war came with the western allies, the empire which had been conquered with such an expense of blood and treasure would be a hostage to fortune, isolated by allied territory. In April, 1940, he went to Rome to try to convince Mussolini how unready I.E.A was to face a war. According to Ciano, he told Il Duce 'that it is not only problematical whether we can maintain our present position, because the French and British are already equipped and ready for action, but the local population, among whom the rebellion is very much alive, would revolt as soon as they got an inkling of our difficulties.' If this is what he said he can only have been deliberately exaggerating the problems of his position in order to make his point. On both his outward and his return journeys he stayed at both Khartoum and Cairo; it is beyond belief that he could have been impressed by the strength of the British forces at either place, since no impressive amount of strength existed. His warnings had no effect. Within weeks Mussolini believed that he discerned a way of linking Italian Libya with the East African empire without having to fight.

CHAPTER 2 Summer of Discontent

ITALY DECLARED WAR on Britain and France at midnight 10/11 June, 1940. It was not an unexpected development but it added one more disaster to a situation that was already catastrophic. A week earlier 200,000 men of the main British army, a quarter of them administrative personnel, had been evacuated from Dunkirk, leaving 50,000, mostly fighting men, behind. Most of the returning troops had brought their rifles with them but almost everything else had been left behind. There were only 420 field guns in the British Isles and one third of these had been embarked in a vain attempt to prop up the battlefield in western France. It was assumed that the Germans would attempt a cross-Channel invasion in the immediate future and, if they could secure a beachhead, it was the opinion of the Chiefs of Staff that 'our land forces would be insufficient to deal with them'. They believed, however, that the Royal Navy and the R.A.F. would prevent such a beachhead being established. It was clear that little further could be expected from the French army and it was possible that Britain might be faced, in Churchill's words, with France 'not merely out of the war, but actually hostile to us'.

With Italy in the war and France out of it, the future was desperate. Naval dominance in the Mediterranean, hitherto taken for granted, was now in serious doubt and to the U-boat menace was added the threat of more than a hundred Italian submarines at a time when British escort vessels were heavily depleted by the losses at Dunkirk. On land the British would have to face Italy on four new fronts, of which one, in the Western Desert, was of paramount importance. Nothing could cripple British resistance more surely than an Italian thrust across the Suez Canal which would engulf the countries of the

Near East (which was just being retitled the Middle East) and the oilfields on which Britain depended. To resist such an attack General Wavell, Commander-in-Chief, Middle East, had 36,000 men in Egypt who might be reinforced from the 27,500, including a horsed cavalry division, in Palestine. In Libya were not less than a quarter of a million Italian troops backed by an air force at least twice as numerous as the R.A.F. in Egypt. The Italians could easily be reinforced from Italy. There was nothing in Britain that could be sent by the only route available, round the Cape of Good Hope, though some troops could be spared from India and already Australian and New Zealand brigades, magnificent material but under-trained and ill-equipped, were arriving.

Air Chief Marshal Longmore, Air Officer Commanding Middle East, was responsible for an area of 4½ million square miles and had twenty-nine squadrons of all kinds. His most up-to-date aircraft were a single squadron of Mark IV Blenheim light bombers, but most of his strength was made up of obsolete types, Bombays, Wellesleys, Vincents, Furies, Lysanders and Gladiators. Since they were elderly and out of production it was hard to get spares for them and particularly hard in the Middle East. The other services were equally short of equipment. In July the 7th Cruiser Squadron went to sea to engage the enemy off Cape Spartivento with only half their outfit of ammunition. Wavell's only armoured division was short of two regiments of tanks and his artillery was incomplete and obsolete. His medium guns were the 6-inch howitzers and 60-pounders of 1918 while his field guns were either the 18-pounders of the earlier war or a hybrid stopgap, the 18/25-pounder. The first of the new 25-pounders did not reach the Middle East until the end of 1940. All reinforcements and supplies for the army and most of those for the navy and air force* had reached them round the Horn of Africa and through the bottleneck of the Red Sea.

Much of the Horn of Africa and a long stretch of the Red Sea coast was in the hands of the Italians and it seemed probable that the rest of the coast could be in Italian hands within a few weeks. In that case a determined offensive by Axis aircraft could make the bottleneck impassable so that the forces in Egypt would be dependent on the desert tracks from Basra, through Baghdad, in neutral Iraq, to

---

* The oil fuel for the fleet was brought by pipeline from the oilfields to Haifa. From late September onwards aircraft could be flown to Egypt from Takoradi in the Gold Coast (Ghana).

Palestine or from Mombasa and thence by rail and tracks to Juba in southern Sudan from where it would proceed by alternating river steamers and railways on an 1,800 mile journey to Cairo. Either route would be a dubious way of supplying a brigade, let alone a substantial army and airforce.

On paper there was nothing to stop the Italians doing anything they liked in East Africa. On the outbreak of war Mussolini had boasted to Hitler that there were 350,000 Italian and colonial troops there and he probably believed it to be true since he had given orders to that effect. In February, 1937, he had instructed Graziani:

> It is essential that you recruit and begin training the first 100,000 men of the 'black army'. You must aim to be able to mobilize at least 300,000 men by the time our own rearmament is complete [1940–41]. If war breaks out, the mother country will not ask for help but equally will not be able to send help either.

In fact Mussolini exaggerated, since the strength of the Italian army in I.E.A. on 1 June, 1940, was 255,950, to which could be added 9,000 *Carabinieri* (military police), 6,000 civil police and 1,800 men of the *Guarda Finanza* (armed customs service) who, with the frontiers closed by war, had little to occupy them.

182,000 of the army were native soldiers organized either in colonial battalions, brigades and divisions or in *bande* (*Bande Armatedi Confini*), groups of irregulars commanded by Italian officers. Eritrea produced the best of the formed troops, and they were very good indeed, and the *dubats* (white turbans) from Somaliland had a high reputation as irregulars. Many excellent askaris were raised from occupied Ethiopia, especially from Tigre and Galla, and fought well for their colonial masters and even those from the more turbulent Shoa and Gojjam gave good service as long as they were away from their homeland and the war was going well for the Italians.

Of the 74,000 Italian 'national' troops, one third, 26,000, were Blackshirts (*Militzia Voluntaria di Securezza Nazionale*), the private army of the fascist party. They were less well-trained than the regulars and much less well-led since their officers were either party activists or poor-quality regular officers who transferred to the Blackshirts in exchange for a step in promotion which, in most cases, they were unlikely to achieve in their regiments. Roughly half the ranks of the Blackshirts were men conscripted within the empire and formed into the Africa Division, which were noticeably less enthusiastic about fighting than the party volunteers from Italy. The figure of 47,000 regular troops exaggerates their real strength, since many officers and NCOs were required to lead the native troops, regular and irregular, and to take charge of the technical services. Of these the artillery was the most important, having 450 pieces, many of which were 65mm mountain guns, but including 75mm and 105mm field guns and some mediums, among them four formidable if elderly 149mm howitzers. Italians also provided the crews for some sixty obsolete tanks, a third of them mediums, and 126 armoured cars. The combat strength of the regulars lay in a single excellent division, the Savoia, made up of two regiments of grenadiers, each of three battalions, and a brigade of mountain troops, three battalions of Alpini and one of Bersaglieri.

Not all these troops were available against external enemies. According to the official figures, 78,000 men were required *'per ordine interne'*, for internal security, but this figure includes the central reserve, the Savoia and Africa divisions, and a large army headquarters, perhaps 30,000 men altogether. At the outbreak of war the largest field corps faced French and British Somalilands, another, almost as large, faced the Sudan as far south as the Blue Nile, and other corps were deployed facing southern Sudan, northern Kenya and on the western borders of Italian Somaliland.

The *Regia Aeronautica* had 325 warplanes in I.E.A. although 142 of them were either in reserve or unserviceable (or both). Reinforcements of bombers, but not fighters, could arrive by over-flying the Sudan from southern Libya and seventy-five planes actually arrived during the campaign. At the outbreak the hard core of Italian air power comprised thirty-six bombers and forty-five fighters, all of which were more modern than anything that could be immediately brought against them. In particular the Savoia 79 bombers had a maximum speed of 255 mph, 10 mph faster than their most formidable opponents, the Gladiator fighters. They also had a bomb load of 2,750 lbs, almost three times that of the opposing Blenheims and Wellesleys. There were more than 4,000 airmen in the theatre, many of whom later fought as infantry.

Considering that the Italian navy was the third largest in Europe, Mussolini allocated a surprisingly small squadron to his excellent harbour at Massawa, only seven fleet destroyers, two escort destroyers, eight submarines and nine smaller craft, five of them motor torpedo boats. Since he had more cruisers than the combined British and French Mediterranean fleets, he could have spared one or two for the Red Sea, together with a stronger flotilla of submarines, since he had 108 at home against a combined allied strength of fifty-eight. Nothing could have made a more effective contribution to his main offensive, the invasion of Egypt, than a strong and active naval presence in and around the Red Sea.

The great weakness of I.E.A. was its isolation. There were very large stocks of most war stores but no possibility of replacing them once they had been expended. The main deficiency was of motor tyres and it was unfortunate that when a shipload of Japanese tyres slipped into Kismayu through the blockade they were found to be of the wrong size. There was some hope in London that the Italian empire could be strangled by blockade, a hope nurtured by the erroneous calculation that there was only petrol for five months, but starving I.E.A. would, in practice, have been a very prolonged business. Equally, initial British estimates of Italian military strength were far wide of the mark. In June, 1940, it was thought that the Duke of Aosta had only 130,000 troops, although this estimate was almost doubled in the following month. On the other hand he was believed to have 200 light tanks, a figure probably reached by adding the number of real tanks to that for armoured cars.

Any weakness in East Africa did not enter into Mussolini's calculations as he saw no prospect of a long war. He had always intended to join Hitler in arms as soon as his preparations were complete but, like the rest of the world (including the German High Command), his calculations were upset by the speed of the German breakthrough in France. On 13 May, the day on which the *panzer* spearheads crossed the Meuse, he said:

> Some months ago I said that the Allies had lost the victory. Today I tell you they have lost the war. We Italians are already sufficiently dishonoured. Any delay is inconceivable. We have no time to lose. Within a month I shall declare war. I shall attack France and Great Britain in the air and on the sea.

He made no mention of attacking on land, although a month earlier, when discussing what Italy should do when eventually she declared war, he had insisted on an attack on Jibuti. Now he saw this as unnecessary. In fact his first orders to East Africa called for no offensive on land, in the air or on the sea. Instead he formulated his minimum demands in the armistice talks with France – the cession to Italy of Corsica, Tunisia and Jibuti – only to find them vetoed by Hitler who was insistent that only minimum demands should be made

so that as few Frenchmen as possible would find the terms unacceptable. 'Under these conditions,' wrote Ciano, 'Mussolini does not feel
inclined to advance claims to territorial occupation.'

The incompetence of Italian intelligence was a contributory factor
in the stand-fast order to I.E.A. If they could describe Wavell's 36,000
men in Egypt, a country in which there were 80,000 Italian residents,
as 'the 100,000 strong Anglo-Egyptian army', it is hardly surprising
that they over-estimated allied strengths in the Somalilands. They
reckoned that the French had 10,000 men around Jibuti and attributed
7,000 to the garrison of British Somaliland. The facts were that the
French had 7,000 men, many of them locally recruited, while the
British had just reinforced the 500 members of the Somali Camel
Corps with a battalion of the Northern Rhodesia Regiment, making a
total of 1,475 all ranks. To add to their fantasy, they claimed that
Somaliland could be reinforced from the 10,000 men in garrison at
Aden where there were no more than two Indian battalions.

In practice the occupation of Jibuti and Berbera would only slightly
have improved Italy's position on the Red Sea until the defeat of
Britain opened the sea-lanes and a far more attractive option was open
to Mussolini. An advance on Khartoum and Port Sudan, coordinated
with an Italian attack on Egypt from the west, could hardly fail to put
Britain's Middle East command in an intolerable position. In I.E.A.
the Italians had both the strength and the capability for launching such
an attack through Kassala but there is no evidence that such a move
was even considered. Doubtless Mussolini's estimate of the probable
length of the war affected such planning but, once again, his
intelligence service made the prospect daunting. They calculated that
there were 31,000 British troops in the Sudan, most of them to the
north of Gallabat. The actual garrison was three British battalions and
4,500 men of the Sudan Defence Force. If the police and some
irregulars were included the total still fell short of 9,000. There were
no tanks, though the S.D.F. had a small number of armoured cars
made by mounting an armoured body on a standard commercial 30
cwt chassis and topping the construction with a revolving turret
mounting a Vickers M.M.G. and a Boyes anti-tank rifle. Apart from
two saluting guns at Government House, there was no artillery,
although the Sudan Horse was being hastily retrained to man a battery
of 3.7" howitzers. There was, in short, nothing to stop a determined
Italian incursion.

The Duke of Aosta also had to keep in mind a third front, that facing

Kenya, although he discounted it as a scene for offensive operations since, between the Italian and British colonies was 'the most abominable, uninhabited, waterless desolation' stretching for 300 miles, the Northern Frontier District. In Kenya Italy assessed the British strength at 39,000 men, whereas, at the outbreak of war, there were 8,500, made up of two brigades of the King's African Rifles supported by two light howitzer batteries, one from India and one newly raised in East Africa. Unlike the other two East African fronts, reinforcements were on their way to Kenya. Two brigades of West Africans started landing at Mombasa at the end of June and more help was on its way from the Union of South Africa. A makeshift anti-aircraft brigade, a battery of 1918-vintage 3″ guns and two batteries of twin-mounted Lewis guns, arrived at the beginning of June and were soon followed by personnel from the S.A. Tank Corps who took over a dozen obsolete Mark V light tanks discarded in Egypt. Then a field battery arrived and, on 17 July, an infantry brigade sailed from Durban. The Union also provided air support, the first contingent comprising all her four Hurricanes and a squadron of Hartbeests (known elsewhere as Hartebeests), single-engine biplanes with a bomb load of 568 lbs, a maximum speed of 145 mph and a range of 450 miles.

On each of the three fronts all the British could do was to hang on and hope. All pre-war planning had been based on the French alliance and on the possession of Jibuti as a base for operations against Ethiopia. After consulting his French colleagues in June, 1939, Wavell had reported that 'a ground offensive on any large scale could only be undertaken from Jibuti in the general direction of Harar and Jijiga' and this remained the overall plan though great reinforcement would be required before such a stroke could be mounted. Wavell had also agreed that everything should be done to stimulate a rebellion 'in the west and south of Abyssinia'. The defeat of France clearly made the use of Jibuti as a base impossible and gravely hindered the work of encouraging dissidents inside Ethiopia. The 'Gentlemen's Agreement' (Anglo-Italian Joint Declaration) of 2 January, 1937, between Chamberlain and Mussolini contained a clause discouraging activities liable to impair relations between the two countries and this had been taken to bar Britain from sending agents into I.E.A. The subsequent *Bon Voisinage* agreement effectively prevented any useful intelligence being received from the British Consulate General (previously Embassy) in Addis Ababa, so that in June, 1940, Britain was ignorant of the situation inside I.E.A. and, on the civil side, not anxious to remedy the situation. Up to the declaration of war by Italy, Wavell complained bitterly that:

The Governors [of Kenya and the Sudan] were obstructive in the matter of my passing agents. . . . They suspected me of trying to stir up trouble on their borders and making things difficult for them.

Such subversive activity as had been undertaken was the work of the French who had chosen to operate across the Sudanese border where they had the connivance of British officials who kept Khartoum in ignorance. The moving spirit was Colonel Paul Robert Monnier, a man with a distinguished record in both the Great and Spanish Civil Wars, who had the support of the indomitable Georges Mandel, then Minister for the Colonies. Entering Ethiopia in June, 1939, he made contact with the persistent rebels in Gojjam and Beghember before dying of fever in November. All subsequent operations in that area stemmed from his work and it was not until June, 1940, that a British mission was authorized to undertake the same task.

In the summer of 1940 it was quite clear that the British could undertake no offensive action on land. In the words of G.O.C. Sudan:

It was useless to launch a mere thousand soldiers armed with rifles, and two or three machine guns to a company, in two or three packets into the mountains of Abyssinia, against a European-led enemy vastly superior in the air, in ground numbers and armament, on nebulous information with no known local chieftains to rely on for support and insurrection.

In the air and at sea gestures at least could be made. In the small hours of 11 June R.A.F. bombers made it clear to the Italians, many of whom seemed unaware of what was going on, that war had been declared. Single-engined Wellesleys (designed 1931; bomb load 1,061 lbs) from 254 Wing in the Sudan attacked airfields at Asmara, Guru and Massawa, setting light to 780 gallons of petrol. Mark I Blenheims (bomb load 1,000 lbs) from Aden attacked Assab and Diredawa, while from Nairobi four Junkers 86, taken over by S.A.A.F. from South African Airways and converted to carry 1,160 lbs of bombs, attacked a camp of *bande* near Moyale. These attacks were largely a matter of defiance and did little more damage than the reprisal raids which the *Regia Aeronautica* carried out against Kassala, Port Sudan, Atbara, Kurmuk and Gedaref.

At sea there was more substantial success. A Norwegian tanker was torpedoed south of Aden and a task force led by the cruiser *Carlisle* immediately searched for the submarine. She was soon found and attacked with depth charges which it was believed had damaged her. The armed trawler *Moonstone* was left on guard but after two days the submarine *Galileo Galilei* surfaced and set about the trawler with torpedoes and her deck-gun. Unperturbed, *Moonstone* replied with her antique 6-inch gun and scored two hits on the conning tower, killing her captain and forcing her to surrender. It is fair to her crew to add that they were suffering from gas poisoning, due to her long submersion and because of this they failed to destroy her papers which included the sailing orders for four of her consorts. Two of these were located and sunk, one of them in the Persian (or Arabian) Gulf, while a third was found already to have wrecked herself near Port Sudan. The remainder stayed quietly in Massawa until the following February when they put to sea again and, after an epic voyage, reached Europe.

The Italian surface ships kept a very low profile, although, by Christmas, 150,000 soldiers and vast quantities of stores had sailed past them subjected to nothing worse than high-level and very inaccurate bombing. Only once did the destroyers put to sea when, on 20 October, they made a foray against a convoy of thirty-two ships. As soon as they realized the strength of the escort they made for home and, attempting to negotiate the entrance to Massawa harbour, the *Francesco Nulli* (1,058 tons, 4×4.7″ guns) ran ashore and was bombed to destruction by Blenheims from Aden. Not that the British got away unscathed. The cruiser *Kimberley* was hit in the engine room by a shore battery and had to be towed to Port Sudan. Thereafter the Italian navy relapsed into five months' inactivity while, after 4 November, the air attacks on convoys also ceased. Nevertheless the very presence of a squadron at Massawa served a useful purpose since it forced the United States to declare the Red Sea a war zone and thus out of bounds to their shipping. This threw an added and unwelcome burden on British merchant tonnage and was crucially to affect Wavell's strategy.

Meanwhile the Italian army had shown some tentative signs of activity. On 4 July a force of 6,500 men, including two squadrons of tanks and ten batteries of artillery, advanced on Kassala, a place of some sentimental regard to the Italians since they had held it for some years until, at the end of 1897, they had handed it over to the Sudan since it was too much trouble to retain during the Mahdist years.

Although the garrison consisted of only 320 men of the S.D.F. and the police, they stood their ground all day, inflicting, according to Italian accounts, casualties of forty-three dead and 114 wounded. During the night the garrison slipped away, having lost one dead and sixteen missing, several of whom later rejoined. On the same day an attack by a battalion and some *bande* dispossessed a platoon of the Sudan Defence Force of Gallabat and another seized the northern frontier post at Karora. Three days later sixty Sudan police were evicted from Kurmuk. These petty advances were trumpeted as great victories on Italian radio and caused some concern in the Sudan but they did not foreshadow the advance on Khartoum that had been feared by the civil government. They were merely intended to block convenient sally ports which the British might use for transporting arms to the rebels inside I.E.A. None of the places seized was defensible and only Kassala was important, since, apart from being the obvious starting point for an invasion, its capture interrupted the southern part of the Sudan railway system which, for reasons which were certainly not military, had been built in a vast circle.

At the same time the Italians started to nibble away at their southern frontier. By some anomaly of frontier-drawing, Kenya had a single toe-hold on the Ethiopian highlands. This was the little mud-walled fort of Moyale, perched on the escarpment and facing, at a range of half a mile, a similar fort at Moiale (better known as Italian Moyale) across the border. Inconveniently sited at the end of 300 miles of dusty track, there was no point in holding Moyale beyond a desire not to lose face. The fort was surrounded with barbed wire and some concrete pill-boxes had been built, but, apart from a small storage tank, the only source of water was outside the perimeter and the garrison consisted of 180 men, a company of 1/K.A.R., a platoon of machine-gunners (3/K.A.R.) and some sappers. All was quiet, apart from some desultory bombing, until 28 June when mountain guns started firing at the fort. Many of the rounds failed to explode but two days later there was heavy bombing and some signs of ground troops. The garrison suffered four casualties before, on 1 July, the enemy inexplicably withdrew. The water supply was immediately replenished and the fort was reinforced with a troop of mountain guns while another company of K.A.R. was stationed outside the perimeter as a counter-attack force. At this stage the Italians launched a full-scale attack under cover of darkness. This was beaten off by the garrison and the 3.7″ howitzers although the counter-attack force got lost in the dark and was withdrawn. The place was then besieged for a week before the Italians again withdrew, but they reappeared after twenty-four hours and launched another unsuccessful attack under a heavy barrage. On 14 July, the water supply having become critical, the garrison evacuated the place with their weapons during the night. They left behind three wounded who, it was thought, could not be carried but two of them managed to escape under their own steam.

The K.A.R. had fought well at Moyale, which was something of a relief since an earlier episode had shown them in a less favourable light. Brigadier C. C. Fowkes, commanding the northern of the two defending brigades, was a naturally aggressive commander and decided that a two-company attack should be mounted against the frontier post of El Uach. Air support was available in the form of an elderly (1928) Hawker Hart of the Rhodesian Air Force and it was arranged that this should fly over the village after the assault to ensure communications. In practice the troops were late and the first the enemy knew of the attack was the arrival of the old aircraft. Being only a handful of irregulars, they took fright and dispersed into the bush, leaving El Uach to be seized unopposed by a company each from 1 and 5/K.A.R. These unfortunately were not properly under control and took to looting the Italian stores, an occupation they were still pursuing when a colonial battalion mounted a brisk and efficient counter-attack, at which the askaris, in their turn, took to the bush, leaving their British officers and NCOs to fight their own rearguard action. It was not an encouraging debut for the army in Kenya, made worse because the Hart had to make a forced landing and was abandoned. Italian radio claimed that the action had frustrated an invasion of Somaliland.

The only other activity of the Italian army in the early days of the war was undertaken against Jibuti. Although Hitler had forbidden the annexation of French Somaliland, the armistice with France had authorized Italian control of Jibuti port and of the railway to the Ethiopian frontier. This, however, required the cooperation of the French on the spot and their military commander, General Paul Le Gentilhomme, was determined not to cooperate. It had been agreed that he should command both French and British Somaliland and his orders were 'to resist sufficiently long to enable a revolt to be raised in Abyssinia . . . and to tie down enemy forces on the ground and, particularly, in the air which might otherwise be used against Egypt.'

These orders he was determined to fulfil, deciding, with British agreement, to concentrate on securing Jibuti port. He had available seven battalions of Senegalese and Somali infantry, three batteries of field guns, four of A.A. guns, a company of obsolete light tanks and a squadron of very elderly fighter planes. The approaches to Jibuti were suitable for defence and had been fortified, the weakest point being the frontier with British Somaliland and, since the British had so few men, this was strengthened by putting a French battalion across the border at Jirreh.

18 June was the day on which Pétain broadcast to the French people, telling them that 'the fighting must cease'. On the same day the Italians made their first attack on French Somaliland, an advance down the railway line towards Ali Sabieh, which was repulsed. Next day they struck from the north and, although they took an outlying fort, they were held on the main French position at Dadatte while a counter-attack seized a small Italian fort. On 21 June a heavy air raid killed twenty civilians and three soldiers without damaging the port, while four Savoia bombers were brought down by the A.A. guns and on the following day they made another unsuccessful attack on Ali Sabieh. The Franco-Italian armistice came into effect on 25 June and Le Gentilhomme received orders to cease firing against the Italians though he was authorized to retain his battalion in an active role at Jirreh until the British were able to relieve it. Certain that he could rely on his troops, the General ignored these orders and replied to all Italian approaches, as was technically true, that he had not been officially informed of the armistice. This notification eventually arrived on 10 July and still Le Gentilhomme played for time until he was undermined by the civil government which, on 19 July, voted unanimously to remain loyal to Marshal Pétain. It was not until 23 July that a senior officer, humiliatingly transported in an Italian aircraft, arrived to supersede him and Le Gentilhomme slipped across the border into British territory to join de Gaulle's forces in the Middle East. The battalion at Jirreh was withdrawn five days later, having been relieved by a detachment of the Camel Corps.

By that time Mussolini had realized that Britain was not going to surrender unless the Germans launched a successful invasion and decided to use the time profitably by filching British Somaliland. In the interim the British had had time to consider, and reconsider, the merits of defending the territory. On the face of it there was little to be said for committing scarce troops and scarcer supplies to retain it. The protectorate consisted of thousands of square miles of sand, scrub and rock, waterless for most of the year and supporting a sparse population of fierce nomads with a deserved reputation of causing nothing but trouble to any occupying power. Its only export, myrrh, had long since ceased to be a commercial proposition and the only port, Berbera, was so primitive that it took ten days to unload a 3,000-ton ship using lighters. Such a harbour would be an inadequate base to support any substantial military operation and, at pre-war Anglo-French talks, it had been decided that the place must be regarded as expendable so that all available troops could be used to protect Jibuti. The Somali Camel Corps, 500 men under Colonel Reginald Chater, Royal Marines, were to fight a delaying action against any invader and, to assist them, the Colonial Office had made available the princely sum of £900 to provide reserve water tanks and a few isolated pill-boxes.

Not everyone was happy about abandoning without a fight a territory that had been held for more than half a century and in particular A.O.C. Middle East and C-in-C East Indies (who was responsible for naval matters in the Red Sea) protested that its loss would give the Italians more air bases for attacking convoys. These recommendations gradually persuaded Wavell to change his mind and, in December, 1939, he recommended that an East African battalion should be sent to reinforce the Camel Corps and that the approaches to Berbera should be fortified. This proposal led to extended debate between the War Office, the Colonial Office and, since the effect on Italy had to be considered, the Foreign Office, and it was not until 15 May, 1940, that 1 Northern Rhodesia Regiment began disembarking at Berbera. Meanwhile the mechanization of the Camel Corps had been approved and funds for defence works were allocated. As it happened, the War Office assumed administrative control of Somaliland on 1 June (they had had operational control since January) and the money vanished into some bureaucratic morass.

In June Wavell had, at Le Gentilhomme's request, sent a British battalion, 1 Black Watch, to Aden to be ready to move to Jibuti and, when Vichy eventually assumed control there, the battalion was warned for duty in Somaliland since Wavell had now swung over to defending it. Chater was promoted to brigadier and his force was increased by two Punjabi battalions (1/2 and 3/15) and 2 K.A.R. with 1 E.A. Light Battery, a newly raised unit armed with four 3.7-inch howitzers.* It was a dubious decision to take so late in the day. Even assuming that British Somaliland was worth fighting for, it was questionable whether this small and hastily assembled force, five battalions (including the Black Watch), four small guns and air support dependent, apart from the over-worked Blenheims at Aden, on a handful of Gladiators based on two small and vulnerable air strips, could hold any part of British Somaliland. It was a very inadequate force to resist an enemy immensely stronger in men, armour, artillery and aircraft who had three usable lines of approach. Close to the frontier of French Somaliland the Italians, basing themselves on the railway, could advance on the seaside town of Zeila and then swing south-east along a bad track leading along the coast to Berbera. On the other flank there was a road of kinds through Odweina and Burao before crossing the Assa hills at the difficult and easily defensible Sheikh Pass. Between these two approaches was the best road in the Protectorate which linked Berbera with Harar by way of Hargeisha, crossing the Assa range at the Tug† Argan gap. To hold this gap, the best defensive position available, required not only a deployment ten miles wide to secure the heights dominating the road, but a subsidiary force guarding the Jerato Pass five miles to the east. Even if enough men could be found for these two positions, the surrounding country, while impassable to vehicles, was ideal for infiltration by infantry.

Even with adequate artillery, the defence of Tug Argan alone would have overstretched Chater's entire force and, at the last moment, Wavell further confused the situation by deciding that the force was too large to be commanded by a brigadier. He therefore appointed Major-General A. R. Godwin-Austen, then sailing from Palestine to Kenya, where he was to command a division. It is no disrespect to that officer to say that, as the timing turned out, it would have been better to leave the command to Chater, whose gallantry was well established from the First World War and who knew the country well. In the event Godwin-Austen was still at sea when the Italians invaded and

* The 3.7″ howitzer was designed to be mule-borne (and was so employed at Keren by 1 Jammu & Kashmir Mountain Bty in Feb–Mar, 1941) but in I.E.A. was normally carried in trucks. It threw a shell (H.E., shrapnel, smoke or star-shell) weighing 19½ lbs to a maximum range of 6,000 yards. In the summer of 1941 a 'supercharge' was authorized, thus obtaining an additional 700 yards of range. In the high altitudes around Gondar, 'meteor effect' gave ranges of more than 7,000 yards.
† Tug=a (dry) watercourse.

the British defence was arranged entirely by Chater and based on Tug Argan. There he stationed 2/K.A.R. and 1 N.R.R. (less one company) with 3/15 Punjab in reserve. Most of 1/2 Punjabis were at the Sheikh Pass while the remainder supported the Camel Corps posts in front of Zeila. Most of the Camel Corps were deployed as a screen to cover the roads to Odweina and Hargeisha and at the latter place they were supported by the detached company of Rhodesians. In the situation, it is hard to see that any other commander could have made more effective dispositions.

The Italians had collected at least 26,000, perhaps 30,000 men for their invasion. On their left two brigades, including one regular and one Blackshirt battalion, with six batteries were sent to take Zeila whence a separate force under different command consisting of one Blackshirt and one colonial battalion with a battery were to move down the coast to Berbera. The main attack was to be delivered down the Hargeisha–Berbera road, the only one that would stand heavy traffic, and was commanded by General Carlo de Simone who had with him eleven colonial battalions, fourteen batteries, a squadron of tanks and some armoured cars. His right was covered by a third column consisting mainly of *bande*, but including one colonial battalion and a battery under General Bertello, whose task was to tie down the troops at the Sheikh Pass. There were four battalions and two batteries in reserve behind de Simone's column and twenty-seven bombers, twenty-three fighters and a flight of reconnaissance planes were allocated to support the invasion.

All three columns began to cross the frontier on 3 August, the day before Wavell was to fly to London for consultations. Before leaving Cairo he reaffirmed his decision to defend at least Berbera and ordered a number of reinforcements to be despatched. The Black Watch were to go from Aden with two A.A. guns, all that could be spared from the port's defences, and he asked the Government of India to send a battalion, a field battery and some sappers who were on the point of embarking for the Middle East. From his own command he moved most of another field regiment, two 2-pounder A/T guns and the mechanized cavalry regiment of Fourth Indian Division. None of these units, except those from Aden, arrived before Berbera fell.

Both the Italian flanking columns started well, that on the left taking Zeila without difficulty, although the coastwise advance ran into trouble, largely through heavy and accurate bombardment from the sea. On the right Bertello took Odweina and then sent his *bande* to skirmish against Sheikh Pass while taking his regulars to his left to help de Simone who was not having everything his own way. Before reaching Hargeisha his advance guard fell foul of the Camel Corps' A/T rifles which accounted for three armoured cars and tanks had to be brought up before they could fight their way into the town on 5 August. The General then halted for two days while supplies were brought forward. This caused a spate of messages from Addis Ababa and Rome demanding haste, to which de Simone replied that, since he was 165 miles from railhead at Diredawa to which he was linked by a single disintegrating road, some pause was imperative before advancing to meet the main British strength. His aircraft reported that the enemy were organizing a defensive position at Tug Argan, fifty miles ahead, and he started to move towards them on 8 August. By that time bombing had forced the surviving Gladiators to abandon their airstrips and any future air support must come from Aden, 200 miles away. In other ways the defenders had slightly improved their situation. The Black Watch had disembarked and been put into reserve behind the gap, allowing 3/15 Punjab to strengthen the main position. The navy had produced an anti-tank gun in the form of a 3-pounder saluting gun with thirty rounds of ammunition. Mounted on an oil drum, it was manned by a petty officer and two ratings from HMAS *Hobart*.

Four battalions with minimal artillery support could have no chance of holding Tug Argan indefinitely against the strength de Simone was leading against them, the more so when Bertello took his detachment against the Jerato Pass on Chater's left. It is greatly to the credit of Chater's men that they stood their ground for five days and inflicted very heavy loss on their assailants, a loss greatly increased because the Italians started by attacking in heavy formations reminiscent of the nineteenth century, in one instance being urged on by a general 'wearing a black jacket, white riding breeches and black top boots, and riding a fine white horse'.

The first attacks came on 11 August and that evening Godwin-Austen reached the front, not that there was much he could do to affect the course of the battle. Some outlying positions were lost but most were retaken by counter-attacks, although two howitzers had to be abandoned after they had been spiked. More seriously, the Italians, learning that frontal attacks did not succeed, took to infiltration round the flanks. By 14 August the defenders were exhausted and Godwin-Austen signalled to General Maitland Wilson, Wavell's deputy, that they had the choice between fighting to a finish and a prompt evacuation. Wilson authorized evacuation on the following morning which was not a moment too soon since that afternoon a very gallant Italian attack captured Observation Hill and with it the saluting gun and its crew. Another casualty was Captain E. C. T. Wilson of the East Surreys, serving with the Camel Corps, whose dogged defence with a machine gun earned him a posthumous VC, an award he was lucky enough to receive in person since he was found to be alive and a prisoner.

That night the defenders fell back through a rearguard position held by the Black Watch and two companies of K.A.R. at Barkasan, sixteen miles behind the gap. The Italians were very slow to follow and the rearguard had plenty of time to ponder the weakness of their position, strung out across a valley two miles wide and without commanding the heights on either side. To support them they had a single Bofors 37mm A.A. gun that had just arrived and a 25mm Breda A/T gun which, with five rounds, had been captured. The morning of 16 August was quiet and the first troops who approached their position turned out to be two platoons of Punjabis who had been cut off. True to their peacetime training, they had meticulously collected their spent cartridge cases and brought them with them. They were soon followed by a platoon of Italian motor-cyclists, backed by a dozen lorries loaded with infantry. These were easily driven off but for the rest of the day the rearguard was very heavily pressed and frequently had to counter-attack with the bayonet. On one occasion a Black Watch platoon drove the enemy back 600 yards before they were recalled. Even an attack by six medium and twelve light tanks was held off, but by dusk the Italians were round both flanks although little inclined to exploit this advantage. By that time, however, the job was done and they were able to slip away by truck, reaching Berbera on 18 August.

Meanwhile the Royal Navy was carrying out the evacuation with its usual competence and the *Regia Aeronautica*, which had lost two Savoias raiding the port on 15 August, seemed content to let them go quietly. All white civilians, several hundred Ethiopian refugees and such of the police and Camel Corps as wished to leave were embarked on the night 16–17 August and the troops followed the following evening, 2 K.A.R. augmenting itself with a company of Nyasas from the Camel Corps. HMAS *Hobart*, with Godwin-Austen on board, remained in the roads until the morning, when, as a Parthian shot, she shelled the government offices before leaving. The Italians marched in that evening and, as was to be expected, made great propaganda play with their victory. They admitted to 1,800 casualties, a figure they later amended to 2,052.

The British had lost 140 killed and wounded with 120 missing, most of whom became prisoners of war. It was this slim casualty list that focused the Prime Minister's attention on the campaign. His first reaction had been mild enough, remarking that the loss of the Protectorate was 'strategically convenient' even if it was 'enforced on us by the enemy'. When he found that only 260 men had been lost, he took it into his head that not enough had been done. He sent an intemperate signal to Cairo demanding that Godwin-Austen, by that time commanding a division in Kenya, should be suspended and that a general officer should be sent from India to conduct an inquiry. Wavell refused to cooperate.

> I sent a reply refusing to suspend Godwin-Austen . . . saying that a court of inquiry would be disastrous to morale and that the troops had fought very well and hard, as was evidenced by the 1,800 casualties admitted by the Italians (it was lucky for me that they were publishing their casualties at this period of the war); and ending with the remark that 'a big butcher's bill was not necessarily evidence of good tactics'.

The C.I.G.S. remarked that this last comment made Churchill more angry than he had ever seen him but the matter was not pursued.

It can only be a matter for speculation whether Churchill would have been even more angry if British Somaliland had been evacuated without a fight, as the Channel Islands had been. To defend it gave the Italians the chance of claiming that the routed British had fled to their ships. Evacuation would have enabled them to boast that they dare not face the invincible fascist legions. Wavell, as so often, was faced with a problem to which there was no correct solution and the only criticism that can legitimately be levelled at him is that he failed fully to adopt either of two wrong answers. At the last moment, too late, he started to move substantial reinforcements to Berbera but it is far from certain that, even had they arrived, they would have checked the Italians. It is doubtful whether, if they had arrived, the port would

35

have been able to sustain them. A field regiment of artillery would have been of the greatest assistance in the defence of Tug Argan but only if sufficient shells could have been landed and brought up to the gun lines. If that proved impossible the guns would, at best, have been an embarrassment, at worst, a glittering prize to the enemy.

CHAPTER 3 Interregnum

LIKE ALL BRITISH military operations, the planning of the East African campaign was liable to the whims of Winston Churchill. One facet of his indomitable, irreplaceable leadership was his constant pressure for action, irrespective of the merits of the action. As the D.M.O. at the War Office wrote, he 'thirsted for action, and his head was full of projects that had no attraction for the Chiefs of Staff. He fretted at the delays which are inseparable from the preparation of modern fighting forces, and he pressed us incessantly to "grapple with the enemy".' To Churchill a soldier was a soldier and, as such, should be available on the instant to be thrown into battle irrespective of his state of training, the incompleteness of his equipment and the fact, deplorable but inescapable, that more than half any modern army is composed of men and women who have no place in the firing line but perform the routine task of making it possible for the fighting men to fight. He regarded the large total of soldiers as if it was the return of an eighteenth century army which could neatly be divided into 'muskets and sabres' all of whom could be employed in the field.

His desire to 'grapple with the enemy' was laudable but, in the summer of 1940, impractical on any but the smallest scale. Soldiers were there in plenty but it was difficult to find them even a rifle each. Of twenty-six infantry divisions in the United Kingdom in mid-July only three had their full complement of field artillery and fifteen had less than half their establishment, while the figures for anti-tank guns were even more depressing. There were shortages in various degrees of machine guns, mortars, bren-gun carriers, anti-tank guns and, above all, of tanks, while many of the weapons which the troops had with them were obsolete or, as in the case of the Boyes A/T rifle, had been shown in France to be inadequate. The army in Britain was scarcely equipped to fight a defensive battle; it had no hope of taking the offensive. In the Middle-East, far from the centre of supply, the situation was far worse. By mid-August Wavell could deploy one incomplete armoured division and two infantry divisions for the defence of Egypt but they were deficient, apart from tanks for two regiments, of 124 field guns, thirty-two medium guns, 230 A/T guns, 2,100 A/T rifles and 461 bren guns carriers.

Such considerations did not inhibit Churchill from demanding action and not least for action in East Africa. Acknowledging that the force in the Sudan was too small for an immediate offensive, he proposed a sea-borne invasion of Eritrea to be launched from Britain. On 27 July Lieutenant-General Marshall-Cornwall, commanding III Corps in Shropshire, was summoned to spend the night at Chequers where he was closely interrogated on the condition of his two inexperienced Territorial divisions. Churchill believed them both to have '50 per cent in field artillery, anti-tank rifles and machine guns' and the fact that they actually had far less than this poor provision was not allowed to interfere with the Prime Minister's plans. After dinner, Marshall-Cornwall, with the C.I.G.S. and General Ismay, were taken aside by Churchill who unrolled a large-scale map of the Red Sea.

> The PM placed his finger on the Italian port of Massawa. 'Now, Marshall-Cornwall,' he said, 'we have command of the sea and the air; it is essential for us to capture that port; how would you do it? . . . I looked hard at the map for a moment and then answered, 'Well, Sir, I have never been to Massawa; I have only passed out of sight of it, going down the Red Sea. It is a defended port, protected by coast defence and anti-aircraft batteries. It must be a good 500 miles from Aden, and therefore beyond cover of our fighters. The harbour has a very narrow entrance channel, protected by coral reefs, and is certain to be mined, making an opposed landing impracticable. I should prefer to wait until General Wavell's offensive against Eritrea develops; he will capture it more easily from the land side.' The PM gave me a withering look, rolled up the map and muttered peevishly, 'You soldiers are all alike; you have no imagination'.

In fact the soldiers had more than enough imagination to realize what would happen if two divisions of undertrained, ill-equipped troops were sent on a six-week voyage at the end of which they would be expected, in temperatures of 100°F and upwards, to undertake an opposed landing for which no landing craft were available. There was no lack of offensive spirit among the generals but, unlike the Prime Minister, 'We wished to do nothing that would postpone decisive action; we considered it rash to risk unnecessary reverses merely for the sake of doing something.'

The chances of 'doing something' in East Africa were minimal. Nothing could be attempted from Kenya until the problem of transporting a large fighting force across 300 miles of desert could be solved. In the Sudan the logistic difficulties were less severe since the great loop of the railway gave at least a basic supply line but there were no troops who could launch an attack. The Kaid (Commander-in-Chief), Major General William Platt, had the S.D.F. which had been chiefly trained to maintain internal order, and three British battalions with which to protect a frontier with I.E.A. which stretched for 1,200 miles and it was hard to see any reinforcements which could be sent to him. Egypt, in particular, seemed a most unpromising source especially after mid-September when the Italian army lumbered over the western frontier, took Sidi Barrani and settled down to organize its supply lines for a further advance. It was Wavell's expectation that they would move on again in October and that such a move would be coordinated with a thrust from Kassala into the Sudan. Platt's force was inadequate to resist the kind of attack that might have been made but all that could immediately be sent him was a battalion of Mahrattas (2/5) from Aden and the regiment of field guns, 4th, which had been directed, too late, to Berbera. The only other source of troops was India where two brigades, six Indian battalions, designated Fifth Indian Division, were ready to be embarked. Unfortunately the War Cabinet, despite the objections of the Commanders-in-Chief of both India and the Middle East, had decided that the division should be sent to Basra to protect the oil fields against a possible Russian attack. It was not until the end of that month that they could be persuaded to release them for service in the Middle East, and Wavell, bravely in view of his shortage of troops in Egypt, directed them to land at Port Sudan. They started arriving there early in September and strengthened Platt's hand not only by six battalions but by two further field regiments and a divisional (mechanized) cavalry regiment. After their arrival there were fair grounds for believing that the Sudan, or at least Khartoum and Port Sudan, could be protected against invasion.

Taking the offensive was quite another matter, particularly against country as naturally strong as western Eritrea. There were not enough troops, the administrative system was undeveloped and the doctors entered a very strong *caveat* against operations in I.E.A. Medical intelligence warned that in Eritrea more than one in five of the population suffered from tuberculosis, that dengue fever was endemic in Massawa, that 80% of the native population 'had either syphilis, gonorrhoea or soft chancre, the first being the commonest'. In addition, malaria, typhus and enteric were widespread throughout the country, and there was a significant incidence of epidemic meningitis, relapsing fever, leichmaiasis, leprosy, brucellosis, myiasis, tropical ulcer, smallpox, trachoma, diphtheria, worm infections, rabies, typhoid, paratyphoid, and both bacillary and amoebic dysentry. It seemed that disease would be as formidable opponent as the Italian army.

Meanwhile Churchill, after his consultations with Wavell, had despatched (21 August) a directive to the commanders-in-chief in the Middle East. Naturally most of it dealt with events in the Western Desert where 'a major invasion of Egypt must be expected any time now'. In East Africa he laid down a defensive attitude in the hope that the Italian empire would collapse from economic pressures. In particular he opposed any reinforcement of Kenya.

> The defence of Kenya must rank *after* the defence of the Soudan. There should be time after the crisis in Egypt and in the Soudan is passed to reinforce Kenya by sea and rail before any large Italian expedition can reach the Tana river. We can always reinforce Kenya faster than Italy can pass troops thither from Abyssinia or Italian Somaliland.

It is hard to see where these reinforcements 'by sea and rail' were to come from, but Churchill, having convinced himself that they could be found, proposed that the South Africans in Kenya should be sent to Egypt and the two West African brigades to the Sudan, thus releasing Fifth Indian Division for Egypt. Wavell commented that 'I carried out such parts of the directive as were practicable and useful and disregarded a good deal of it.'

What Wavell did decide would be practicable, useful and desirable was the clearing of the Eritrean coast so that the Red Sea would no longer be a combat zone and would become accessible to American shipping. In his present situation he was forced to rely largely on a rebellion within the Italian empire, but he was determined that there must also be offensives from both the Sudan and Kenya to tie down the main strength of Aosta's army. He realized too that, however much trouble could be stirred up within Ethiopia, it was unlikely that any significant revolt could be stirred up in the key area, Eritrea, where both history and Intelligence suggested that the inhabitants would prefer to remain under Italian rule to being subjected to the Amhara empire. He thus retained all the South and West African troops in Kenya and put Fifth Indian Division into the Sudan, knowing that he would have to reinforce it before it could attack.

Fomenting revolt within Ethiopia was no easy matter, since the relations between the various dissident groups within the country were known to be deplorable and communications worse. Wavell had, however, taken early steps to plan a rising, and, in September, 1939, had secured the services of Colonel D. A. Sandford whom he had set to work devising such schemes as were permitted. Sandford, who had been Consul in Addis Ababa in 1914, had gained a DSO and bar as a gunner in the First World War, after which he had been for a time in the Sudan Political Service. Later he had settled as a farmer outside Addis Ababa where he had become the friend and confidant of Haile Selassie. Driven from the country by the Italian invasion, he had reverted to his clerical roots – his father had been a Canon of Exeter Cathedral – and at the outbreak of war, then aged fifty-eight, was Treasurer of the Guildford Cathedral Building Fund. His efforts on Wavell's behalf had been much hampered by the insistence of the civil government on a strict adherence to the 'Gentleman's Agreement' (see p 25) but he had contrived to make some contacts with dissidents in Gojjam and Beghember and had begun to give wireless training to some Ethiopian refugees in Khartoum, although, to conceal their presence from Italian spies (and possibly the Governor), he had to insist that they wore the tarboosh. He envisaged the stimulation of the revolt in three stages. In the first, Metemma and Gubba would be seized as points of entry for the supply of arms. Then raiding parties would disrupt communications, while attacks were made on small Italian posts and depots, thus expanding the area of revolt and encouraging the desertion of the Italian colonial soldiers. Only in the final stage would attacks be made on substantial Italian centres which, thanks to the earlier operations, would by then be isolated. As soon as Italy declared war Sandford sent across the frontier letters, signed by General Platt, addressed to eleven supposedly rebel chieftains, offering arms to those who would send to Gallabat to fetch them. It was unfortunate that the only arms available for distribution were single-shot rifles, half a century old, which were far inferior to the Italian weapons which the more enterprising rebels had already stolen for themselves. At the same time work started on establishing a line of supply dumps on the frontier and a new unit of S.D.F, the Frontier Battalion, was raised to guard them.

This was the state of affairs when, on 25 June, Emperor Haile Selassie arrived at Alexandria by flying boat. He came unannounced and his appearance horrified the British Ambassador to Egypt, Sir Miles Locker Lampson, who, while complaining violently to the Foreign Office, insisted that he should not be permitted to land and must spend the night in his aircraft. This order was disregarded and he was landed secretly to spend the night at R.A.F. headquarters which, until a few days earlier, had been the Italian Yacht Club.* Next morning Sir Miles had him flown to Khartoum, but the Governor, warned by telephone, refused to allow him to move further south than Wadi Halfa and appealed to the Governor of Kenya to relieve him of his unwanted guest.

The Emperor's unheralded arrival in Egypt was a direct result of Churchill taking control in Downing Street. For months the Foreign Office had been agonizing over whether Britain should try to restore him to his throne. The official view, as expressed in a minute of 20 May, 1940, was that:

> We have no indications that there is any demand among the native rebels in Ethiopia for the return of the Emperor.

This is unsurprising since the Foreign Office, like the Governors of the Sudan and Kenya, had gone to great lengths to ensure that they had no contact with the 'native rebels'. On the other hand there was a superabundance of advice from Britons who had lived and worked in Ethiopia before the Italian invasion and their advice reflected the area in which each adviser had lived. Those who had spent their time in Addis Ababa strongly favoured the Emperor's return. Those who had been in outlying areas, especially those which the Amharas had conquered, regarded his return as a disaster for the country.

---

* In his *Haile Selassie. The Conquering Lion*, Leonard Mosley quotes George Stead, who was in the Emperor's party, as saying that Haile Selassie had to spend the night in the cloakroom, but in his own account, Stead asserts that it was to the cloakroom that the portrait of Mussolini had been hastily removed to get it out of the Emperor's sight.

Meanwhile Haile Selassie had abandoned his home of exile at Bath and moved to the Great Western Hotel at Paddington from where he wrote to the Foreign Secretary putting himself at the disposal of the allies. Since Lord Halifax and his officials were still deciding what to do, it was two weeks before he received even an acknowledgment. On 8 June, two days before Italy declared war, he wrote again and this time his letter was referred to the War Cabinet on 18 June. Churchill took an immediate decision. France was on the point of collapse and there was a choice between flying the Emperor to the Middle East immediately or having him out of play for at least six weeks while he was shipped round the Cape. The decision was to send him immediately, Churchill ruling that 'All problems can be decided on the spot'. It was unfortunate that, when the Foreign Office passed on this decision, they gave Haile Selassie the impression that, on his arrival in the Sudan, the British would have prepared an expeditionary force ready to recover his empire with full air cover.

It was at Wadi Halfa that he learned how hollow these assurances were. Sandford spelled out to him the resources actually available. There were insufficient men to defend the Sudan and none for taking the offensive. There were 1,600 Ethiopian refugees in Kenya and Somaliland who were being enlisted and a few hundred more were expected from Palestine. Including 5,000 which had already been offered to the Gojjami rebels, 17,000 rifles were available for the Ethiopians, although they were of several different calibres and ammunition was short. No artillery was available but four mortars had been supplied. Four hundred Hotchkiss light machine guns – the type that had been used for horsed cavalry until superseded by the bren – were due to be landed at Mombasa during July. There were no anti-aircraft guns and the aircraft available were few and obsolete. Haile Selassie's first reaction, expressed privately, was, 'It would have been better had I never left England.'

He soon recovered his calm confidence and, after a week at Wadi Halfa, was allowed to move to a small palace twenty-eight miles outside Khartoum. Not that he could feel that he was a welcome guest. The Governor, soon to be replaced, was no admirer of Ethiopians of any rank and General Platt was too concerned with defending the Sudan – Kassala and Gallabat fell just after the Emperor's arrival – to concern himself much with schemes which would deprive him of irreplaceable equipment to further nebulous operations inside Ethiopia. Haile Selassie was, however, partially mollified by a meeting with Wavell who painstakingly explained to him the facts of military life in the Middle East. The General, on the other hand, found the meeting heavy going.

> Discussion with the Emperor at this and subsequent visits was always a complicated business. I think H.I.M. understood either French or English pretty well but he would not admit it; and he would never speak anything but Amharic. As the only interpreter of Amharic could only speak Arabic as his medium of interpretation, conversation had to filter through at least three languages – on one occasion four when it was found that the interpreter of Arabic knew no English, only French.

At least Haile Selassie persuaded the British to stop referring to the Ethiopian dissidents as rebels and to call them 'patriots' and more practical moves were started. The Ethiopian refugees were brought to the Sudan from Kenya and Palestine and, once the civil authorities could be induced to release them from prison, they were formed into infantry battalions and trained by British and Sudanese NCOs. A number of Operational Centres were formed, each consisting of a British (or Australian) officer and five NCOs with some thirty Ethiopians, the intention being that they should be attached to patriot groups inside Ethiopia and give them arms and advice while using a wireless set to co-ordinate their movements within the overall rising. It was also decided that Sandford's organization, entitled 101 Mission, should cross the frontier. Haile Selassie was most anxious to accompany them but Wavell forbade accepting such a risk. The mission split into three parts. The first, crossing the frontier near Gedaref on 6 August, was led by Sandford himself and made for the isolated Mount Belaya. His chief staff officer followed three weeks later and the third party, led by a sixty-three-year-old Australian senator, left ten day afterwards only to be ambushed and killed by irregulars.

From many points of view it is unfortunate that, by taking all its senior staff into Ethiopia, 101 Mission had practically disbanded itself as an organizing body in the Sudan. The gap was filled on 6 November when Major Orde Wingate arrived in Khartoum. A figure of controversy forty years after his death, Wingate is likely to go down to history as a flawed genius. He came from a strictly non-conformist background, his grandfather having thrown up a profitable business career to devote himself to the conversion of Hungarian Jews to

Christianity. Both his father and maternal grandfather were soldiers who joined the Plymouth Brethren, the former taking his religious convictions to such lengths that, while on active service, he had refused to march his company on the Sabbath. At Charterhouse and the Royal Military Academy, Woolwich, Orde was an undistinguished student and a lonely man since, at all stages in his life, he went out of his way to antagonise his seniors, his equals and, frequently, his subordinates by expressing, arrogantly and at length, opinions which he knew to be obnoxious to them. The resulting hostility convinced him that the rest of the world was in league against him. Commissioned into the Royal Artillery in 1923 he was an undistinguished regimental officer until, in 1928, he secured, through the influence of a cousin, a posting to the S.D.F. and it was in the following five years that he first visited Ethiopia and developed an admiration for the Amharas.

Most accounts of Wingate before the war make him appear intolerably arrogant, opiniated, bullying, subject to 'melancholic depressions' and made no more agreeable by his passion for eating raw onions and, instead of bathing, for scrubbing himself with a dry brush. On the other hand, he could be generous, charming and attractive, especially to women and children, and was happily married. After his Sudanese service, he was brigade major to a Territorial A.A. Brigade and passed his entrance examination for the Staff College at the second attempt, although not well enough to secure him a nomination. Once more he believed that he was being victimized but, after a personal appeal to the C.I.G.S., he was given a job as an Intelligence Officer in Palestine, then on the brink of the Arab revolt against the increased Jewish immigration resulting from Hitler's pogrom in Germany.

Almost immediately after his arrival in September, 1936, Wingate embraced Zionism with a passion which astonished even his Zionist friends. Such fervour embarrassed the civil government, which was trying to protect the indigenous Arabs, thus laying itself open to accusations of anti-semitism, and the army, which was attempting to hold the ring openhandedly. Not so Wingate who openly preached that a Jewish State should immediately be established as part of the British Empire, covering not only Palestine but Transjordan (now Jordan) and, for preference, Syria and the Lebanon. Moreover this new state would raise a large all-Jewish army ready to fight Germany in the war which was rapidly becoming inevitable. The trainer and eventual commander of this army would, of course, be Captain Orde Wingate.

He had an opportunity to lay the groundwork when Wavell took over Palestine Command in September. By this time gangs of Arabs, based for the most part in Syria, were crossing the frontier to sabotage the oil pipe-line to Haifa and conventional military tactics were doing little to check them. Wavell agreed to Wingate raising a number of Special Night Squads composed of picked British soldiers and Jewish settlers, the latter, though this was not known to the authorities, being recruited through Hagana, the illegal Jewish defence organization. These squads were strikingly successful and his powers of leadership and remarkable courage earned Wingate the DSO. By this time Wavell had left Palestine and his successor, while admiring his work with the S.N.S, was increasingly alarmed by Wingate's open advocacy of Zionism, an activity which he undertook on several occasions to renounce, but never did. When he was seriously wounded late in 1938, he was posted back to England to the staff of another anti-aircraft brigade and, soon after his arrival, he received a copy of his annual confidential report, a document which every officer must initial before it is sent to the War Office. This document said that he was an officer of exceptional ability but that his addiction to Zionism made him unsuitable for employment on the staff in Palestine since his enthusiasm for his chosen cause distorted his obedience to both army and government. It seems astonishing that any long-serving regular officer who had behaved as he had done could expect to escape some censure, if nothing worse, but to Wingate the report seemed a monstrous injustice. Without further ado, he reached for the ultimate method of obtaining redress, an officer's right of direct appeal to the Sovereign, claiming that not only was the report unfair but that, since the award of the DSO five months earlier, he had received no recognition for his services. This Complaint (as it is officially known) was still being discussed by the Army Council when war with Germany broke out and it was not until early in 1940 that Wingate was induced to withdraw it, having received assurances that 'your merit is thoroughly known' and that nothing in the contentious report would prevent him being employed 'for the good of the service'. Meanwhile he continued to serve with his A.A. brigade until after the fall of France when he was sent to raise a body of irregular anti-invasion troops in Northern Command.

Some writers have expressed surprise that the army should have wasted the time of such a brilliant soldier by keeping him in a routine staff post throughout the first nine months of the war. On the contrary, it is a matter of congratulation that the army should have retained the services of a man who, apart from being insubordinate and disobedient, was usually badly turned out, with dirty hands and unkempt hair and the habit of doing business while stark naked. It says much for the tolerance of senior officers that Wingate should have earned the approval of Field-Marshals so diverse as Deverell, Ironside and Wavell. It was at the request of the last of these that he was despatched to the Middle East in September, 1940.

He was sent to Khartoum on the heels of Anthony Eden, Secretary of State for War, who, with Wavell, had been conferring with General Smuts and Generals Platt and Cunningham. He had also had talks with Haile Selassie, who was inclined to complain about lack of support for his Patriots. As Eden wrote in his diary on 29 October:

> It is clear that the rebellion [in Ethiopia] goes better than we dared to hope, and no less clear that there is a sad lack of co-ordination and, I gather, to some extent perhaps, of interest on the part of the military here. Wavell not satisfied either. As a result, we had a meeting of all concerned after dinner which was at times a stormy affair. Wavell began the indictment and I followed up. I fear they must have regarded me as intolerable.

It is hard not to feel sympathy with Platt and his senior staff officers, who were doing their best to defend the Sudan and plan for an offensive with wholly inadequate resources, to be berated for failing to give adequate support to fostering a revolt about which reliable information was unobtainable and about which they received ambiguous advice from both the Foreign Office and the Sudan government. Equally, Eden, with his background in international affairs, was in no doubt that Britain owed a debt of honour to the exiled Emperor and that to pay that debt would earn prestige in the neutral world, not least in the United States. As a result Platt was ordered to make more resources available to the patriots and to enable him to do so he was given a credit of a million pounds – the annual budget of the Sudan was only five million – and sent a trained staff officer, the first to reach Khartoum since war with Italy began, and Major Orde Wingate.

Wingate's appointment was only that of liaison officer to 101 Mission, but, since Sandford and his senior officers were already inside Ethiopia, he was virtually in command of its work in Khartoum and he stirred up its somewhat lethargic operations in his first two weeks there, inspecting the two embryo battalions of Ethiopian infantry, visiting the Operational Centres and organizing the purchase of 18,000 camels on whom, with their hired drivers, the whole enterprise depended. He also called on the Emperor and explained to him his plans for making the Patriot movement viable and effective, asking in return for his 'complete trust and confidence'. Then he set out to visit Sandford, flying to a tiny airstrip at Faguta, thirty miles south of Lake Tana, in a Vincent biplane (maximum speed 135 mph) with an intrepid pilot. Sandford was depressed. It was difficult to differentiate between Patriot activity and brigandage; two Patriot leaders on whom he was relying refused to cooperate with each other; supplies, even of obsolete arms, were arriving only in a trickle; his radio link with Khartoum was weak and intermittent; the air support he had been promised had failed to materialize due, in fact, to the most successful of all the Italian air raids which, on 16 October, had destroyed the eight Wellesleys and two Vincents allocated to him on the ground at Gedaref. Wingate was able to cheer him with news of the preparations under way and of the increased level of supplies and arms that would soon be available. The two men agreed on the desirability of the Emperor's re-entry into his country as soon as a bodyguard had been trained for him but they differed on which of them should control the distribution of arms. Nevertheless, when, at the third attempt the pilot succeeded in coaxing the Vincent into the air, they parted on good terms.

Back in Khartoum Wingate pressed on with his arrangements and, as usual, succeeded in making a large number of unnecessary enemies. Some men he accused of pro-Italian sympathies, others of seeking staff posts to avoid facing the enemy. On at least one occasion he flatly refused to attend a meeting with General Platt and his relations with government officials were disastrously bad. As always he regarded any opposition to his wishes as being deliberately engineered to thwart him and he put it about that his mission had been personally and unreservedly backed by Churchill.

The authorities in the Sudan still had plenty to worry them apart from Wingate's bloody-mindedness. While on the east they had a 1,200-mile frontier with Italian East Africa, they had in the north-west one half as long with Italian Libya, which, even in peacetime, had seen Italian patrols pushing south from Kufra. On the west there was a vast border with French Equatorial Africa and, in the summer of 1940 and especially in the aftermath of the shelling of the French fleet at Mars-el Kebir, it was far from sure that the Vichy Government might not ally itself with the Germans. Fortunately, in August the Governor of Chad, a negro from Martinique, declared for de Gaulle and his example was followed by the rest of F.E.A. and by the French Cameroons. Even then the danger in that quarter was not over. In December, 1940, General Huntziger, who had signed the armistice on behalf of France in June, was negotiating with the Germans for authority to send an expedition to recapture Chad and General Falvy was released from a German prison camp to command it. These talks, of which the British were well aware, were broken off with the temporary eclipse of Laval but were re-started by Darlan as late as November, 1941.

There was even a remote possibility of trouble over the common frontier with the Belgian Congo where the authorities were divided in their loyalties between their King, who had allowed himself to become a German prisoner, and the Government, which had disavowed him and gone into exile. Fortunately the doubts in the Sudan were resolved in August when a Belgian lieutenant arrived at Yei, in the extreme south, on a bicycle, having apparently 'pedalled over the Nile-Congo watershed' to arrange co-operation. Even within the Sudan internal peace was not to be relied upon, for, although the Muslim north had undertaken to support the war effort, the heathen tribes of the south had a long tradition of feuding and cattle raiding which had to be kept in check by such parts of the S.D.F, mostly recruits and pensioners, as could be spared from the eastern frontier.

All these alarms showed General Platt at his best. He was not a great field commander but he was determined and aggressive and had a gift for retaining the loyalty and affection of the Sudanese who, in the early stages, made up so high a proportion of his soldiery. He was 'as aggressive as they come, a regular little tiger, a fine, upright, fiery (often testy) capable soldier' and the last thing he wanted to do was to fight a defensive war. In the early months, when there seemed to be nothing except lack of determination to prevent the Italians striking up to Khartoum or Port Sudan from Kassala, he felt obliged to keep his three British battalions guarding the main towns and had to leave the frontier to a half-a-dozen companies of S.D.F. These, however, mercilessly harried the Italian posts and created the impression that the area was swarming with aggressive troops. This impression Platt heightened by deception schemes which created cantonments, dumps and airfields where they could be seen by reconnaisance planes. Such ruses were, as it happened, scarcely necessary since the Italian Intelligence officers were quite capable of inventing their own chimeras. When, in August, Platt thought it necessary to move a British company to guard the vital Butana bridge, south-west of Kassala, they were accompanied by two bren-gun carriers which were reported as a large armoured force. In fact the Italians only made one incursion into the Sudan. In October Colonel Rolle led a group of Shoan *bande*, about 1,500 men, in a raid towards Roseires. Their only opposition consisted of a few policemen and some irregulars hastily raised by a local chief but they had chosen the wrong time of year, before the crops had been harvested, and the highland Shoans were unversed in desert ways. They were attacked by some Vincents, the only aircraft available, but, when they had penetrated about eighty miles they were driven back by thirst, not realizing that water might have been found a few feet below the surface of the sand. They lost more than a quarter of their strength. Nor, apart from the raid on Gedaref, were the *Regia Aeronautica* as effective as they might have been. In the first three months of war they 'raided the Sudan sixty-five times; total casualties, mostly civilians, have been eighteen killed and seventy wounded.'

The situation was changed by the arrival in September, 1940, of Fifth Indian Division. Since it had only two brigades, the third was created by adding the three British battalions. It was therefore made up to a full-strength division with a field regiment of artillery attached to each brigade, which consisted, as was usual in Indian formations, of one British and two Indian battalions. This mixed formation was orginally adopted to add a stiffening to the Indian units, but in this case the situation was reversed. All the three British battalions were regular units but they were well below even peacetime strength in regulars, having been found to be a useful quarry for officers and NCOs for the staffs and training schools of Middle East Command, to say nothing of the rapidly expanding headquarters of the Sudan itself. The numbers had been made up with reservists and recruits. 2 West Yorkshires, for example, had been completed by a draft of 200 men, drawn from the York and Lancs and the Durham Light Infantry. The other two units, 1 Worcesters and 1 Essex, had been brought up to strength with drafts from their home areas; thus both had large numbers from Birmingham and East London who were resentful at being stationed idly in the Sudan while their homes were being bombed. To make matters worse, none of the units were well commanded and their training, since the war began, had fitted them more for the parade ground than the battlefield. In Fifth Indian Division it was the Indian units which stiffened their British comrades.

Not the least advantage from the arrival of the Division was the presence of the divisional Motor Cavalry Regiment, Skinner's Horse. Owing to the dearth of armoured cars in India it had been equipped with what was available and reached the theatre of war as a cross between a reconnaissance regiment and a battalion of motorized dragoons. The main body of three squadrons consisted of foot soldiers – they would not have cared to be described as infantry – mounted in 15cwt Chevrolet trucks. They also possessed a dozen Boyes anti-tank rifles, which were effective against Italian light tanks, and they should have had thirty-six bren-gun carriers and six mortars. These, however, did not reach them until mid-February, 1941.* Improvised as their equipment was, it gave Platt a mobile unit which, boldly handled, implanted in the mind of the Italians the idea that Britain had a large highly mechanized force. He used it as the basis of 'Gazelle Force' whose other components were two motor-machine-gun companies of S.D.F. and a battery of 18-pounders (replaced by 25-pounders in December), while parts of other units were attached for particular operations. The command of this mechanized commando was given to Colonel Frank Messervy, an officer of the Indian cavalry who had been G.S.O.1 of Fifth Division, and he set about making the frontier between Kassala and Gallabat untenable to the enemy. No small Italian post could henceforward feel itself safe and even their larger positions were kept in a state of constant alarm. They could never assess where the elusive Gazelle would strike next.

Masservy's most ambitious scheme, executed in November, was an attempt to beat up a colonial battalion stationed at some wells in the hills south-east of Kassala and for this move the force was reinforced by two platoons of Indian infantry. During the approach march a camel convoy escorted by a company of Eritreans crossed their spearhead and was attacked. The escort retreated and, with reinforcements, made a stand in a good position, only to be overwhelmed,

* The cavalry regiment of Fourth Indian Division, Central India Horse, had their carriers and mortars when they reached the Sudan in January, 1941.

partly due to some bombing from the *Regia Aeronautica* which did more harm to their friends than to their enemies. Leaving twelve dead and 263 prisoners behind, the Eritreans then fell back on their main position which, by this time, was fully alerted. Seeing that an assault would be costly even if it succeeded and finding that the Italian aircraft had discovered who they were meant to be bombing, Messervy withdrew but his aim was achieved since the colonial battalion was withdrawn to the rear.

While this was going forward, a more ambitious attempt was being made further south. Urged by Wavell to make a substantial attack, Platt and Major-General L. M. Heath of Fifth Division decided to recapture Gallabat and to seize Metemma, the town which faced it across the frontier. The operation was entrusted to 10th Indian Brigade consisting of 1 Essex, 4/10 Baluchis and 3/18 Garhwal Rifles and commanded by Brigadier W. J. Slim, then an almost unknown Indian Army officer. In support was a regiment of field guns and, brought from Egypt specially for the operation, a squadron of 4 Royal Tank Regiment armed with six Mark III (A 13) cruisers and six Mark VI light tanks. The R.A.F. contrived to collect six Wellesleys, ten Gladiators (six of them from S.A.A.F.), four Rhodesian Hardys, two Vincents and six Gauntlets.*

The old British fort at Gallabat stood on a hill and was constructed of mud and stone. It had been strengthened by the Italians and was 'now surrounded by a ham-shaped outer area about six hundred yards long and four hundred wide. The perimeter of this enclosure was a stout wall of logs and stone, mud-cemented, with a barbed wire entanglement in front of it and, beyond again, a most awkward thorn zariba'. The approaches to this perimeter had been cleared of cover. A thousand yards east of the fort, beyond Gallabat village, was a dry watercourse which marked the national frontier and close to it was the town of Metemma which had been fortified and wired. A colonial battalion, reinforced by an extra company, held Gallabat and two more were stationed in the dry *khor* where they had the support of two machine-gun companies of Blackshirts, a platoon armed with Boyes A/T rifles (captured in British Somaliland), a mortar company, a detachment of artillery and a small *banda*.

---

* Hardys were obsolete light bombers, biplanes with a maximum speed of 156 mph and a bomb load of 500 lbs. Gauntlets were the predecessor of the Gladiator fighter with a maximum speed of 225 mph.

Slim realized that he would have to rely on surprise and succeeded in getting his guns and tanks into position secretly, thanks largely to the elephant grass which, beyond the cleared area, grew to eight feet high. His intention was that under the heaviest artillery and air bombardment that could be mounted the Garhwalis should take Gallabat with the tanks and that the Essex should then go straight through and seize Metemma while the third battalion secured the flanks. Since the Italian airforce was known to have forty Fiat fighters stationed within range and they could out-perform the Gladiators,★ it was arranged that the British fighters should only be flown *en masse* rather than attempt to keep continuous patrols overhead.

At dawn on 6 November the Wellesleys accurately dropped their bombs on Gallabat and the guns opened their barrage while the tanks led the Garhwalis from their start line a thousand yards from the fort, crushing the zariba and the wire. Then the bombardment lifted on to Metemma and the Indians fought their way into Gallabat against stiff opposition from the Eritreans. The Essex came forward to their assaulting positions on the reverse slope of the hill on which the fort stood and some batteries moved forward to shorten the range. From that time everything went wrong. First the tank commander reported that five of his cruisers and four light tanks had lost tracks, some due to mines, more to rocks. It would be at least four hours before his spares truck could be got forward and repairs carried out. This forced a postponement of the second phase since one cruiser and two light tanks would be insufficient to help the Essex across the *khor*. Next the air plan miscarried. A pair of Gladiators flew serenely over the battlefield and were promptly shot down. The R.A.F. liaison officers urged the airfield to fly only in substantial formations but Gladiators continued to arrive in pairs until six had been shot down and another had to make a forced landing. All fighter cover was then discontinued and the Italian bombers had a clear run, opposed only by small arms. Packed on to Gallabat hill were two battalions in a space so small that company areas were only about fifty yards square and, since the ground was rocky, no amount of digging could produce more than a scrape six inches deep. Casualties could only be evacuated by loading them on to bren-gun carriers and sending them to the rear and, during the first heavy burst of bombing, an ammunition truck exploded in

★ The Italian fighters had a maximum speed of 270 mph, compared to the Gladiator's 245 mph.

the middle of the troops. The rear companies of the Essex were seized with panic and fled, some of them seizing vehicles and driving off at high speed, shouting that the Italians had retaken the fort and that a retreat had been ordered. One group which had the misfortune to encounter Slim assured him that they were the sole survivors of the battalion, that their colonel was dead, as, they added, was the brigadier. It was quite certain that the Essex were in no condition to mount an attack and, to clinch the matter, a bomb destroyed the truck carrying the spares for the tanks. Slim held on to the fort for thirty-six hours but the bombing was incessant in the hours of daylight and, on the night of 6–7 November, he pulled the troops back to the surrounding hills. The Italians never reoccupied Gallabat and admitted to losses of 428 men. British losses amounted to 167, those of the Essex being fifteen killed or died of wounds, forty-seven wounded and six missing.

Gallabat-Metemma was a clear Italian victory and, for the British, a humiliating one. Given particularly unfortunate conditions, even the best troops can panic and the unfortunate Essex, ill-led, ill-trained and subjected to the horrors of unopposed bombing on their first contact with war, can only be regarded as unfortunate. They were withdrawn from the line, retrained, reorganized and in time became a worthy battalion. The action also high-lighted faults in liaison with the R.A.F. and the fact that cruiser and light tanks had serious limitations on Ethiopian terrain.

*   *   *

It was perhaps inevitable that, in the early months of the war, attention in Kenya should be focused on the northern frontier. The capture of Moyale was the only substantial Italian incursion into the colony. Moreover, in that direction was the only common frontier with Ethiopia across which supplies could be passed to the Patriots, a task that would have been eased by the existence of the mountain oasis of Marsabit, a staging post in the *cordon sanitaire* of desert. In fact, there was little future in campaigning to the north. The Ethiopian highlands were broken and roadless, almost trackless, and the inhabitants unlikely to rise on behalf of Haile Selassie. They had suffered too long from Amhara oppression and, if they had to have a foreign overlord, they marginally preferred the Italians. To operate north from Kenya would yield the minimum of strategic gain with the maximum of logistic difficulty.

General Dickinson, G.O.C. East Africa, had orders to secure Kenya and tie down as many Italian units as possible. Believing that the vital point to be defended was the port of Mombasa and the railway that ran north-west from it through Nairobi into Uganda, he based his defence on the River Tana on his right, while, on the left, he secured the two main sources of water in the desert, Wajir and Marsabit. Since his defensive perimeter ran from Lake Rudolf to the sea, some 850 miles, he felt that he had insufficient troops, the more so since both his East and West Africans were initially almost immobile from lack of transport. For reinforcement he could look only to South Africa. Even if Britain had had support to send to Kenya, Churchill would not have sent it. Anxious as he was to 'grapple with the enemy', he failed to see the offensive potential of Kenya, a country he had visited more than thirty years earlier.

> What was the sense of keeping twenty-five thousand men, including the Union Brigade of South Africa and two brigades of excellent West African troops, idle in Kenya? I had ridden over some of the country, north of the Tana River, at the end of 1907. It is a very fine-looking country, but without much to eat. The idea of an Italian expedition of fifteen or twenty thousand men, with artillery and modern gear, traversing the four or five hundred miles before they could reach Nairobi seemed ridiculous. . . . On account of our superior communications it was our interest to fight an Italian expedition as near Nairobi and the broad-gauge railway as possible. For this large numbers of troops were not required.

Churchill was right in assuming that the Italians would not attempt to force their way across the desert. He was wrong in extrapolating that the British could not do so.

Before any such British offensive could be undertaken men and resources must be obtained from South Africa and, at the outset, neither existed. It had been the settled policy of the Government that, in the event of a European war, 'the existing relations between the Union of South Africa and the various belligerent countries will, in so far as the Union is concerned, persist unchanged and continue as if no war is being waged.' This ostrich-like policy was reversed by a surprise vote on 4 September, 1939, which narrowly (80 votes to 67) brought General Smuts to power and caused war to be declared on

Germany two days later. Nevertheless the means for waging war were those which the previous Government had judged sufficient for neutrality. The defence budget for 1939–40 amounted to only £2¼ million compared to Britain's £381 million for the same year. The navy comprised a token volunteer force and both army and air force were far below their planned strength. The Permanent Force consisted of 313 officers and 3,040 other ranks, including a single infantry battalion. The Active Citizen Force, roughly equivalent to Britain's Territorial Army, was supposed to be able to field twenty-seven battalions each of 926 men but had a total strength of 14,632. The Defence Rifle Associations, heirs to the commando tradition, which supposedly gave compulsory training to all able-bodied males, were thought to be able to provide 18,300 men. In infantry alone the deficiency was estimated at 39,000 men. There were only sixty-five medium and field guns, all, like the anti-aircraft guns, of 1918 vintage, the only modern pieces being two 2-pounder A/T guns. The S.A. Tank Corps had two obsolete medium tanks, two armoured cars, bought in 1925, and two locally built experimental models. Unit transport consisted of horse-drawn carts of Indian pattern. Moreover, as the vote of 4 September had shown, the country was far from united for war, although, in Smuts' view, there was more apathy than opposition. South African troops were enlisted for service 'in any part of South Africa whether within or without the Union' which was taken to mean in any part of Africa south of the equator. When it was decided to send a brigade to Kenya it was necessary to alter these terms to include the whole continent, a change which resulted in 350 men leaving the brigade, which was drawn from the Active Citizen Force, a volunteer body.

Despite these handicaps the Union made a vast contribution to the campaign in East Africa. 1st (S.A.) Brigade with its supporting arms started to land at Mombasa early in August and the other brigades of First (S.A.) Division were there by the end of November. They were short of men* and of much equipment, having more Lewis guns than brens, but, with their field guns, they gave East Africa command the strength to plan for offensive operations as

---

* Against a war establishment of a battlion of 926 all ranks, roughly 900 exclusive of officers, 1st brigade averaged on landing 882 for each battalion, 2nd Brigade 720 and 5th Brigade 691.

soon as the logistic problems could be solved and in solving them two branches of the South African army were invaluable. The first was the 'Q' Services Corps which was responsible for transport. The problem facing Headquarters East Africa was how to get two or three divisions across up to 300 miles of desert and then supply them when fighting on the far side. The only answer was an enormous provision of trucks and the resources of the Union were harnessed to providing them. Not that building the trucks was more than half the answer since sea transport was available for less than one in six of the trucks needed. The remainder, 13,000 of them, had to go to Broken Hill in Northern Rhodesia (Zambia) by rail and continue on their own wheels on the 1,200-mile journey over unmetalled roads to Nairobi. The safe arrival of so many is a tribute to their drivers, nearly all coloured, who had to be recruited and hastily trained for the task.

At least as important was the work of the South African Engineer Corps which made it possible to employ this vast fleet of trucks. At the outbreak of war S.A.E.C had consisted of 426 all ranks, mostly scattered in half-a-dozen Active Citizen Force companies. By the end of 1940 there were in Kenya alone five field companies, seven road construction companies, three works companies, two field parks, a forestry company, and a field survey company. More engineers, mostly for railway and port operating, were to follow, but already they had built a network of metalled roads to support the army's defensive position, fortified the main points and built camps for three divisions, constructed airfields – for one of these alone 675,000 square yards of scrub had to be cleared without mechanical aids – and mapped the country on both side of the frontier. Much of this work had to be done in intolerable conditions. North of Marsabit, for example, a 21-mile stretch of road had to be built across 'a vast, flat, white waste of soda and soft lava dust, totally devoid of vegetation and mercilessly reflecting the scorching sun' at temperatures of up to 141°F.

Above all S.A.E.C provided 42nd Geological Survey Section and 36th Water Supply Company whose work made the coming campaign possible. The temperatures in Northern Frontier Region were such that both men and vehicles needed great quantities of water even when in static positions. One doctor reported that his ambulance boiled so freely that it required a gallon of water every five miles. Any attack across such terrain needed either much transport to be devoted to carrying water, thus reducing the size of the assault force, or water to be conjured up from the desert. At this the Geological Survey Section, known as the Water Diviners, were adept. When, using science and instinct, they had sniffed out an underground source, the Water Supply Company would move in with their drills, sinking shafts up to 360 feet deep. Sometimes they were disappointed, but in most cases the Water Diviners had divined right and a new well could be opened.

Late in October 1940 Lieutenant-General Alan Cunningham, brother of the famous A.B.C, C-in-C Mediterranean Fleet, took over the command from Dickinson who was exhausted and who had never managed to establish a good working relationship with the South Africans. Where Dickinson had looked north towards Galla-Sidamo, Cunningham, with the enthusiastic support of Smuts, turned his attention towards Italian Somaliland. The initial logistic difficulties would be the same but the eastward thrust gave the possibility of capturing Kismayu and its harbour. It was not much of a port but even the unloading there of 1000 tons of cargo would save three hundred trucks making a round trip, including the return journey, of 600 miles.

Soon after his arrival Cunningham had told Wavell that he hoped to strike for Kismayu in January, 1940, but a month later he had reluctantly to report that, unless many more trucks could be provided or water could be found in the desert between the Tana and Juba rivers, the operation would have to be postponed until May or June, after the spring rains. This, as was to be expected, irked Churchill who complained bitterly of '70,000 troops now virtually out of action in Kenya' and pressed for both the South and the West Africans to be removed. Fortunately his attention was diverted soon afterwards by the spectacular victory in the Western Desert and Wavell kept seven brigades in the colony while making a concession to the Prime Minister by moving a newly raised battalion of K.A.R. to the south of the Sudan. Cunningham meanwhile disposed his men into three divisions, Eleventh and Twelfth African, each with a brigade each from East and West Africa and supported by gunners from the Union, and First (S.A.) Division.

To give his troops practical experience Cunningham planned a large-scale raid as a dress rehearsal of the Kismayu attack. The objective was the frontier villages of El Wak and its Italian neighbour El Uach. These had been turned into a fortified area with wire and

1. General Sir Archibald Wavell, G.O.C.-in-C. Middle East.

2. Lieutenant-General Sir William Platt, the "Kaid el 'Amin" (Commander-in-Chief) in the Sudan, with Sudanese soldiers of his personal bodyguard.

3. Lieutenant-General Alan Cunningham, commanding East Africa Force, which advanced from Kenya to Addis Ababa and beyond.

4. Brigadier F. W. Messervy.

5. Agordat: Mount Cochen seen from Lacquetat. Gibraltar spur projects from the foot.

Railway Bridge | Cameron Ridge | Brig's Peak | Sanchil | Dongolaas Gorge | Pinnacle | Fort Dologorodoc | Pimple | Zeban

6. Panorama of the Italian position in front of Keren, looking north-east.

mines and were believed to have a garrison of three battalions, although the actual strength was one battalion, some *bande* and fifteen pieces of artillery. Although it commanded one of the four tracks which connected Kenya with Somaliland, it had been neglected by the Italian command and the senior officer on the Juba frontier, Lieutenant-General Gustavo Pesenti, had never visited the place. To reach El Wak required an approach march of more than a hundred miles from Wajir, the nearest source of water, and, to gain experience of this kind of move, Cunningham deliberately used a very large force, taking a steam hammer to crack a nut or, in the words of the South African official historian, 'using an elephant gun to shoot a hare'. Five and a half battalions* were supported by a company of light tanks and two of armoured cars, three batteries of artillery and two field companies of sappers, the force being commanded by Major-General Godwin-Austen. Naturally there were problems in moving so large a force of inexperienced troops across a hundred miles of largely trackless scrub and thorn-covered desert but the attack itself on 16 December, Dingaan's Day, was a great success. Most of the garrison took to the bush leaving behind thirteen guns, forty-four prisoners and, by their own figures, 208 dead, of whom eight were Italians. The raiding force suffered negligible casualties and withdrew without interference.

It could not be claimed that the fighting at El Wak made it a memorable action but it was an invaluable training exercise which taught the attackers many useful lessons, not least in the matter of water discipline. Even more important was the effect on the enemy whose morale slumped as they realized that the wide desert did not make them invulnerable. The colonial troops, regular and irregular, brought back horrifying stories of the strength of the obsolete light tanks (which in practice were all but useless) and a rumour circulated, quite without foundation, that the Gold Coast soldiers ate their prisoners. Confidence was further undermined by reports, intercepted and circulated by the British, that the colonel commanding at El Wak had led the retreat of his men in a mulecart. So widespread did this story become that Rome asked the Duke of Aosta for explanation and received the reply that 'even if it were accepted that he took to flight, it would be absurd to believe that he fled in a mulecart

* 1st (S.A.) Brigade, 24th (G.C.) Brigade, less 2 Gold Coast Bn, and two companies of 1/6 K.A.R.

when he could have done so by car'. Worst of all, though less well publicized, was the reaction of General Pesenti who was so shaken by the raid that he recommended Addis Ababa to seek an immediate armistice as a prelude to the surrender of the whole of I.E.A. He was dismissed and replaced by de Simone, the conqueror of British Somaliland.

CHAPTER 4 Limited Offensive

WHEN WAVELL DESCRIBED the campaign in Ethiopa as 'an improvisation after the British fashion in war' he had in mind not only the way in which administrative services were improvised from whatever resources lay to hand, but the whole concept of the operations. In January, 1941, it was not envisaged that the whole of I.E.A. would be subdued in one continuing double-handed stroke – in view of the great disparity between the apparent strengths of the British and Italian forces, such a concept would have been foolhardy – but to the way in which a limited offensive was exploited as successes occurred until it brought down the whole structure of Italian rule.

An overall plan had been devised in October, 1940, when Eden had visited Khartoum and had discussions with Wavell, Smuts, Platt, Cunningham and Haile Selassie (see p. 44). It was not a happy time for Middle East Command. The Italians had already invaded Egypt and taken Sidi Barrani. There seemed every probability that, in the near future, they would resume their advance and take Mersa Metruh, possibly threatening Alexandria and the Canal. As the generals were coming to the conference news arrived of the Italian invasion of Greece, making it a virtual certainty that Churchill would insist on British troops being sent to Greece to honour Britain's legal and moral obligations to that country. Wavell fully recognized these obligations but realized that honouring them would make it impossible to reinforce the Sudan sufficiently to enable Platt to take the offensive and would encourage the Prime Minister in his demands to thin out the troops in Kenya. Since there was no viable alternative, it was decided at Khartoum to give priority to supporting a Patriot revolt in

Gojjam and Beghember. Platt's operations would have to be restricted to taking Gallabat and Metemma in November, to be followed by the recapture of Kassala in February. On the Kenya front Smuts, who was anxious for a victory to bolster public opinion in the Union, persuaded Cunningham to agree to attack Kismayu in January.

By the beginning of December this plan was in ruins. Despite Sandford's skilful and dangerous work, there was no sign of a serious rising inside Ethiopia and there seemed to be no prospect of inducing the patriot leaders to work together. It was clear that any major revolt would follow rather than precede victories by regular British forces. Such victories seemed a remote prospect. The Gallabat attack had failed miserably and the Kismayu offensive had been postponed for four months or more. The possibility of taking Kassala and of making a limited advance into Eritrea seemed unlikely to give any great stimulus to Patriots in Ethiopia. Wavell, however, was still anxious to clear the Red Sea coast and, being a secretive as well as a resilient commander, had not mentioned that, as early as 21 September, he had discussed with Generals Wilson and O'Connor the idea of a counter-offensive in the Western Desert – Operation Compass. This was due to start early in December and on 2 December he told Platt that, as soon as the first stage of Compass, the recapture of Sidi Barrani which was scheduled for early December, was complete Fourth Indian Division would be switched from Egypt to the Sudan, its place being taken by an enthusiastic but untried and under-equipped Australian division. It was a bold move since it deprived him of his only experienced infantry in the desert and exposed him to another tirade from Churchill about wasting troops in East Africa, but it made military sense since the mountain-trained Indians would be far more at home in the rocky country of Eritrea than the inexperienced Australians. Platt was therefore to continue to plan a limited advance in February while Cunningham was ordered to dominate the desert no-man's-land, try to stir up Patriot activity in Galla-Sidamo and plan for his Kismayu offensive.

Operation Compass was launched on 9 December. Screened by Seventh Armoured Division, Fourth Indian with a regiment of Matilda tanks seized all the forward Italian positions and, by 11 December, had collected 38,300 prisoners, 237 guns and seventy-three tanks. On that day, with the enemy in full retreat on Bardia, the Indians were astonished to be taken out of the line and sent back to the canal. By a fortunate coincidence the desirability of their move also occurred to Churchill. Before he heard of Wavell's order to switch the Division, he signalled:

> The Sudan is of prime importance, and eminently desirable, and it may be that the Indian brigades can be spared without prejudice to the Libyan pursuit battle.

The Duke of Aosta, even before he was actively threatened, had appreciated that he would have to defend I.E.A. against a threefold offensive, in the north, in the south and from within and believed that the most serious attack would come from the Sudan. In Eritrea, where General Luigi Frusci commanded, he stationed three colonial divisions and three independent brigades while their flank was covered, from the Setit River to beyond Gallabat, by three more brigades backed by five Blackshirt battalions. Ten brigades were allocated to the southern border, of which the stronger half were under de Simone on the Juba frontier. Four brigades were considered sufficient to contain the Patriot activity being stimulated by Colonel Sandford, roughly the same garrison which had been in the area before war was declared on Britain. Each of these field forces was supplemented by *bande* and, after garrisons had been provided for key points, there was the central reserve – the Savoia and Africa Divisions – at Addis Ababa.

Pratt's intention was to clear the Sudan–Eritrea border and the advance was planned to begin on 9 February, a date dictated by the timing of the move of Fourth Indian Division from Egypt. Nothing spectacular was contemplated. As Wavell wrote later:

> The ruling idea in my mind was that the fomentation of the Patriot movement in Abyssinia offered, with the resources available, the best prospect of making the Italian position impossible and eventually reconquering the country. I did not intend a large invasion from Kassala towards Asmara and Massawa, or from Kismayu to the north. The two operations to Kassala and Kismayu were designed to secure our flanks and I intended that our main effort should be devoted to furthering and supporting the rebellion by irregular action.

On the face of it, any considerable advance into Eritrea must face great difficulties. The countryside, which an Italian described as 'a tormented landscape like a stormy sea moved by the wrath of God' was wholly in favour of a defender and the Italians had a considerable numerical advantage. Having disposed First Colonial Division to hold the northern frontier, Frusci had allocated the defence of Kassala and the adjacent frontier from the River Anseba in the north, to Fourth Colonial Division which had been made up to a strength of four brigades. On their left, covering the main road from Tessenei through Aicota to Barentu, was Second Colonial Division (three brigades); 43rd Brigade closed the gap between them and the Setit River (which is called the Takkasse when it leaves the Sudan). In support behind Kassala were two companies of tanks and there was a liberal supply of *bande*. Having left a brigade to guard Port Sudan and another to watch Gallabat, Platt could only bring four brigades against eight and, although his field guns were superior in open country, they were liable to be less effective than the enemy's mountain guns once sharp slopes were encountered. His great advantage was that he had been promised a squadron of Matildas, tanks which, as had been shown at Sidi Barrani, no Italian A/T gun could penetrate.

Two roads led eastward from Kassala and he planned to advance on both of them with Fourth Indian Division (5th and 11th Brigades with Gazelle Force under command) on the left and Fifth (29th and 10th Brigades) on the right. It was hoped to push forward to the line Aicota–Keru, which would overrun the airfield at Sabderat, but the advance would be limited by the extent that the forward troops could be supplied. As soon as the line to it could be restored, Kassala would be railhead but beyond that every round of ammunition, every ration and every other of the multifarious items which an army needs to enable it to fight must be ferried forward by the inadequate number of elderly and infirm trucks available. Nor was this the whole of the supply problem. The real supply base for the operation was neither Khartoum nor Port Sudan but Cairo, more than 1,200 miles by rail and river from Kassala. To oversee the complex administrative arrangements there were very few trained staff officers. Before the Italian war, Headquarters, Sudan had been little more than a brigade headquarters. By January, 1941, it was commanding a corps and there were few trained men available for the extra work. The Quartermaster-General's staff at Khartoum never had more than six officers, two of them staff learners, and two more whose duties kept them almost permanently away from headquarters. The intelligence available, largely from comprehensive radio intercepts, revealed that the enemy had fortified a defensive position based on Agordat and Barentu and prudence suggested that a set-piece battle would have to be fought to achieve a breakthrough. This reinforced the wisdom of halting on the Aicota–Keru line so that stocks, especially artillery ammunition, could be built up before an attack.

In the event the situation changed before the attack started. The news of the Italian débâcle in the Western Desert depressed General Frusci and, early in January, he signalled to Addis Ababa that the chances of a successful defence would be greatly increased if he made an immediate retreat to the Agordat–Barentu position where the ground would not favour the mechanized British forces. The Duke of Aosta sought and obtained (11 January) the permission of Mussolini for this withdrawal and the interchange was duly monitored by the British. This put Platt in a most embarrassing position since Fourth Indian Division was only in process of arriving in the Sudan. 7th Brigade, which was to guard Port Sudan, landed there on 2 January and 5th Brigade, which, with a field regiment, moved overland by rail and Nile steamer, reached Khartoum a week later. 11th Brigade and two field regiments, taking a later convoy, was not complete at Port Sudan until 14 January, some of the divisional 'tail' not arriving at the end of the month. To make matters worse the shipping authorities bungled the landing of B Squadron 4 Royal Tanks, putting the tanks ashore at Port Sudan but taking the crews on to Suez. Even when the two were reunited it was found that the 'flats' of Sudan Railways were too small to carry the 26½-ton Matildas. Despite magnificent work by the railway workshops in constructing enlarged 'flats', more time was wasted.

When he heard of the Italian decision to withdraw, Platt had only three brigades available on the Kassala sector but he was determined not to let the Italians get away unmolested and rushed 11th Brigade down to the front straight off the boat while putting forward the date for his attack from 9 February to 17 January, although being subsequently forced to postpone it for two days. In the interim, 2 H.L.I., who had replaced the Essex in Slim's brigade, moved against the wells at Tessenei on 11 January. Since these were the source from which some of the Italian forward posts drew their water, this thrust ensured that the advanced Italian battalion at Abu Gamal withdrew on 16 January.

The assault on Kassala was an anti-climax. During the night of 18–19 January a patrol of S.D.F. reported that the Italians were still holding the town but when, in the morning, a two-battalion assault was launched it was found that the garrison had slipped away. The pursuit was started immediately with Gazelle Force, strengthened by

4/11 Sikhs (from 7th Brigade), leading Fourth Division up the poor road that led to Keru and Biscia while Fifth took the main metalled road to Aicota. Gazelle found its way obstructed by mines, demolitions and nullahs ten to twenty feet deep across the track which had to be 'ramped' before the trucks could cross. There were also some minor air attacks but forty miles had been covered before enough ground resistance was encountered to justify dismounting the Sikhs from their trucks and even then the enemy decamped before they could be attacked. On this part of the pursuit the greatest excitement was provided by a skirmish, fortunately bloodless, between Skinner's Horse and some armoured cars of the S.D.F.

Dawn on 21 January found Gazelle's leading vehicles probing the mouth of the Keru Gorge where the road, running for a mile and a half between steep cliffs of rock, had been heavily mined and blocked by demolitions. The whole of 41st Colonial Brigade (General Fongoli) had been deployed to hold this defile and Messervy, underestimating the enemy's strength, sent the Sikhs against them, supported by his field battery. It was not enough. The infantry, who suffered 150 casualties, were pinned down short of their first objectives and even the gunners were in imminent danger. While their attention was fixed to the front, they were charged by a squadron of Ethiopian cavalry led by two Italian officers on white horses. There was a moment of stupefaction before trails were swung round and the guns engaged the horsemen over open sights, while parts of Skinner's Horse and the S.D.F. joined in. The cavalry withdrew only to reform and charge again before they were driven off, leaving twenty-three dead and sixteen wounded on the ground.* Meanwhile there was no prospect of Gazelle Force continuing to advance until reinforced, and Savory's 11th Brigade was brought forward as fast as could be contrived with only sufficient vehicles to lift two companies, the remainder having to follow on foot, having dumped their greatcoats, anti-gas capes and blankets, all of which were promptly looted by the liberated inhabitants of Kassala.

On the southern road Fifth Division met no opposition except mines and air attacks before reaching El Gogni, ten miles beyond Aicota, where the Italians made a stand on a low ridge at right-angles to the road. Before dawn on 25 January Brigadier Marriott of 29th Brigade attacked them with 3/2 Punjabis and two companies of

---

* Skinner's Horse, 25 Field Regiment R.A. and the S.D.F. all claim the main credit for beating off this gallant horsed attack which very nearly succeeded. One of the Italian officers was killed by an A/T rifle round in the head, the other survived the war.

1/Worcesters. The attack miscarried. The Worcesters wandered off line in the dark and one company occupied a knoll outside the enemy position, believing that it was on its objective, while the other became mixed up in the Punjabi attack. Since this was behind schedule, the attacking force found itself pinned down on the rock-strewn slopes when daylight came. The gunners saved the day by firing a heavy concentration which kept the enemy's head down until the ridge was seized and held against a strong counter-attack.

Meanwhile Heath had sent Slim's brigade of 5th Division north from Aicota to threaten the rear of Fongoli's men at Keru by means of a track which had more substance on the map than on the ground. It was so bad that the Italians had only guarded it with a small post which was easily swept away. Despite the appalling going and the fact that Slim and his artillery commander were wounded in an air attack, the brigade, now under Lieutenant-Colonel B. C. Fletcher, H.L.I., pressed on and, early on 23 January, reached a point fifteen miles east of Keru where the road to Biscia was commanded by a large hill with a strong garrison. An attack by the H.L.I. failed but the sound of their artillery support showed the defenders of Keru that their retreat was threatened. Fongoli decided to withdraw them but their retreat turned to a rout when the H.L.I. demonstrated against their flank. The brigade commander and his staff were captured and 41st Colonial Brigade was never again fit to take its place in the line.

It took several hours to clear the Keru Gorge of mines but as soon as the road was passable Gazelle pressed forward with Messervy shouting 'Bum on! Bum on regardless!' The battered Sikhs were temporarily replaced by 1/6 Rajputana Rifles and on 25 January they reached Biscia, western terminus of the Eritrean narrow-gauge railway from Massawa. They met no opposition save some high-level bombing from the *Regia Aeronautica*, which did little damage, and some inadvertent machine-gunning from the R.A.F. which did even less. Beyond Biscia the country opens out as the road emerges into the valley of the dry but palm-fringed Baraka River, a dusty plain with a covering of scrub to the south. They were now well beyond their original objectives and were aiming for Agordat, the main Italian centre in western Eritrea. Having advanced more than a hundred miles in a week, neither commanders nor troops doubted that, if the momentum of the advance could be kept going, the Italians could be driven into the Red Sea. This confidence was barely abated when, on a low ridge three miles short of Agordat, Skinner's Horse were attacked by five medium tanks. The Indians' A/T rifles would dent their assailants' armour but not penetrate it and things would have been difficult had Gazelle Force not included a troop of Bofors 37mm A.A. guns which knocked out two tanks and discouraged the rest.

It is at Agordat that the two roads from Kassala rejoin and together skirt the great mass of Mount Cochen, a long rugged feature which rises 1,500 feet above the plain. At its eastern end the road to Asmara, swinging through a right angle, enters a four-mile gorge, the turn being guarded by a line of four sharp hills to the south-east of Agordat town. A mile before reaching this position the road passes through a mile-wide defile marked on the right by a rocky spur running down from Cochen and known, from its shape, as Gibraltar. On the left is a precipitous ridge, Mount Lacquetat, which blocks the space between the road and the railway which runs close to the river. It was obviously a powerful position, known to be fortified, but no one doubted that the Italians could be bounced out of it, although reconnaissance showed that there was no way of outflanking it owing to the tangled mountains. G.O.C. Fourth Indian Division, Major-General N. M. de la P. Beresford-Peirse, sent the briefly rested 4/11 Sikhs against Lacquetat on 27 January. They reached the crest almost unmolested only to find themselves faced with a double apron fence of barbed wire covered by intense fire. Recognizing his mistake, the General withdrew the Sikhs before their casualties became severe and, leaving Gazelle to screen Lacquetat, concentrated his attack on Mount Cochen.

What the British had failed to realize was that General Frusci had decided that he would fight the decisive battle for western Eritrea on the line Agordat–Barentu. This was a grave tactical error since, fifty miles to the east, across land that was not worth fighting for, was the infinitely stronger natural position of Keren. The result was that much time and concrete had been expended in building the Agordat defences. There was a fort at each end of Lacquetat and both there and on Cochen were prepared defences which had been lavishly wired. The defile through which the road ran had been wired and entrenched and work had been started on an anti-tank ditch. The garrison consisted of Fourth Colonial Division (three brigades) under General Baccari with a Blackshirt battalion and twenty-four tanks, a squadron each of light and medium, and seventy-six guns. There was also a company of Germans recruited from merchant ships blockaded in Massawa.

To attack it Beresford-Peirse had only seven battalions, forty-eight field guns, two motor-machine-gun companies S.D.F. and Skinner's Horse. None of these units were at full strength since, apart from 4/11 Sikhs, all had suffered casualties on the move from Kassala, some from air attack, a few from ground action and more from the hardship of a long, sweltering march. 2 Cameron Highlanders, for example, had lost 123 men between Kassala and its arrival on the Agordat battlefield. Nor was 10th Brigade, which had been so useful at Keru, available, having been marched back to its own division to assist in dealing with the 6,000 Italians holding Barentu. On the credit side, it was hoped in the near future to get at least some of the Matilda tanks forward to Agordat.

The plan was to use the two Indian battalions of 11th Brigade to seize the southern crests of Cochen while Lloyd's 5th Brigade, reinforced by the Camerons, broke through in the plain with the help of the tanks. The first phase started on the night of 29–30 January when 3/14 Punjabis scaled the southern face of Cochen without trouble. 1/6 Rajrifs passed through them and almost immediately ran into strong opposition. Fighting hand to hand in total darkness among huge and towering boulders, the Rajrifs found themselves against a force which was quickly reinforced to six battalions and were forced to give ground, becoming separated from the Punjabis. Both these Indian battalions were incomplete, having had to detach one rifle company to act as porters on a supply track that was being hastily improvised by the divisional sappers. It was a scrappy battle in which control was difficult as companies, platoons and even sections tended to be isolated by the ebb and flow of attack and counter-attack. The few obsolete wireless sets available functioned poorly in the mountains and the cables of field telephones were frequently cut by shell-fire. Going forward to assert personal control, Brigadier Savory found that at dawn the Rajrifs, low in numbers and lower still in ammunition, were clinging grimly to a foothold on the crest, suffering badly from the Italian mountain guns. There was little reply which the British guns, with their flatter trajectory, could make, although, on the evening of 30 January, 31st Field Regiment caught sight of gun flashes and, firing twenty-four rounds on a predicted shoot, earned a long period of blessed quiet. Earlier Savory had felt obliged to order both his battalions to make a short retreat so that they could be reorganized under cover. During 30 January two companies of Camerons seized the westerly tip of Gibraltar where it jutted out into the plain and that evening a daring patrol from the Royal Fusiliers examined the entrenchment across the plain. On receiving their report Beresford-Peirse, who had just heard of the arrival of a handful of Matildas, felt able to order a combined attack at dawn on 31 January.

At 5 am low cloud covered the summits of both Cochen and Lacquetat, blinding 'the Italian artillery spotters, as Savory's two battalions reinforced by Bengal Sappers and Miners dashed forward with the bayonet. As they loomed out of the mist they caused panic among the defenders on Cochen. The Italians mounted a counter-attack at company strength which was pressed with such determination that every attacker died on the bayonets of the Indian advanced guard, forty Rajrifs and Sappers. It took less than an hour to seize a firm hold on the south end of the mountain.

In the plain below the poor visibility worked both ways. It shielded Lloyd's brigade from observation but it confused some of them. The Royal Fusiliers, advancing on a three-company front, found their reserve company leading. On the entrenched line they found stubborn resistance but this crumpled when, out of the mist, lumbered four Matildas and the Italians found that no weapon that they had could make any apparent impression on them. To the right of this assault the Camerons dashed forward and seized a group of huge rocks jutting into the plain a thousand yards ahead of Gibraltar. From there they were able to see an Italian counter-attack force, eighteen tanks and the Blackshirt battalion, forming up in a re-entrant of Cochen. As soon as this was reported to him, Brigadier Lloyd recalled the tanks, one of them now having a jammed 2-pounder, and gave command of them to Major Colin Duncan of the Camerons. Using the Camerons' carrier platoon as bait, Duncan drew the enemy tanks from their cover. Then the Matildas opened fire at close range, destroying six medium and five light tanks. The Blackshirts broke and ran under concentrated machine gun fire. Simultaneously 3/1 Punjabis moved through the Fusiliers and seized the line of four hills at the entrance to the gorge. By dusk the main road to Asmara was a mass of fugitives, shepherded and encouraged on their flight by the Matildas. On the battlefield were found a thousand prisoners and twenty-eight Italian guns, some of large calibre. Messervy and Gazelle set out in pursuit at dawn the following morning.

Meanwhile Fifth Indian Division was fighting a hard and unnecessary battle for Barentu, the Italians reisisting strongly and making frequent counter-attacks with fresh troops. They kept Heath's two brigades out of the town but, as was inevitable, they retreated as soon as they heard of the fall of Agordat. This cut off the only serviceable road to their rear and they were forced to withdraw on a poor track towards Aressa on which they had to abandon their weapons and all but their personal arms. A single company of S.D.F. was sufficient to guard against further trouble from this direction. To the south Heath's other brigade, 9th, under Brigadier Mayne, was also on the move. The fall of Kassala had determined the Italians to abandon both Um Hagar and Gallabat. The brigade from the former was pursued by detachments of S.D.F. and a horsed squadron of Spahis, escaped from Vichy-dominated Syria, until a well-timed air strike turned the retreat into a rout. The garrison of Gallabat withdrew towards Gondar with 9th Brigade following but seriously hampered by thousands of mines sown by the enemy to cover their rear. That the brigade was able to keep up a pursuit was largely the work of 2nd Lieutenant Preminda Singh Bhagut, 21 Royal Bombay Sappers and Miners, and the citation for his VC gives the best appreciation of what he achieved:

> For a period of four days and over a distance of 55 miles this officer in the leading carrier led the column. He detected and supervised the clearing of fifteen minefields. Speed being essential, he worked at high pressure from dawn to dusk each day. On two occasions when his carrier was blown up with casualties to others, and on a third occasion when ambushed and under close enemy fire, he himself carried straight on with his task. He refused relief when worn out with fatigue and with one eardrum punctured by an explosion, on the grounds that he was now better qualified to continue his task to the end.

It should be added that mine detectors were still not being employed in the British army and that Bhagut had to rely solely on eyesight and instinct, mines being located by probing and feeling.

Mayne's brigade continued harrying the enemy as far as the village of Uahni where, as the track started to climb the main escarpment, opposition began to stiffen. Since there was no point in a single brigade attempting to storm the Ethiopian highlands, Mayne left a company of S.D.F. to guard the track and pulled his men back to the Sudan from where they set out to rejoin their division.

*　　*　　*

In Kenya the whole situation changed in mid-January when the Geological Survey Section divined a supply of water at Hagadera, almost at the mid-point in the 130-mile stretch of desert between Garissa on the Tana River and the Somaliland border at Liboi. An engineer detachment under Lieutenant A. G. Richardson immediately started drilling but were near despair as their drill approached maximum depth. Then water was struck at 356 feet and, after working round the clock to clear and line the well, 600 gallons were being produced every hour by 20 January. This transformed the situation and, four days later, Cunningham sent, by hand of officer, a pencilled note to Wavell:

> I am proposing to make an attempt at the capture of Kismayu round about February 12. The finding of water at Hagadera has released just enough transport to make it possible, and I am hoping that the enemy morale is sufficiently shaken to make up for any lack of resources.

To reward his enterprise a further well at Galmagalla, a few miles from Hagadera, was opened and started to produce 400 gallons an hour ten days after his message.

Nothing could have pleased the Commander-in-Chief more, as he was, yet again, under pressure from Churchill, who wrote:

> How can you expect me to face the tremendous strain upon our shipping, affecting as it does all our food and import of munitions, in order to carry more divisions from this country to the Middle East, when you seem opposed to taking a South African division [from Kenya] which would have less than half the distance to come?

On 28 January Wavell flew down to Nairobi to discuss and approve Cunningham's plan for an offensive into Italian Somaliland.

While there he took the opportunity of visiting Major-General G. E. Brink, G.O.C. First (S.A.) Division, then comprising 2nd and 5th (S.A.) and 25th (E.A.) Brigades, and with him flew to Dukana where 2nd Brigade was poised for a strike into Ethiopia. This operation was begun on 1 February when the brigade seized the fort at Gorai, whereupon 5th Brigade went on to take El Gumu and Hobok. No progress was made in inciting the inhabitants to revolt and it was soon borne in on Brink that he could not maintain his troops there unless the direct road Marsabit–Moyale–Mega was opened, a need made more pressing by the early start of the rains which reduced the existing tracks to such a state that even the water ration could scarcely be brought up. He therefore planned to take Mega by a two-pronged attack with 5th Brigade coming from the north and 2nd taking a long flank march through El Sod and striking from the east. Starting on the night of 14–15 February, the operation was not an unmitigated success since 2nd Brigade reported that a company, which had been posted in the wrong place, had been over-run by tanks, which turned out to be machines rather less formidable than bren-gun carriers. Thereafter brigade headquarters appear to have lost their nerve and pestered Brink with reports of illusory enemy forces attacking them from unlikely directions. Fortunately 5th Brigade did its part well and took Mega, with 1,000 prisoners and seven guns, three of them 122mm calibre, with little help, the only 2nd Brigade contribution being a single battalion arriving from an unexpected direction and three days late. It was not an operation which gave grounds for much confidence in South African commanders or in the steadiness of some of their troops, although it persuaded the Italians to evacuate Moyale voluntarily. It may also have made the enemy look to their right instead of at their Juba frontier. It also convinced the British that the way to Addis Ababa, or even to an effective Patriot revolt, did not lie through Moyale. They now knew that victory would come, if at all, through Eritrea and Somaliland. Wavell heard of the victory at Agordat on 3 February and signalled to Platt:

Now go on . . . to take Keren and Asmara.

The intention had changed from a limited advance to the total conquest of at least Eritrea.

CHAPTER 5 The Gate

IT HAD NOT needed Wavell's order to get Gazelle Force moving on towards Keren. By 8 am on 2 February they had reached the point where the road and railway crossed the Baraka River on the four-span *Ponte Mussolini*. The Italian engineers had tried to demolish the bridge but had succeeded only in cutting some of the main girders so that the trackway, though sagging, was still continuous. Messervy wanted to push his vehicles across, risking a collapse, but this was forbidden, the engineers ruling that although they could patch the bridge up for use their facilities would be insufficient to rebuild it and the already tenuous thread of a supply line would be jeopardised if the bridge was lost. Gazelle therefore set about searching for places where their vehicles could be coaxed across the wide, dry and, for the most part, steep-sided river bed, a process made no easier by the presence of a small but determined Italian rearguard which included a mountain gun. It took eight hours of intensive mine-clearing and track-building, some of it within three hundred yards of Italian machine guns, before Gazelle could get across and set out on the last forty miles to Keren.

Late in the afternoon the leading trucks of Skinner's Horse began to approach the point, five miles from the town, where the road swings sharply north to enter a cleft in a wall of towering mountains and above them, to their left, they saw the last train chugging hastily along the track into Keren and safety. Ahead of them was the Dongolaas Gorge, nowhere more than three hundred yards wide at its floor. On its eastern slope a splendidly engineered road clung part-way up the cliff while on the opposite wall the railway clawed its way across the western escarpment occasionally vanishing as it tunnelled its way

74

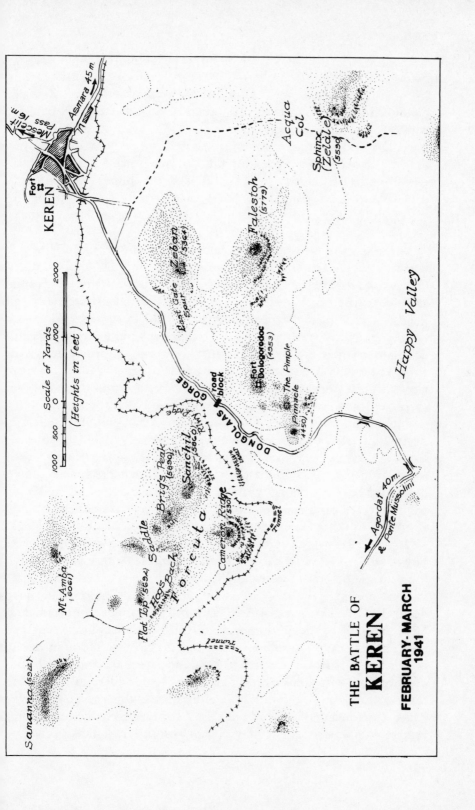

Asmara 45 m.

Mescelit Pass 16 m.

Fort KEREN

Acqua Col

Sphinx (Zelale) (5590)

Falestoh (5779)

East Gate Spur

Zeban (5364)

Fort Dologorodoc (4253)

The Pimple

Pinnacle (4450)

Happy Valley

road block

DONGOLAAS GORGE

Second Rim

Sanchil (5890)

Brig's Peak (5890)

Saddle

Porcupine

Flat Top (5694)

Hog's Back

Cameron Ridge (5530)

Tunnel

Mt Amba (6091)

Samanna (5921)

← Agordat 40m. & Ponte Mussolini

Scale of Yards
(Heights in feet)
1000   500   0   1000   2000

THE BATTLE OF

KEREN

FEBRUARY - MARCH
1941

through a spur. Above the road the entrance to the gorge is dominated by Mount Dologorodoc, rising 2,500 feet above the valley and crowned with a fort, and pushing sub-features southward. East of Dologordoc is the long mass of Mount Falestoh, 800 feet higher and, between both these heights and Keren town, Mount Zeban, scarcely lower than Falestoh, interposes itself. On the other side of the gorge the natural defences are even more formidable since Mount Sanchil, round which the railway winds, rises sheer to a hundred feet higher than Falestoh and is itself only the eastern end of a long pinnacled *massif* which, at its centre, towers 3,400 feet above the valley by which Gazelle was approaching.

As the Chevrolets of Skinner's Horse, believing themselves to be pursuing a routed enemy, nosed up towards the foot of Dologorodoc, there was a series of large explosions followed by rocky rumblings and a cloud of dust which rose from the gorge. The Italians had blown a hundred yards of the roadway down into the gorge and, to make assurance doubly sure, had brought a corresponding length of cliff down on to where the road had been. The days of 'bumming on' were over. The enemy had slammed the gate and brought the British face to face with the most powerful natural defensive position they were to encounter outside I.E.A. in the Second World War.

The position astride the Dongolaas Gorge had everything that a commander tied to the defensive could pray for, including utterly secure flanks, perfect observation and, comparatively speaking, easy access from the rear. The astonishing fact is that the Italians only decided to hold it at the very last moment. Since the beginning of the war General Frusci had convinced himself that the main attack on Eritrea would come from the north on the line Port Sudan – Massawa, an appreciation which credited the British with almost supernatural powers for supplying a substantial force across 300 miles of notably inhospitable desert. To resist any incursion from the west he pinned his faith on the Agordat – Barentu line and, if that should fail, he had decreed a last-ditch stand at Ad Teclesan, thirty miles from Asmara. How the potentialities of the gorge escaped him is inexplicable but the fact remains that it was not until Beresford-Peirse started to threaten Agordat that orders were given to prepare a covering position in front of Keren and two colonial brigades were ordered there to conduct a rearguard action. Simultaneously Addis Ababa, which seems to have had a clearer view of the realities than Asmara, despatched from the central reserve a regiment (three battalions) of Grenadiers of Savoy and some Alpini to Eritrea, a four-day journey which they only completed hours before Gazelle Force started to probe the mouth of the gorge.

Early on 3 February a second reconnaissance of the gorge was made by Skinner's Horse, reinforced by two Matildas and taking with them a sapper officer who reported not only that the road was completely impassable but that, as far as could be judged from an inevitably distant view, it would take ten days' work to reopen it. By this time Brigadier Savory had joined Messervy and two battalions of his 11th Brigade had arrived in trucks – the third battalion was toiling up on foot. Deciding on the textbook solution of seizing the high ground on either side of the road, he ordered the Rajputana Rifles to take Dologorodoc while the Cameron Highlanders captured the Sanchil massif.

The Rajrif attack never started as no forming-up place could be found, but the Camerons made a magnificent start of the battle. Despite their orders which laid down that 'the high ground to the west of the gorge must be taken and held at all costs', they committed only a single company, commanded by two second-lieutenants, to the first phase.* Their objective was 'a big unnamed feature marked "1616"' which pushes out southward from Sanchil though separated from the massif by a wide dip. They set off at 1 pm, having first to cross a mile of open ground where they attracted only some sporadic and inaccurate shelling, though their march was in full view of the enemy. By three o'clock, after a hard struggle up a steep and rocky slope, they were able to report that they had reached the railway where it enters a tunnel which took it through into the gorge itself. So far they had met no enemy but, as they climbed up towards Point 1616, they were engaged by small parties of grenadiers supported by Eritrean marksmen. These had only just reached the spot and, with a fine example of 'fire and movement', the Scotsmen were able to dispossess them of the Point, which was thereafter known as Cameron Ridge. They were able, with the last rays of the setting sun, to report this success by heliograph and, during the night, beat off three half-hearted counterattacks. They also heard from below a great subterranean rumble as

* Some authorities have said that the first attack was made by two companies, C and D, probably because the Regimental History edits together the War Diary for 3 and 4 February. From the running narrative in that work and from 2/Lt Cochrane's fascinating account *Charlie Company* it is clear that only C Company advanced on 3 February.

the Italians blocked the railway tunnel by derailing a number of trucks loaded with rock inside it. By dawn another company of the battalion had joined them and it was possible to extend a tenuous front across the whole width of the ridge.

The seizure of Cameron Ridge was a magnificent achievement and the fact that the enemy suffered eighteen casualties while the Camerons had only one man wounded is a tribute to their skill in fieldcraft. Hindsight suggests that a splendid opportunity was lost by employing only a single company. If a complete battalion could have been pushed up on to Sanchil that afternoon the whole of the feature might have been wrested from the Italians and the whole agony of the Battle of Keren averted. Hindsight, however, is always unfair to the people on the spot. There was no way in which the British could have known that Frusci had made an astonishing tactical blunder and neglected the possibilities of the defence of the gorge, possibilities which, it might be supposed, would be obvious to the youngest subaltern. It would have been absurd to assume, as was the fact, that Sanchil was defended by two companies of Grenadiers who had reached the height only as the Camerons started to climb it. A slightly more valid criticism might be that it would have been better to use both available battalions against Sanchil rather than send the Rajrifs to attack Dologorodoc, with the long, dangerous approach march, since it was dominated by Sanchil in any case.

What Cochrane's company had actually achieved with such skill was a precarious lodgement on the southern extension of the massif, an extension which was commanded by heights 500 feet higher and separated from them by a sharp ravine 1000 yards across. Sanchil itself overhung the ravine but, 500 yards to the north-west of it, was a long ridge rising to three peaks, a ridge which itself commanded Sanchil and was named on the map as Forcuta. The right-hand peak, thirty foot higher than Sanchil, was no more than 'a line of jagged knife-edged pinnacles' on which there was scarcely space to site a section. To the left of it, separated by a slight col, was a lower pinnacle, known as Centre Bump and, going left again, was a similar protuberance, about 150 yards long, nicknamed Sugarloaf. From the British side the whole Forcuta feature was extremely difficult to reach – 'it had to be climbed almost on hands and knees' – and, even if captured, did not give scope for deploying more than four platoons in defence. On the afternoon of 4 February Lieutenant-Colonel Anderson of the Camerons pointed to the right-hand, the highest, of the pinnacles and said, 'That's the peak the Brig wants', and towards evening a platoon was sent to seize what was thereafter known as Brig's Peak. They were fractionally too late. As they scrambled up the final slope of the ravine – 700 feet in 500 yards – Italian reinforcements were seen to arrive in time to drive them back.

By this time 3/14 Punjabis had marched up from Agordat and Savory sent them up to Cameron Ridge. During the night of 4–5 February they surged across the ravine and, by dawn, they held all the peaks of Forcuta and caught a glimpse of Keren town before the storm broke on them. The Italians now had four battalions, two of them 'national troops', on Sanchil and Dologorodoc and a great advantage in artillery. The 18-pounders of 31 Field Regiment R.A. and a battery of 60-pounders from 68 Medium Regiment were the most powerful on the field* but their trajectory was so flat that they could not reach to the Italian positions tucked in behind the sharp crests, a task for which the Italian 65mm mountain guns were ideal as were the 3.7" howitzers of the newly converted battery of Sudan Horse, if they could be got to within their 6,000 yards range (see p 31 fn). Above all it was ideal mortar country and each Italian battalion had six mortars while the British units had only two. The Italian bomb was smaller, 7¼ lbs compared to the British 10 lbs, but their range was 4,429 yards against the 1,600 yards which was all that the British 3" model could then attain. These Italian advantages were greatly magnified by their possession of positions from which they could observe every move made by their opponents whereas the British could only look up to the concealing crests and send Forward Observation Officers (F.O.O.) with their advancing troops and hope to gain a view point. On 5 February two out of four F.O.O.s became casualties.

On Forcuta the Punjabis were totally exposed. They were too thick on the ground for the scanty cover available and there was no chance of digging in. All they could do was to build themselves sangars of piled rocks which were of little use against the relentless bombardment to which no effective reply could be made since the guns and mortars firing at them could not be located by the British observers. Most of their officers were killed or wounded before a charge most gallantly executed by a Grenadier battalion drove them back to

---

* Most of the British batteries from India were equipped with 1918-type 18-pounders with a range of 9,800 yards, although 1 Field Regt (4 Div) and 4 Field Regt (5 Div) had the modified version (18/25-pounder) with a range of 11,800 yards. The range of the 60-pounder was 15,100 yards.

Cameron Ridge where they helped the Scottish battalion to drive off a determined Italian attack which at one time gained a foothold on the ridge. It was dark before the position was safe and during the night the Punjabis, who had suffered 116 casualties, were relieved by their 3/1 battalion from 5th Brigade. The Rajrifs had meanwhile been brought up to the tunnel as a reserve.

Seeing no easy way through the gorge, Beresford-Peirse used his divisional cavalry regiment, the Central India Horse, to search for a way round but, probing east and west, they found none. The only chance seemed to be a track, five miles east of Dongolaas, which led over the ridge east of Falestoh through Acqua Col but dominated on the right by a mountain known from its shape as Sphinx. If the col could be forced there was a chance that the defences of Falestoh could be taken from the left rear and, if Zeban could be neutralized, the track would lead straight to Keren town. It was a plan which raised many difficulties, not least that the only possible forming-up place, behind a low hill, Point 1216, south of the bridge which carried the main road up the gorge, left a four-mile approach march up a bare stretch of baked and sandy scrubland, known ironically as Happy Valley, to the col. Since this stretch was impassable to vehicles the attacking battalions would have to use one of their rifle companies for porterage and carry their machine guns, mortars and rations for three days with them. The maps available were both small and inaccurate and no detailed reconnaissance could be made. This unpromising task was allocated to Brigadier Lloyd and 5th Brigade.*

The intention was for a single battalion, 4/6 Rajputana Rifles, to seize the crest of the col whereupon the other two would pass through them to Keren but only surprise could have made it succeed and, even if the Italians had not seen the troops on their long approach march, they received sufficient warning from the switching of the artillery fire eastward to be able to ensure that the two colonial battalions guarding the ridge were alerted. A single company of Rajrifs managed to get a foothold on the objective but they were quickly encircled and could neither be relieved nor supplied. By dawn they were out of ammunition and Subedar Richpal Ram led the nine survivors back to the battalion through a ring of enemies. The Rajrifs held on to an

---

* The Brigade was without 3/1 Punjab which, as has been seen, had been sent up on to Cameron Ridge and they were replaced by 4/11 Sikhs from Gazelle Force which was now disbanded.

exposed position near the foot of the ridge throughout 8 February but were then withdrawn to the south side of Happy Valley.

Unsuccessful though this venture had been, Beresford-Peirse intended to renew it on 10 February but postponed the attack for twenty-four hours on hearing that 29th Brigade was moving over from Fifth Division at Barentu and would be available as a follow-through force although, on Platt's orders, it was not to be committed unless the Acqua Col was firmly held by 5th Brigade. This time blows were to be struck on both sides of the gorge and operations were to be started by 11th Brigade capturing Brig's Peak, thus giving the gunners an O.P. for their support of the more easterly attack. Thus at midday on 10 February a very heavy concentration of artillery – two field regiments and two medium batteries, including one newly arrived from Egypt – started to fall on the Sanchil – Forcuta heights and continued until just before dusk when 3/1 Punjabis went forward with all four companies in line. The garrison of Forcuta, 97 Colonial Battalion, was too shaken to offer resistance and, although a company of Bersaglieri which had been rushed to the spot put up a tough defence, all three peaks of Forcuta and the saddle to the left were in Indian hands. By this time, however, the Punjabis were running short of ammunition and they could only be supplied by the men of their headquarter company carrying it across the wide, mortar-swept ravine from Cameron Ridge. A counter-attack re-took Brig's Peak but it was promptly seized again and at dawn 1/6 Rajrifs were moving up to reinforce the Punjabis who were now down to 179 all ranks. The return of daylight decided the matter. The Italians saturated the whole of Forcuta with accurate shell and mortar fire, and, reinforced by a battalion of Alpini, were able to mount flanking attacks from both Sanchil on one flank and Mount Amba on the other. Seeing that if they stayed on the pinnacled ridge, both battalions would be destroyed, Brigadier Savory recalled them to Cameron Ridge where the Punjabis, having lost 198 men, were reorganized into two weak companies. For the time being 11th Brigade was a spent force.

Even though the O.P. on Brig's Peak had not been retained, Beresford-Peirse allowed the second attack on Acqua Col to go forward on 11 February. Despite their earlier losses Lloyd again sent 4/6 Rajrifs against the col itself but this time had 4/11 Sikhs attack Sphinx on their right and kept the Fusiliers in reserve. A heavy artillery preparation, switched from Forcuta, preceded them but it was not enough, the defenders having excellent cover and ample warning of attack. Both battalions dashed forward with extraordinary courage but both were halted by machine gun fire and a hail of 'red devil'* grenades. Some parties reached the crest of the col only to be counter-attacked repeatedly. Once again Richpal Ram distinguished himself, continuing to command his company though unable, through a wound, to walk. He received the second Indian VC of the war but, sadly, it was a posthumous award. One Sikh company attacked eighty-seven strong but brought only seventeen unwounded men out of action. The attack was called off, the brigade brought back and Happy Valley left to a screen of Central India Horse.

The first attempt to capture Keren had been a costly failure. The two brigades involved had been fought to a standstill and of the seven battalions committed six had suffered losses equivalent to at least one of their rifle companies. Losses in officers had been particularly severe with, for example, 3/1 Punjabis losing their commanding officer, second-in-command, three company commanders and six other officers. All that had been achieved was a tenuous hold on a sub-feature of the dominating mass of Sanchil. Dologorodoc and Acqua Col appeared unapproachable and Sanchil itself impregnable. There was no way round. The only course open, short of abandoning the advance, was to bring forward Fifth Indian Division, a move which would more than double the strain on the supply line which already, by any Staff College assessment, was stretched beyond endurance. This dictated a pause while stores, especially artillery ammunition, were dumped immediately behind the front, but this pause could not last long since, before the end of March, the rains were due and they would make the track which formed the supply line impassable. During this pause Platt directed that Fifth Division, held back near the Sudan frontier to reduce its demands on transport, should undergo a short but intensive course in mountain warfare. Fourth Division was left with the unenviable task of clinging to its conquest, Cameron Ridge.

*   *   *

Not the least of the reasons for this initial failure at Keren was a serious and all-pervasive underestimate of the fighting qualities of the

* Painted bright red, these grenades were extremely light, about half the weight of a British Mills Bomb (36 grenade), and could be thrown much further. The injuries they inflicted were unlikely to be fatal but were sufficiently disabling to require that the victim be evacuated from the battlefield.

enemy. The uselessness of Italians as soldiers had been an accepted truth in the British army since the débâcle at Caporetto in October, 1917, and had been underlined by their disastrous defeat in the Western Desert, a defeat in which Beresford-Peirse and Fourth Indian Division had played a most prominent role. Their poor defence of Agordat followed immediately by news of their spectacular desert defeat at Beda Fomm convinced Beresford-Peirse and his men that they would not stand against constant heavy pressure. It overlooked the fact that, like the soldiers of many nations, Italians vary in quality. As a generalization it may be true that southern Italy does not produce good infantry but those from the north-west compare well with any in Europe. Napoleon did not make a mistake when he placed special confidence in his north Italian troops and it was universally acknowledged that Italian gunners were as competent and as steady as any in the world. The 'national' troops at Keren – Grenadiers, Bersaglieri and Alpini – were *élite* units and fought as such and while there was considerable desertion among the colonial troops – 1,500 are said to have crossed the lines by mid-February – the askaris from Eritrea were magnificent fighters and would press home counter-attacks again and again. The defenders of Keren were not soldiers to underrate.

Moreover the odds were stacked in Italy's favour. It was a magnificent natural defensive position and its advantages were magnified since its convolutions were inaccurately shown on the small maps available to the British. They had a clear numerical advantage and, although much of their equipment would have been obsolete in European warfare, their mountain guns, old as they were, were more suited to the intricate terrain than the more modern, flat-trajectory British guns. Their mortars were superior in range and numbers and, for both guns and mortars, they had the advantage. of superb observation. Their supply problems were simple, since a railway led from Massawa to the battlefield itself and there were good metalled roads leading to Asmara and Addis Ababa, whereas the British were fighting at the end of a single deteriorating road leading back 209 miles to railhead at Kassala over which everything had to be hauled in an inadequate fleet of decrepit trucks.

Naturally the Italians had their problems, many of their own making. Frusci's inexplicable blunder in deciding that, once Agordat had fallen, the army should fall back to the far less formidable position at Ad Teclesan meant that there was no time fully to fortify the Keren barrier. He chose the immensely able General Nicolangelo Carmineo, a 53-year-old veteran of the 1935–36 campaign and of the Spanish Civil War, to command the covering action at Keren. He reached the town, bringing with him a colonial brigade, only on the morning of 1 February to find two battalions of askaris guarding the gorge supported by four mountain batteries and two squadrons of native cavalry. Just arrived in the town were three battalions of grenadiers, debussing from their journey from the capital. The little town itself was chaotic as fugitives from Keru and Agordat flooded in. He deployed the 6,500 formed troops available to him to deny the gorge and its bastions to the first British attack and had his engineers blast away the road through the gorge just in time to prevent Beresford-Peirse's handful of Matildas cutting their way through. He ignored Frusci's order to fight only a rearguard action and set his men to digging themselves cover with the aid of plentiful supplies of explosives which, by a fortunate chance, happened to be stored nearby and, wherever possible, deploying quantities of barbed wire. He narrowly frustrated the first assualt of 11th Brigade and, by 7 February, deployed twelve battalions between Sphinx on his left and Mount Amba on his right. In reserve were two more battalions and a company of light tanks. He even converted Frusci to the idea of defending Keren and, on 8 February, the senior general issued an order of the day calling on every unit to 'constitute a strongpoint and be prepared to live or die in apparent isolation'. Two days later Frusci demanded from Carmineo a colonial brigade and the Alpini battalion to counter a thrust into Eritrea from the north.

Frusci had always regarded an attack from the north as the chief threat to his command. This line of approach had few attractions to the British. From railhead at Suakin to Massawa is 300 miles of sand, crossed by a track which was not always identifiable, and, very occasionally, a well. Communications between Kassala and Keren were deplorable; between Suakin and Massawa they were non-existent. Moreover, having committed almost all the available troops and trucks to the advance through Kassala, there was little left for a second offensive, only two battalions of 7th Indian Brigade* (Brigadier H. R. Briggs) which had been assigned to guarding Port Sudan and keeping the Italian reconnaissance aircraft occupied by building real and make-believe camps and supply dumps. While it was admitted that supply considerations would mean that only a small

---

* 4/11 Sikhs had been detached to Gazelle Force.

force could operate south of Suakin, it was unrealistic to suppose that two battalions without artillery and with very few vehicles could make any significant advance into Eritrea. The situation changed early in the New Year when there arrived at Port Sudan the Free French *Brigade d'Orient*, commanded by Colonel Monclar, and consisting of 14me *bataillon* of the Foreign Legion, which had fought in Norway, and an improvised unit from Equatorial Africa, 3me *bataillon de marche (Tchad)*, known, after its commanding officer, as *Bataillon Garby*. These two brigades, making, with supporting troops, less than 6,000 men in all, could not be supplied by the number of vehicles available, so that, if any operation to the south was to be undertaken, the first objective must be some kind of harbour, not that, in the accepted military sense, any sea transport was available. The deciding factor was the information that the resistance likely to be met would be very slight. Most of the garrison of that part of the colony had been requisitioned by Carmineo for the defence of Keren and all that was left were a few *bande* and 112 Colonial Battalion, which was stationed 120 miles south of the frontier at Cub-Cub, the only source of water in the area.

The advance started on 2 February when 1 Royal Sussex moved against the captured frontier post of Karora supported by about 100 Sudanese tribesmen organized as Meadowforce. Their presence was fortunate since, when two companies of the Sussex, mounted in all the available trucks, attacked the post, they ground to a halt in the soft sand and it was left to the Sudanese to evict the garrison of 200 irregulars and customs men. Once the post was secure, Briggs launched his mobile force against the port of Mersa Taklai. It was not a very formidable force, a company of the Sussex with their carrier platoon and that of 4/16 Punjabis – but their objective was not a very impressive port. It was no more than a fishing harbour consisting of a bay about 130 yards wide on one side of which a breakwater ran out to the coral reef. On the other side there was what the R.A.F. had left of a jetty. In the deeper parts of the harbour there were seven feet of water and the village consisted of a lighthouse, half-a-dozen buildings of masonry and a scatter of huts. The nearest fresh water was ten miles inland.

It took the mobile force twenty-four hours to cover less than fifty miles from Karora but when they arrived Mersa Taklai fell with little more than a skirmish which yielded sixty-five prisoners who were put to improving the port facilities. On 16 February the first convoy sailed in, consisting of six dhows, which, as soon as they had been unloaded by the prisoners, returned to bring forward *Bataillon Garby*, who could bring only their rifles and l.m.gs as all their heavy weapons had to be brought up in trucks when these became available. Soon the sea transport was augmented by two small Egyptian coastal steamers but these could not pass the coral reef and had to unload their cargoes into the dhows to enter the harbour. All stores had to be manhandled off the breakwater or jetty and the most welcome reinforcement was a company of the Sudanese Labour Corps who not only supplemented the prisoners in the unloading but, wholly by manual labour, succeeded in sinking some usable wells.

Meanwhile the Sussex were pushing on and coming close to Cub-Cub and were close enough to Fourth Division facing Keren for wireless touch to be established between the two forces, conversations being conducted by two Indian Army officers in Pushtu to avoid the necessity of using code. It was this threat that induced Frusci to demand reinforcements from Carmineo who, after a delay, parted reluctantly with a colonial brigade. This was not in time to save Cub-Cub which Briggs took on 22 February, using the Sussex on one flank and *Bataillon Garby* on the other, while the place was bombarded by a battery of 25th Field Regiment which had just completed the 800-mile drive from Kassala by way of Port Sudan. Cub-Cub yielded 400 prisoners, a large depot of stores and, most valuable of all, a plentiful supply of water. Next morning 4/16 Punjabis took over the lead and for twenty miles advanced unopposed until, as they were approaching the 4,000-foot Mescelit Pass, their carrier platoon was engaged by Italian light tanks. The fact that the carriers induced the tanks to retreat is a telling commentary on the inadequacy of the tanks. It took the Punjabis only two days to fight their way through the formidable natural defences of the pass, but on 26 February, when they were within seven miles of Keren town, their progress was decisively blocked by the 7,000-foot-high Mount Engiahat which was the right rear of Carmineo's main defence and was strongly garrisoned.

Nor was this threat to their rear the only source of anxiety to the command in Eritrea. They had lost command of the air since the opening of the Takoradi route by which aircraft could be shipped to the Gold Coast (Ghana), erected at Takoradi and then flown by way of Lagos, Kano, Maiduguri (NE Nigeria), Geneina (SW Sudan) and Khartoum to Egypt, a journey of 3,697 miles flown in six stages of between 378 and 754 miles. It will be noticed that this route would have been impracticable if the Italians had successfully invaded the Sudan and very difficult to use if French Equatorial Africa had decided to throw in its lot with Vichy since for 600 miles the aircraft had to overfly Chad. In fact this route had been in use for a commercial trans-Africa service since 1926 and weekly fights from Takoradi to Khartoum had been flown since 1936. Not that this meant that the airstrips used were capable of handling heavy military traffic and, no preparations having been made before the fall of France, intensive work was needed to get the route into operation, not the least the establishment of an assembly plant in the Gold Coast. The first draft of airmen landed there on 21 August and the first flight of planes, having been uncrated and erected, took off on 20 September. It comprised one Blenheim and six Hurricanes.

The result of this trans-continental ferry service began to be seen in the Sudan when, in December, 1940, a start was made with re-equipping 1 Squadron S.A.A.F, the main source of fighters in support of Platt's army, with Hurricanes, of which they eventually received ten, in place of their out-classed Gladiators. On 16 December Captain K. Driver, S.A.A.F, shot down a Savoia Marchetti 79 bomber and the pendulum of air superiority began to swing towards the attackers. As soon as Platt's advance had captured the airfields at Sabderat, Agordat and Barentu, the elderly bombers were able to attack all the Eritrean airbases with Hurricane escort and the Hurricanes made many successful sweeps on their own. In late January, 1941, 1 Squadron S.A.A.F, made dawn raids on the airfields at Asmara and Guru destroying fifty Italian aircraft on the ground. There was also a marked decrease in Italian attacks on troops on the move but the *Regia Aeronautica* did not give up the struggle. In two raids on Agordat (8 and 9 February) they destroyed seven planes, one of them a Hurricane, and damaged six (two Hurricanes). The proof of air superiority lay in the fact that during the Keren battles it was possible to supply the fighting troops along 200 miles of road almost devoid of anti-aircraft guns, without serious interference from an enemy air force which was numerically superior. More than that, the R.A.F. and S.A.A.F. under Air Commodore L. H. Slatter gave the army close support on demand in a way that it was going to take other commands a long time to learn and this despite the official policy of the Air Staff in London which still regarded army co-operation as an improper use of air power.

This was a hopeful sign for the future but did not directly assist with answering the crucial problem of how to tackle the Keren defences. Already Wavell, increasingly pressed for men and aircraft, was calling for speedy action. He signalled to Platt on 12 February:

Essential to continue the campaign . . . until northern Eritrea up to Massawa captured.

It was on that day that General Erwin Rommel reached Tripoli.

CHAPTER 6 The Backdoors

TWO DAYS AFTER Platt launched the Indian divisions into Eritrea Haile Selassie returned to his country. On 20 January he was flown to an airstrip near Um Iddla where a dry watercourse marks the frontier with the Sudan. Accompanied by Wingate, both men wearing unfashionably large sun helmets, he was saluted by a company of S.D.F. before descending into the river bed; on reaching the far bank a company of 2 Ethiopian Battalion⋆ presented arms with their Springfield rifles, part of a consignment sent by the United States to Britain to arm the Home Guard. Then he hoisted the Ethiopian flag with his own hands and left by truck for a camp that had been prepared for him thirty miles from the border. Despite the hardships and dangers that faced him, he was glad to escape the suffocating idleness of his stay at Khartoum.

On crossing the border he issued a proclamation to his people:

> From one end of Ethiopia to the other, raise your arms against the enemy who has come to destroy your race, to rob your property, to belittle your glory, to pollute your blood. Wipe him from the face of Ethiopia!
>
> Italy is seized in the grip of the great English, by sea, air and land power. The Italians in Ethiopia will not escape from my trusty warriors.
>
> In our own name and in your name, We thank before the world the Government and the people of Great Britain for their touching and unforgettable charity and hospitality to Us during Our bitter trials.†

⋆ 1 Ethiopian Battalion had been broken up to provide the Ethiopian personnel for the Operational Centres (see p 44). 3 and 4 Battalions were still under training.
† This was putting a charitable gloss on his feelings. The Emperor believed that he had recently frustrated a plot to detach his Galla subjects from his empire and establish a British protectorate over them.

At the same time he made a generous appeal to the Ethiopians:

> I reason with you to receive with love and care those Italians who fall into the hands of Ethiopian warriors, whether they come armed or unarmed. Do not mete to them according to the wrongs which they have committed against our people. Show that you are soldiers of honour with human hearts. Do not forget that, because the soldiers of the Adowa campaign brought to their Emperor the Italian prisoners, that has been to the honour and good name of Ethiopia.
>
> Especially do I ask you to guard and respect the lives of children, women and the aged.

This appeal was heeded more than might have been expected but the Italians continued to dread the reprisals which they saw as inevitable if they were defeated. They had never believed that Menelik had dealt as generously as was possible with his Italian (as opposed to his Eritrean) prisoners after Adowa. Their dread was to be a potent factor for the rest of the campaign.

The plan, agreed by Sandford and Wingate at their November meeting, was to start by raising a revolt in western Gojjam, the most isolated of the accessible provinces, but, since the escarpment which marked the border of that province lay more than a hundred miles from the Sudan across inhospitable terrain, an intermediate base would be needed. To secure this a company of the Frontier Battalion, S.D.F, with a convoy of 160 camels carrying 1000 rifles, 250,000 rounds of ammunition and 70,000 Maria Theresa thalers had set out from Roseires on the last day of November to secure a position on Mount Belaya, a massif which rises 7,000 feet out of the plain between the frontier and the escarpment. The company commander, Bimbashi Peter Acland, had orders to hand his stores over to Sandford, to co-operate with the local Ethiopian magnate, Fitauri Taffare Zelleke, to carry out active patrolling which would discourage Italian activity, and, last but far from least, to clear an airstrip 1,000 yards square to the north-east of the mountain. For this task he had, exclusive of camel drivers, 180 men and, since such things were short in the Sudan, no wireless set.

It took Acland seventeen days to reach Belaya. The track, never good, had become overgrown with thorn, scrub and tall grass and loaded camels could not use it until the Sudanese had cut a way through the undergrowth with their pangas and, with shovels, graded the way through the steep-sided gullies. Their route took them through the country of the Gumuz, backward tribesmen who were

7. A Wellesley on its way to Keren.

8. The Emperor Haile Selassie in conversation with Major Orde Wingate.

9. The Emperor Haile Selassie hoisting the Ethiopian flag near Um Iddla, 20 January, 1941.

10. Consultation in Gideon Force: *left to right* Brigadier D. A. Sandford, the Emperor, Lieutenant-Colonel Orde Wingate.

11. The pontoon bridge over the River Juba at Yonte.

12. The Marda position. The road winds over the ridge in the left centre with, on the left, Observation Hill and part of Saddle Hill. To the right are Marda's Breasts and Camel Saddle Hill.

13. The Marda Pass, showing the crater blown by the Italians in the Via Imperiale.

antipathetic to Italians, Amharas, Britons and, most of all, Sudanese and it proved impossible to obtain food on the way, so that, in the latter stages, the column lived largely on the meat from their dead camels. When they reached Belaya they found Fitauri Taffare amiable and willing to help, but his own men had little food and there were no mules. This was most serious since camels are pernickety in their diet and die in mountainous country. This fact was to affect the whole conduct of operations but its immediate result was that Acland's men had to manhandle the arms and ammunition up the steepest part of the mountain. Then the surviving camels set out on the return journey taking with them a report from Acland saying that he saw no prospect of building an airstrip with the manpower available and that, although they were glad to receive rifles, Taffare's men were unwilling to take offensive action without the support of regular troops.

In Cairo on 6 December Wavell had called a conference of the East African commanders and at one session Wingate, though still only a major, was invited to address the meeting for ten minutes. He extended this time to half an hour and gave a greatly exaggerated account of the way in which guerrilla operations could 'cause the Italian Empire to waste away from within'. He claimed that if most of the British troops were withdrawn, leaving only enough to hold the ring, his own activities would bring about an Italian surrender by May, 1941. None of the senior officers who were present believed his optimistic claims but all were impressed by his dedication and sincerity* and he was authorised to take the Emperor into Ethiopia:

> The ultimate object [being] to seize an Italian stronghold in Gojjam, preferably Dangila, install the Emperor nearby, and from this centre to widen the area of revolt and desertion.

Many of his preparations were already well advanced. 18,000 camels had been assembled at Roseires where the experts of the Sudan Veterinary Service

> sweated the day long in the scorching sun, serving and sorting the convoys, turning away immature animals, repairing the gaping wounds that rutting camels inflict on each other, settling the countless queries of their drivers, arranging pay and conditions.

* There is no evidence to support the story, possibly based on Wingate's subsequent unguarded talk, that he blackguarded the assembled generals (See, for example, Leonard Mosley's *Gideon goes to War* pp 108–09). Any such behaviour would have ruined his chances and Wingate was acute enough to recognize the fact.

Fortunately there was available a cadre of men who had seen service in the Sudan Camel Corps before it was mechanized and who, being used to discipline, were invaluable in sorting out 'the chaotic herds of grunting, gurgling, snuffling and groaning animals' into manageable groups. It was unfortunate that government saddles were only in sufficient supply to be issued for the regimental transport – a mass demand for camel saddles had not been foreseen – which meant that only native saddles capable of carrying 250 lbs were available, whereas with a government saddle a camel could carry 450 lbs.

Apart from 2 Ethiopians, scarcely a highly trained unit, the regular content of the force consisted only of the Frontier Battalion, S.D.F, but this was a very remarkable unit. It had been raised in May, 1940, and, although the ranks had been filled with recruits, the Sudanese officers and NCOs were picked men from the whole of the S.D.F. and the training had been intensive. The British officers included a few regulars but were mostly drawn from the Sudanese Civil Service and the Cotton Syndicate and its excellence derived largely from the character of its commanding officer. Hugh Boustead was, in a very different way, as remarkable a man as Wingate. The outbreak of the First World War had found him serving as a midshipman in an elderly cruiser on the Cape Station but, after July, 1916, when the German cruiser *Königsberg* had been sunk off German East Africa, he had convinced himself that he would see no action during the war and deserted his ship to enlist in the ranks of the South African Scottish. He was a captain by 1918, having served in Egypt and on the Western front, when he volunteered for the military mission being sent to Denikin's army in southern Russia and it was while he was serving against the Bolsheviks that he received a royal pardon for his desertion from the navy. Having spent a year reading Russian at Oxford, during which he won the army lightweight boxing championship and was a member of the British pentathlon team in the 1920 Olympics, he was given a regular commission in the Gordon Highlanders, only to seek secondment to the Sudan where he rose to command the Camel Corps after having taken part in the Ruttledge expedition which attempted Everest in 1933. At the end of his secondment he was offered and accepted a post of District Commissioner in the Sudan and was thus the obvious choice to command the Frontier Battalion when it was raised.

Wingate had met Boustead during his service in the S.D.F. and both men had considerable respect for each other, but, while both were eccentrics and adventurers, they were very different types of soldier. While Wingate was passionate and usually scruffy, Boustead was cool and fastidious about both his appearance and his food. Their relationship was difficult from the start due to the anomalous command structure of 101 Mission of which Wingate was in command by default since his seniors were inside Ethiopia and, for most of the time, out of touch, although he was still only a major while Boustead was a colonel* and knew more than Wingate about the problems of command, staff work and fighting. Things were made no easier when, at their first meeting in Khartoum, Wingate demanded to know why the Frontier Battalion was idling away its time in Roseires (where its companies had just been brought together for the first time) instead of fighting in Ethiopia.

Nevertheless it was Wingate who was going to lead the advance into Gojjam and at Christmas he flew down to Roseires to explain his plans to the older man. The Frontier Battalion was to follow in Acland's path to Belaya while 2 Ethiopians were to escort the Emperor to the same destination if, as seemed certain, he could not go there by air. What worried Boustead was that Wingate and the Emperor were to make their journey by the shortest possible route, marching on a compass bearing, but he raised no objection until he had persuaded the R.A.F. to fly him low over the area and had convinced himself that the direct route was impracticable. Then he flew up to Khartoum, where he found Wingate reading *Pride and Prejudice* in a cold bath, and tried to argue him out of undertaking a march which seemed likely to prove impossible. Wingate was not to be moved, asserting that he and he alone was responsible for the Emperor's safety.

The Frontier Battalion, hampered by a convoy of camels, took two weeks to cross the Sakkala wilderness using the track that Acland had improved. They had been on Mount Belaya for a week and had all but completed the airstrip when the solitary figure of Wingate 'rode in . . . bearded, dishevelled, filthy and worn on a drooping horse' on the last day of January. He had the generosity to admit that he had been wrong about the direct route but, having covered the first part of his ride, he sent back word to Haile Selassie and his entourage that the way was

---

*His Sudanese rank was *Miralai*, equivalent to colonel although wearing the crown and three stars of a brigadier. The other British ranks in the S.D.F. were *Kaimakam* (lieutenant-colonel) and *Bimbashi* (major) and in each case they wore the distinctions of the next rank higher in the British service.

passable and that they should set off in the hired market trucks which formed the imperial transport. Had he delayed this message for twenty-four hours, it would never have been sent for the last forty miles of the journey turned out to be across a tangled countryside of thick thorn interspersed with rocky ridges and stream beds and was impassable to camels and far more so to vehicles. It was 6 February before the indomitable but exhausted Emperor was escorted into Boustead's position astride the Burgi valley north-east of Mount Belaya.

So far there had been no sign of the enemy apart from some ineffective bombing. The only Italian post in the plains had been a small garrison at Gubba which had been frightened away by Patriot threats, lively feints by Acland's men and two sharp air attacks. Above the escarpment the defence of Gojjam was in the hands of Colonel Torelli who had sixteen colonial battalions, four Blackshirt units and two groups of *bande*. These he had deployed in a series of fortified towns on the main road which crossed the Blue Nile at Safartak to Bahrdar Giorgis at the southern end of Lake Tana which was in touch, mostly by boat, with the garrison of Gondar. The road being good, passable in all weather except for the stretch between Bahrdar and Enjibara, Torelli was able to move his troops laterally to counter any threat, and the countryside, a lush and rolling plain between the western escarpment and the Chokey (Ciocche) mountains, was unsuitable for guerrilla activities. The *bande* were posted forward to act as a screen on the natural barrier where the ground rose very sharply from the Sakkala wilderness and this was the weakest point in the defence since the operations of Sandford and news of the Emperor's approach were sapping the loyalty of the irregulars and leading to desertion. To counter this the Italians had sent to Debra Marcos their most influential Ethiopian collaborator, Ras Hailu.

Now in his early seventies, Hailu was descended, albeit illegitimately,* from the hereditary rulers of Gojjam and had been Governor of that province for almost a quarter of a century from 1908. He had always been an opponent of Haile Selassie and had been a focus of the disaffection felt by reactionary elements, clerical and lay, against the Emperor's attempts at reform. At the same time he was a very cautious man, particularly attached to the splendour and luxury in

---

* The ease of divorce and remarriage in Ethiopia, a practice of which Ras Hailu was a notable exponent, made considerations of legitimacy largely irrelevant.

which he lived in his capital of Debra Marcos to which he brought in pieces, a Rolls Royce and, while it was being assembled, constructed a paved street on which it could be driven. Nothing could be proved against him until 1932, while leisurely negotiations were in progress for the marriage of his daughter to the Crown Prince, when he was shown to be implicated in the escape of the putative Emperor Lij Isayu (see p 10), who had for a short time been his son-in-law. This earned him a fine of 300,000 thalers and banishment from Gojjam. When the Italians invaded he was brought to Addis Ababa lest he should collaborate with them and when Haile Selassie had to leave his captial in May, 1936, Hailu, more or less under arrest, travelled on the same train. On arrival at Diredawa the Emperor came under the protection of the small French garrison (see p 10), but while France, with British assistance, was prepared to ensure the Emperor's safety, they declined to extend their protection to his state prisoners. Hailu therefore took the next train back to the capital and made his peace with the conquerors. His great ambition was to be restored to the governorship of Gojjam – as the Emperor's son-in-law, Haile Selassie Gugsa, had been restored to Eastern Tigre – but he was too tricky a character to be allowed back to his old power base. As the Viceroy, Marshal Graziani, claimed to trust him, even pardoning some notabilities on his recommendation during his savage purge, he allowed him to recruit a private army, but he was constrained to live in Addis Ababa. In February, 1941, the Duke of Aosta, realizing that a crisis was approaching, sent him and his 6,000 men back to Gojjam as the only man whose influence might enable him to compete in respect and popularity with Haile Selassie. A British officer who saw him at Debra Marcos thought that the old man had 'something of the obese but royal dignity' of the Hogarth portrait of Simon, Lord Lovat, who was executed for his support of the Young Pretender in the rebellion of 1745. In fact his part in events was more reminiscent of the Earl of Derby during the Bosworth campaign of 1485 as he managed to sit on the fence to the bitter end.

Ras Hailu had no doubt that, with his private army, he could defeat Haile Selassie and the thin gathering of Patriots who had rallied to him, but fighting the British was quite another matter, the more so since Italian intelligence was, once more, contriving to represent their army's position as untenable. At Debra Marcos it was firmly believed that the British were moving on Gojjam with two regular brigades supported by artillery and 10,000 irregulars. The logistic problems involved in moving such a host across the Sakkala wilderness and getting them up the escarpment do not appear to have occurred to them. The result was that both Hailu and Torelli were convinced that they were threatened by an immensely powerful force and, true to his nature, Hailu decided that procrastination was the better part of valour. He stayed at Debra Marcos and waited to see how things turned out.

The British were having their own difficulties with the command of 101 Mission and, as soon as the Emperor had reached Mount Belaya, Khartoum issued a directive aiming to make sense of the situation. Sandford was promoted brigadier and appointed political and military adviser to the Emperor while Wingate was made a lieutenant-colonel and given command of the British and Ethiopian forces 'Serving with the Emperor in the field'. This, at least, gave him command over Hugh Boustead (although the latter was still a rank senior) but further confused his relations with Sandford since he was told to obtain the latter's agreement to all military operations and to consult the Emperor through Sandford even though Wingate was with the Emperor and Sandford was, for the most part, away from him. There was no chance of such an arrangement working smoothly and on 11 February, the landing strip having been completed, both men flew back to Khartoum for consultations with Platt. Their orders were clear enough – to disrupt Italian communications to the north, west and south of Addis Ababa, but doing no damage to the few existing roads, and to tie down as many enemy troops as possible. No progress was made on the vital questions of their co-operation. All that was done was to lay down a system that might have worked if the two men had been experienced bureaucrats with plenty of secretarial support but was absurd when applied to two individualists, one of whom was notoriously averse to accepting orders, operating without staffs in broken country in the midst of a large enemy force.

During the Khartoum meeting Boustead and the Frontier Battalion were looking for a way up the escarpment, 'a cliff-like rampart rising over three thousand feet above the plain'. These probings greatly alarmed the Italians who voluntarily evacuated the strongpoint of Enjibara and, when a platoon of S.D.F. fought a small action with a patrol near Tuma, pulled the garrison of Dangila back northward to Bahrdar Giorgis thus decisively breaking the line of fortified posts across the province. Meanwhile others of the Frontier Battalion had discovered a passable track that led to the plateau near Makatal and was unguarded.* By this time Wingate was back from Khartoum and announced his arrival by abandoning the prosaic title of 101 Mission in favour of the more dashing Gideon Force, a name that reflected his Zionist proclivities, and decided to strike at once while the enemy was off-balance. He estimated that there were 14,000 colonial troops, apart from *bande*, around Bahrdar Giorgis and 17,000 more between Burye and Debra Marcos where there were also Hailu's 6,000, while Gideon Force was less than 2,000 strong and had the still luke-warm support of about 3,000 Patriots. But he believed that, by maintaining a bold front, he could stampede the enemy out of Gojjam. There was one unavoidable difficulty. Despite the efforts of Sandford and the Emperor's emissaries, mules were not to be had and thousands were needed. It followed that, despite their unsuitability, camels would have to be taken into the highlands well knowing that it would certainly kill them.

By 19 February Gideon Force had reached the top of the Makatal Pass without casualties, except among the camels, and Wingate detached No. 2 Operational Centre with a company of the Frontier Battalion and about 1000 Patriots to keep the Italians round Bahrdar in check. As soon as enough supplies had been brought up the escarpment he led the rest of his force, 2 Ethiopians and the Frontier Battalion, both less one company, southwards aiming for the bridge over the Blue Nile at Safartak. Between Gideon and their objective lay two substantial fortified towns, Burye and Debra Marcos, and a number of smaller strongpoints, and Wingate planned first to contrive the fall of Burye by threatening the fort at Mankusa, six miles beyond it. This, in theory, was the classic guerrilla tactic of using a small mobile force to menace the retreat of a larger static enemy. As it happened, the commander at Burye, Colonel Natale, had already made up his mind to retreat to Debra Marcos as soon as a convincing show of force allowed him to claim that honour was satisfied. The threat to his rear had the effect of delaying his withdrawal.

The flank march from Enjibara to Mankusa showed Wingate's limitations. Pistol in hand, he led the column in person, followed, for political reasons, by 2 Ethiopians. It was a long column since it included, apart from the Sudanese, No 1 (Australian-led) Operational

---

* It is not clear why the finding of the Makatal Pass came as a surprise to both the Italians and 101 Mission. It had been found five years earlier by Maj. E. Chapman Andrews who was serving with Sandford. He had published an account of it in *Lake Tana and the Blue Nile* (1936)

Centre, a platoon of four mortars and a long column of camels. The march was chaotic.

> There was no estimate how far this four-mile camel column could march before daylight, no plan for a day camp, no reconnaissance for cover from the air, or defence on the ground, over open downland where no near cover was available for a force of this size. . . . Chance led our going, chance covered our day move, and some tolerant Deity protected us. . . . The blocks, halts and telescoping continued through the night. It was already past midnight when the force was held up by a blown bridge. Steep double banks led down to a rushing stream, bordered by a strip of fringing forest. The ramping of this crossing and the slow progress of leading 700 camels over singly in the black darkness was clearly impracticable.
>
> The sorting of this inconceivable tangle of camels was a long and exasperating performance. It was broad daylight before the last lagging camels were in and the companies concealed in tiny groups, when the familiar hum of Caproni bombers rose and swelled in the morning air. They flew low over the tree-tops searching the flanks of the main road. They circled round for ten miles while the whole force froze into stillness.

Wingate had hoped to cover thirty miles during that first night but had only managed fifteen and the next night's march was certain to be more difficult as he had to abandon the road and by-pass Burye. To reduce the problems he decided to lead with a group of thirty Ethiopians who would light guiding beacons on each successive ridge. This had the effect of throwing the intervening valleys into even deeper shadow so he stationed more men at intervals who were to guide the column by whistling a pre-arranged signal. None of this stopped part of the force wandering off into the night.

> The Ethiopian soldiers left by Wingate to make the call sign by whistling were quite unable to make a sound through their pursed lips. They stood in frozen stupidity, making a sibilant hiss which could be heard five yards away with difficulty. The scene culminated in one enthusiastic fire tender spreading a grass fire that lit a huge area of downland, effectively obliterating all beacon lights.

Once more Gideon Force failed to cover the distance Wingate had estimated and throughout the following day they had to shelter and take some much-needed rest in woodland within five miles of Burye but Natale sent out no patrols and relied on aircraft to locate his enemy, which they signally failed to do. Wingate, who had never commanded more than a company, was having to learn from his own mistakes, but he had every assistance from his opponent who showed a barely credible timidity and lack of initiative.

Reconnaissance showed that the defences of Burye consisted of a central fortified hill encircled by four smaller hills, entrenched and cleared of cover on their approaches. It was a much stronger position than Gideon Force could attempt to storm and even a serious attack on the far less formidable Mankusa could only have succeeded with unacceptable casualties. Since Natale showed no sign of withdrawing, Wingate decided to send the Ethiopian battalion far beyond both places so as to cut the road to Debra Marcos while harassing Burye and Mankusa with the Frontier Battalion and such few Patriots as were prepared to take active part. A number of feints, supported by mortars, were made, the Sudanese, despite the restraint of their officers, tending to press their attacks too far and drawing heavy retaliatory fire, most of it aimed too high. Natale used his cavalry to counter-attack and, on different occasions, almost succeeded in capturing both Wingate and Boustead. There was little appearance of anything being achieved and the two men were frequently on the verge of a serious quarrel. Then the R.A.F. attacked Burye. Natale was not to know that, owing to the demands of the Eritrean front, this was the last air support that Gideon was to receive but finally made up his mind to retreat. He was haunted by fears for the safety of the Italian women and children in Burye and he had convinced himself, wrongly, that Mankusa was on the point of surrender. On 4 March:

> The clotted Italian column, twenty files across wherever there was order in it, swarmed down the road. Disorderly *bande* protected the flanks. Four armoured cars and an Italian officer with a flag led the 4,000 regular [colonial] troops. Two regiments of cavalry brought up the rear. With the troops were the men and women and children of a long occupation and the Ethiopian chiefs who feared vengeance.

Harassed by attacks from low-flying aircraft, the Frontier Battalion clung closely to the Italian rear but the only hope of stopping Natale's column lay with 2 Ethiopians and, since they had no wireless, they could not be warned that 7,000 Italians were rushing at them. Their commander, Major Boyle, an amateur soldier from Kenya, had 400 men with him and had just returned from a sweep in the hills to the road north of Dembecha when his outposts warned him of Natale's approach. He took up the only defensive position available, a very bad one, and stood to block the road. With the Sudanese snapping at his rear Natale went bull-headed at the obstacle, broke through and dispersed the Ethiopian battalion with a hundred dead and wounded. It was a victory of a sort but a dearly bought one. Two hundred and fifty dead were left on the road, two armoured cars were disabled by a single Ethiopian corporal with an A/T rifle, and, it was claimed, a bomber was brought down by small arms fire. 2 Ethiopians had done all that could be expected of them, but, for the time being, they were finished as a fighting unit and the Italian column went on to Debra Marcos.

*   *   *

On 11 February, while Fourth Indian Division was failing in its second attack on the Acqua Col, Boustead's men were completing the airstrip at Mount Belaya and First (S.A.) Division was fumbling its way into Mega, Cunningham attacked Italian Somaliland. By any standards it was a risky enterprise made possible only by the discovery of water at Hagadera three weeks earlier, thus releasing sufficient trucks to make a striking force of four brigades mobile, and by the radio intercepts which convinced Cunningham that morale inside Somaliland was collapsing. The assembly of this striking force left a gap of 300 miles between its left and right of the South Africans at Mega, a gap that was guarded by only two battalions (1/2 and 1/4 K.A.R.) and, while it was unlikely that the enemy would launch a serious offensive from Dolo and Lugh Ferrandi, a very damaging raid by *bande* could not be discounted. Fortunately the Italians themselves showed how the gap could be covered. Their intelligence, alarmist as always, reported the arrival of Australian troops at Mombasa, an illusion due in all probability to the slouch hats worn by the African troops, so 'Fourth Australian Division' was put into the line with headquarters at Wajir. Orders were sent to it *en clair* to mount a two-pronged attack aiming at Bardera and Mandera. The division consisted of four South African officers, a handful of wireless sets and signallers and sixty dummy tanks.

On the Italian side De Simone had been in command for so short a time that he had been unable substantially to modify his predecessor's inadequate plan for defence. This was based on the assumption that the wide stretch of desert would make the movement of large forces from Kenya impossible so that only raids had to be guarded against. He had therefore laid out a linear defence based on the River Juba from

Dolo to the sea, a line of some 360 miles as the river winds. De Simone, who did not discount a powerful attack, guessed that Cunningham would aim to cut the Kismayu – Mogadishu road by a sweep through the Jelib – Bardera sector. He therefore stationed the smaller of his two divisions, the 101st, with three battalions at Bardera, supported by a *bande* group fifty miles to the east at Dinsor, while holding Dolo and Lugh Ferrandi with a single battalion apiece. His main strength, the eight battalions of the 102nd Division, was concentrated in the quadrilateral Kismayu – Afmadu – Jelib – Jumbo behind a screen composed of two groups of *dubats*. In reserve was his only mobile force, 15th Amhara Brigade, which included some 'national' troops; and this he posted on the coast at Brava from where all-weather roads led to Kismayu and Jelib. He had a slight superiority in numbers but the demands of defence meant that his troops were very dispersed and, as on the Eritrean front, the arrival of Hurricanes swung superiority in the air to the British to such an extent that the newly arrived Fairey Battle light bombers could be used successfully though they had proved lethally obsolete to their crews in France in 1940. On 31 January the Duke of Aosta reported to Rome that the British were now clearly superior in the air 'as far as numbers of aircraft and their quality is concerned'. He anticipated that the *Regia Aeronautica* would be ineffective within two weeks and started forming his airmen and their ground staff into infantry units. Three days later a raid into Somaliland by the S.A.A.F. destroyed seven bombers and two fighters on the ground.

De Simone had miscalculated his opponent's first objective. Cunningham already had Mogadishu in his sights but his overriding need was the port, inadequate though it was, of Kismayu, which, from the Italian point of view, was inconveniently sited on the western side of the Juba. So important was this that he laid down in his orders that, if it was not seized within ten days, his troops would have to retreat to the Tana. His plan was for the three brigades of Twelfth African Division (Major General Godwin-Austen) to advance from Garissa and Wajir and strike at Afmadu. From there one brigade would continue east to Bulo Erillo and force a crossing of the river, taking Jelib and obstructing the movement of Italian reinforcements froim Bardera. At the same time a second brigade would move south to take Gobwen and its airfield before making a second crossing of the Juba. The capture of Kismayu would be the responsibility of Eleventh African Division (Major General H. E. de R. Wetherall), effectively consisting of the Nigerian brigade and one Rhodesian battalion, which would set off later from Bura and was scheduled to reach the port on 17 February. S.A.A.F. would have as its first priority the neutralization of Italian airfields and the Royal Navy provided a task force including an aircraft carrier★ which would bombard the reserve brigade at Brava before sailing down the coast shelling the coast road and any army camps within range. If all went well Eleventh Division was to be prepared to make a dash for Mogadishu while Twelfth turned north to Bardera.

The preliminary operations started on 4 February when Brigadier Fowkes' 22nd (E.A.) Brigade supported by a troop of Rhodesian armoured cars, a South African field battery and a troop of light howitzers, drove the Italians out of Beles Gugnani at the point of the bayonet, thus further easing the water situation although the well there produced water with a 'faint unpleasantness' later traced to the floating body of a *dubat*. By 7 February all Fowkes's battalions were established in woods within sight of Afmadu but, with the inertia that characterized all Italian moves in Somaliland, the garrison neither attacked the intruders nor sent patrols against them. They must have known that they were there since a carelessly tended cooking fire started a bush fire which drew the attention of a Savoia 81 which dropped its bombs at the wrong end of the conflagration. There was no response when the South Africans registered their guns.

Nevertheless Afmadu was no negligible fortification, being entrenched, heavily wired and garrisoned by a regular colonial battalion (94) with a battery of guns and several mortars. It could have caused the K.A.R. battalions unacceptable casualties but the S.A.A.F. settled the matter. On the afternoon of 10 February the place received five airstrikes, three of three Ju86s and two of three Battles, a total of 16,440lbs of bombs. When the K.A.R. attacked at 5.30 am the following morning they found that their Bangalore torpedoes had failed to breach the wire but that the garrison had fled. They were received by a single dazed Italian who remarked, 'You have only to make a noise like an armoured car and you will be in Mogadishu in a fortnight.'

★ The world's first custom-built aircraft carrier, *Hermes* (1919), with 814 Squadron, F.A.A. (Swordfish) embarked. The rest of Force T (Captain J. H. Edelsten R.N.) consisted of H.M. Cruisers *Shropshire, Hawkins, Capetown* and *Ceres* and the destroyer *Kandahar*.

By noon 24th (Gold Coast) Brigade (Brigadier C. E. M. Richards) had passed through Afmadu and set off on the sixty-mile journey to Bulo Erillo which they stormed against appreciable resistance on 13 February, taking a battery of 65mm guns, four armoured cars and 140 prisoners. They were, however, unable to seize a bridgehead across the Juba and grab Jelib. The third brigade, 1st (S.A.) (Brigadier D. H. Pienaar), had to wait before Afmadu was sufficiently clear of traffic before setting off south for Gobwen which it was due to capture on 14 February before seizing the Italian pontoon bridge and crossing to Margherita. It was dusk before they set out, and since the brigade had with it four field and one medium batteries, twelve light tanks, a squadron of armoured cars, a field company of sappers and a field ambulance, the column had 1,200 vehicles and occupied fifteen miles of road. There were many problems with road discipline, not least since the drivers, who had already made the long approach march from Wajir, tended to fall asleep at the wheel. 13 February found the whole column lying up under cover near Eyadera where they heard explosions and other sounds indicating that Kismayu was being evacuated. Pienaar's orders specifically forbade patrolling and insisted on wireless silence to ensure surprise for the next day's assault. As a result the port's garrison escaped unmolested and, although Gobwen was duly seized, with a loss of two killed and nineteen wounded, the pontoon bridge, now useless to the Italians, had been demolished.

Eleventh Division's move from Bura to Kismayu was not due to start for another three days so 22nd Brigade was switched south from Afmadu to occupy the vital port. After a hectic drive, on which Brigadier Fowkes insisted on leading his armoured cars in his staff car despite reports of *bande* attacks, they raced into the town on the evening of 14 February.

> The town was *en fête*, uproariously and drunkenly so. It might have been the relief of Mafeking or the end of World War I. The entire population must have been in the streets to welcome us and several hundred of them, in a long line, were dancing the Conga, dragging looted cinema film behind them and chanting wildly.

There were twenty-five ships in the harbour and stored round the town were vast quantities of fuel – 222,000 gallons of petrol and half that amount of aviation spirit, a find which greatly eased the logistic problems. The harbour itself was a disappointment. Only one jetty was usable and the road leading to it soon disintegrated under the unaccustomed weight of traffic. Nevertheless the first freighter arrived on 19 February, two days before the crucial date on which the campaign would have had to be abandoned. By keeping the supply line across the desert going there would be just enough stores to justify a further advance, particularly since enemy morale seemed to be even lower than had been predicted.

The immediate problem was obtaining a bridge over the Juba and it was at once clear that at both Gobwen and Jelib the enemy was strongly dug in to resist a crossing. On the morning of 16 February Brigadier Pienaar flew above the river in a Hartbeest and saw near Yonte, fifteen miles upstream, a place where tracks led to the river from both sides, suggesting that there might be a ford between them. There were, moreover, plantations on either side to give cover for the approach. He therefore left a battalion and a battery to occupy the enemy opposite Gobwen and moved the rest of the brigade to Yonte where, on 17 February, two platoons of Natal Carbineers paddled across in canvas assault boats without having a shot fired at them. This peace was not to last, for, as the Transvaal Scottish crossed to support them, the enemy appeared and the rest of the crossing was carried out under a heavy fire which was only moderated by the machine guns of the armoured cars. Two attacks, both carried out with notable gallantry and determination, were beaten off on the first night but by the afternoon of 19 February a pontoon bridge, brought up on seventy vehicles from Garissa, was across the river. Six armoured cars crossed immediately and put an end to threats to the bridgehead. Next day a force was pushed out eastward to threaten the defeat of the Italians who were holding out at Jumbo, opposite Gobwen. The line of the Juba had been broken.

To the north of the South Africans, 24th (G.C.) Brigade was seeking a crossing place by which to outflank Jelib. One was found thirty miles to the north at Mabungo where the river was only eighteen inches deep and here, under cover of a bridgehead force, the sappers built a causeway of sandbags which, by 20 February, was fit to carry light tanks, armoured cars and guns. The Gold Coasters swung south to deal with Jelib while 22nd (E.A.) Brigade took off, driving through the bush, to cut the coast road near Brava. Behind them came 23rd (Nigerian) Brigade (Brigadier G. R. Smallwood) who made a dash for Mogadishu which they reached, after overcoming slight resistance, on 25 February, an advance of 235 miles in three days.

Once more vast stores, including 350,000 gallons of petrol and 80,000 gallons of aviation spirit, were found intact.

Apart from the infertile and useless north, Italian Somaliland had been conquered in two weeks and, reporting his victory, Cunningham sought permission to press on for another 800 miles to Harar. Wavell approved.

CHAPTER 7 Decision

SUCCESSES IN SOMALILAND and Gojjam were welcome but the heart of the matter was in Eritrea. Not only must the Red Sea ports be captured so that the United States could open that vital seaway to their shipping but London was becoming haunted by the fear that the Japanese, whose belligerence was appearing increasingly imminent, might establish naval bases in East Africa, in particular at Massawa. This chimera of Japanese long-range naval penetration was a real factor in strategic planning and even in January, 1941, almost a year before Pearl Harbor, there seemed to be no limit to their potential expansion. Coastal guns were installed at Dar-es-Salaam, Tanga and Zanzibar and the Italian seaward defences at Kismayu and Mogadishu were quickly restored to combat readiness. On 17 February Churchill was enquiring anxiously:

> What are the arrangements in British Columbia for dealing with the Japanese colony there should Japan attack?

On the previous day the Chiefs of Staffs had signalled to Wavell:

> It is essential at this moment to do everything to deter Japan from adopting a forward policy. We have evidence that an early liquidation of Italian East Africa might have a considerable effect on the Japanese in this direction.

Nor was this the only pressure on Wavell for a quick decision. The *Afrika Korps* was assembling for action in Tripolitania and already the *Luftwaffe*, based on Rhodes, had mined the Suez Canal. Western Desert Force was soon to be dangerously weakened, as on 22–23

106

February an agreement was concluded in Athens for British troops to go to help the Greeks. The first convoy sailed from Alexandria on 4 March and by the end of that month 31,000 Australian, British and New Zealand troops were in Greece. With them were eight R.A.F. squadrons and Churchill was pressing for another ten squadrons to be sent to Turkey. Nor was that the Prime Minister's only demand. On hearing of the fall of Kismayu and while he was unnecessarily urging Cunningham on to Mogadishu, he proposed that one of the West African brigades 'should be transferred from Kenya to Freetown' so that the two British battalions 'now disintegrating there could come forward to the Nile Army'. Wavell was only too aware of his need for the Indian and South African divisions in Egypt but they could only be transferred there by a quick victory at Keren.

The question remained of how Keren was to be taken? The orthodox solution, to seize Sanchil, the high ground dominating the gorge, had been shown to be impossible of execution. The key height, Brig's Peak, could be taken, but, because of the inevitable casualties, the dearth of cover and the difficulties of re-supply, it could not be held. The only way round the bottleneck, the Acqua Col, had been found difficult to approach and impossible to storm. The only remaining option was to take the high ground to the east of the gorge, Dologorodoc and Mounts Falestoh and Zeban. This would give access to the road block in the gorge, but Dologorodoc was commanded at a range of 1,900 yards by Sanchil which towered nearly 900 feet above it. It seemed to follow that Dologorodoc could only be taken and held if Sanchil could be neutralized.

Taking Dologorodoc would require the whole strength of the relatively intact Fifth Division so that the unrewarding task of neutralizing Sanchil had to fall on the two battered brigades of Fourth Division, a hard task to impose on men who had already performed prodigies of bravery over just that ground and who had subsequently endured five weeks, with perhaps one short break at the foot of the hill, of the intolerable conditions described by those who had held Cameron Ridge during the interregnum.

Cameron Ridge was a most uncomfortable place. Brig's Peak and Sanchil completely overlooked it. There was a certain amount of enemy shelling and patrolling. By day it was very hot and there was no shade; by night it could be bitterly cold. Rations had to be carried up by men of the reserve company from the dump a thousand feet below. Both food and water were therefore extremely short.

It was punishing work, since it was a two-hour climb to the forward company, with the water in two-gallon cans, the ammunition and rations (bully beef and biscuits, tea, sugar and condensed milk) in sandbags, and even that provided only a pint of water a day per man. That was little enough in the blazing heat of the day; carrying at least kept one sweating at night, when it was very cold on top. Blankets or greatcoats could not possibly be carried up. On the track from the railway line down to the valley was a very dead mule, stinking if anything worse than the dead men, and hourly swelling to a vaster bulk. One of the paths was covered by a fixed-line machine gun at a point where it was impossible to diverge, and uncertainty over whether the man at the other end was alert or nodding led to some swearing.

Casualties were a problem. From the forward positions they could only be evacuated after dark, which meant keeping the wounded men in the sections long after the initial anaesthetic of shock had worn off. We did our best for them, while they in their turn tried to bottle up their groans as the pain of their wounds bit deep. Carrying a stretcher down the hill at night was worse than carrying rations and ammunition up it. For the wounded men it must have been torment.

We tried to bury our dead, but explosions dug them up again, while the Italian and Indian and British dead in the ravine in front of the ridge just lay there swelling. The normally loose uniform of shirt and shorts filled to bursting point, every seam strained, the skin shining as it stretched tighter and tighter.

The whole place was alive with flies which had been attracted by the dead bodies and the general filth of war. . . . The energetic lively ones were a nuisance, but the sluggish bloated ones were a horror. Tobacco was a help. At least it irritated the flies when one puffed at them, whilst cigarette smoke inhaled to the very bottom of one's lungs over-rode for a moment or two the heavy smell of the dead.

Once again Savory's brigade was detailed to attack the tallest feature. The Camerons, reduced to seventeen officers and 362 other ranks, had Brig's Peak as their objective while, on their left, 1/6 Rajrifs went for Sugar Loaf and Hog's Back. 2/5 Mahratta L.I., who had been brought from the Sudan to replace 3/14 Punjab, were to attack Flat Top. In the second line were the Royal Fusiliers and 4/6 Rajrifs whose task was to pass through the Camerons once they were on the Peak and take Sanchil. Away to the left 4/11 Sikhs and 3/1 Punjabis were to pin down the Italians around Mount

Amba by attacking Samana. They were joined by a newly arrived unit, 51 (Middle East) Commando, a tough amalgam of Arabs and Jews from Palestine serving in apparent amity under British officers.*

The attack on Dologorodoc across the mouth of the gorge was entrusted to 9th Brigade, now commanded by Messervy,† and reinforced by 2 Highland Light Infantry. It was hoped that the brigade would not only be able to seize the fort but exploit beyond to seize Falestoh and Zeban whereupon 29th Brigade would go through them and take Keren town. The reserve for both attacks consisted only of two battalions from 10th Brigade. The available artillery, ninety-six guns of which sixteen were 60-pounders, were so sited that, without moving, they could support each division in succession.

Fourth Indian was to attack at 7 am with the Fifth advancing three and a half hours later. The timing of these attacks was the subject of much heartsearching but at that stage of the war all armies, British, Italian and German, were reluctant to attempt night attacks and this battleground, with its tumbled, steep, rocky terrain, made movement by night especially hazardous while darkness in any case ruled out the chance of air support and reduced the effectiveness of the artillery. Nor could an attack at dawn be favoured since, by a topographical mischance, the sun rising over Sanchil would blind the O.P.s who at the best of times had a very limited view. The best hope seemed to be to attack immediately after the dawn 'stand to' when the defenders might have relaxed their vigilance and be arranging their breakfast.

The logistics for a two-divisional battle at the end of a single road stretching almost 200 miles from railhead were the stuff of nightmare although it was fortunate that the *Regia Aeronautica* was able to make only a single, ineffective raid on the huge depots established at Kassala and, before the battle was renewed, a forty-mile stretch of line was laid to the east. Another blessing was that the Italians had done little damage to their railway line which ran from Biscia to the battlefield and, while they had remembered to remove their locomotives, they had left a good deal of rolling stock. Diesel

---

* An Indian account of 51 Commando described them as 'the sweepings of Palestine, Jews and Arabs who were thieves and murderers'. (Skinner p. 143)
† Brigadier Mayne had been promoted major-general but was to return to command Fifth Indian Division within a few weeks.

engines of suitable gauge had been prepared in the Sudan but there were inevitably delays in getting them across the gap between Kassala and Biscia and, in the meanwhile, loaded trucks were hauled up the line by 15cwt trucks and it was found possible to let them run free, guided only by brakemen, on the return journey. Camels were used for the transport of petrol and since the indigenous population could find no use for the stuff, they could go unescorted without fear of pilfering which, for other stores, required constant vigilance. The main burden of transport fell on the road. Three MT companies, manned by Cape Coloured drivers, arrived from South Africa on their own wheels, having only a 30% loss of vehicles on the journey, and two more companies were raised in the Sudan. By omitting all but the most routine maintenance it was found that a truck could make a round trip from Kassala to the forward troops every three days, while, to increase the number of vehicles available, Fifth Division was kept near Kassala until the last possible moment so that its trucks could be used on the ferry service. It was even found possible, by using special priority vehicles, to provide fresh fruit and vegetables to the Fourth Division units which were resting out of the line. The amounts of stores required were enormous. With only two brigades forward, 140 tons were needed daily for current consumption and it had been decided to accumulate at the front fourteen days' supply for five brigades to say nothing of 50,000 rounds of artillery ammunition. Inevitably snags were encountered. Two days before Zero hour – the term H hour came later in the war – someone remembered that wire cutters were essential. They were flown down from Cairo with twelve hours to spare. Even though the start of the attack was brought forward by six days, everything was ready in time.

While the British supplies were being assured, everything possible was done to disrupt those of the Italians. Two raids by Wellesleys, on the second of which they had Hurricane escorts, effectively put out of action the main servicing facility for the *Regia Aeronautica* in I.E.A., the Caproni repair plant at Mai Edega. Hurricanes regularly shot up the airfields at Asmara, Massawa, Guru and Makalle and the airfield and supply depots at Massawa were pounded by two squadrons of Albacores (bomb load 1,500 lbs) flown from H.M.S. *Formidable* as she sailed up the Red Sea on her way to the Mediterranean. The roads and railway leading to Keren were frequently attacked.

Faced with what had to be a battle of attrition against an enemy in superior numbers, it is hard to criticize Platt's plan except in details. The deliberate avoidance of a night attack was shown within twenty-four hours to have been unnecessary but he was faced with having to undertake a frontal attack and with achieving victory in a hurry. Not only was Wavell anxious to get the troops involved transferred to Egypt but the Eritrean rains were imminent and, when they fell, the road from Kassala would become impassable to the huge weight of traffic it was having to bear. A stalemate could not be accepted. Anything short of absolute victory would be defeat. Platt had no illusions about the difficulties. To his senior officers, he said,

> Don't let anyone think that this is going to be a walk-over. It is going to be a bloody battle and it is going to be won by the side which lasts longest.

When Wavell, visiting the front, asked him, 'What will you do if it doesn't come off, William?' He replied, 'I'm damned if I know, sir.'

★   ★   ★

The attack was finally fixed for 15 March and Fifth Indian Division started moving into the line a week earlier. When the day finally dawned the entire available bomber strength, four squadrons including Wellesleys, Blenheims and elderly Hardys, made repeated attacks on the Italian positions astride the Dongolaas Gorge and on their rear areas, a particularly satisfying explosion marking the disintegration of an ammunition train arriving from Massawa. The massed guns opened on the Sanchil massif at 7 am and as they did so the Camerons plunged down the forward slope of their ridge into the saucer-shaped depression which separated them from Brig's Peak. They were encumbered by grenades and extra bandoliers of ammunition but contrived to move very fast.

> We were all very clear that the only chance of pulling it off was to move as fast as possible down into the ravine and up the precipitous slopes beyond, since we hoped that the very steepness of the hill would prevent the enemy artillery from landing anything on its forward slope. . . . As we ran we could see the whole line of crests before us blotted out in dust from the explosions.

111

The counter-barrage arrived promptly and the right-forward company of the Camerons suffered heavily as they were caught in the open. They were pinned down a hundred yards short of their objective though a few men managed to reach the nearest peak of Sanchil. On their left, C Company moved so fast that most of the Italian shells fell behind them as they started up the steep face of Brig's peak where they were in dead ground from the guns if not to the enemy mortars.

> The noise was shattering but commands were unnecessary – every Jock knew that the only way was on up.

They had to pause just short of the crest to avoid the last of their own barrage but, as soon as it stopped, they clambered on and reached the top, 'clearing half a dozen posts, disarming prisoners and chasing them off down the hill on their own'. There was no cover on the bare pinnacle so the two leading platoons, reduced to one officer and three men, pressed on down the reverse slope only to be disabled by a torrent of fire. The reserve platoon reached the peak and tried to hold it but their supporting company swerved to the left and made an unsuccessful attack on Centre Bump. At the cost of half their strength 1/6 Rajrifs took Hog's Back and, reinforced by two companies of their 4/6 battalion, held it against a series of determined counter-attacks, thereby gaining the first O.P. on the high ground. Beyond them the Mahrattas took Flat Top, but, after defending it against several onslaughts, could not go on to Mole Hill as had been hoped. On 5th Brigade's front the Sikhs got a lodgement on the westerly crest of Samanna but were repeatedly repulsed from the central citadel of the height by 'a palisade of huge boulders linked by knife-rests of barbed wire'. Berseford-Peirse sent first one and then a second company of Fusiliers to reinforce the Camerons on Brig's Peak and Sanchil but no progress could be made and when he ordered all three Fusilier companies to go for Sanchil it was found that the battalion could only put ninety men into the line.

Once again an attack on Sanchil had ground to an expensive halt and from the north of Keren came reports that an attack by Briggs' brigade, timed to coincide with Savory's, had made no progress against Mount Engiahat. Platt, after consulting Heath, decided that the Sanchil attack had created sufficient diversion to justify launching the attempt on Dologorodoc. It was a questionable decision since the leading battalion, the H.L.I., had eaten its breakfast, and suffered casualties, in view of the enemy, so that surprise was unobtainable. At 10.30 am their leading company crossed the start line aiming to take Pinnacle, the stony spike which is the most spectacular of Dologorodoc's foothills. Although the massed guns were now supporting them, their task was hopeless. They had to advance a mile over a sandy plain under a storm of fire from machine guns, mortars and artillery from both Dologorodoc and from the eastern, disengaged face of Sanchil. Only a handful of men and their mortally wounded company commander reached the dubious cover of the rocks at the foot of their objective and, though two more companies struggled forward to join them, further progress was impossible and they had to lie up through a notably torrid day until they could withdraw after dark. A gallant but misguided attempt by their carrier platoon to take water and ammunition to them was repulsed with heavy loss.

It was at this stage that Brigadier Messervy proposed that his other three battalions should attack Dologorodoc that night. The brigade would move up to Milestone 98 on the road as soon as it was dusk, thus taking a line to the right of that used by the H.L.I., and 3/5 Mahrattas would then capture Pinnacle with 3/12 R.F.F.R., who were less than two companies strong,* going through them to seize the intermediate feature known as Pimple. The final attack on the fort would be carried out by 2 West Yorkshires. It was basic to the plan that the whole operation should be completed during the hours of darkness on that very night when the enemy would not be expecting a further attack. It was a tribute to the training of both troops and their commanders that approval was given, orders issued, a new artillery plan drawn up and the troops moved into position in some six hours and the Mahrattas crossed their start line exactly as planned when darkness fell. They had no easy time of it and their first three attacks were repulsed but they were almost at full strength and well-trained mountain fighters. After their fourth attempt their Very light signalled success from the top of Pinnacle and the Rifles, who had started an hour behind them but had closed up during the fighting, went through and grabbed Pimple with little trouble. The Italians,

---

* Each battalion had detached one company to act as porters but R.F.F.R. had, in addition, left a company as part of the flank guard on the Barentu–Gondar road and lent one platoon to act as porters for the gunners.

however, reacted violently and quickly. Two companies of grenadiers and two of Eritreans launched vicious counter-attacks against both the captured positions and were only driven off with difficulty. Meanwhile the West Yorkshires were toiling up to the base of Pinnacle and it is indicative of the steepness of the slope up which the Mahrattas had fought their way that it took the British battalion two hours to climb the 700 feet from the milestone without opposition and having dumped such inconvenient loads as anti-tank rifles on the way.

It was 3am before the leading company reached the foot of Pinnacle and there was little darkness left. Their orders were to wait until all three companies were assembled there but to wait would waste at least an hour and their position would be unenviable if the whole battalion was found there in daylight. They were out of contact with battalion headquarters and immediate decision was imperative. Having ascertained from the R.F.F.R. that the counter-attacks were being held, the company commander, Captain Michael Osborn, decided to push on for the summit at once, moving to the right up a re-entrant which emerged on a bare ridge leading to the fort. In bright moonlight the company set off in single file and, in Osborn's words,

> After fifteen minutes we were out of the re-entrant and climbing up the Dologorodoc feature. The sound of bursting shells above us enabled us to keep direction. The slope became steeper and steeper, and halts were frequent as we waited for stragglers to catch up. After some time the slope began to lessen and I guessed that this was the shoulder running out from the fort. Here I determined to wait until our artillery had lifted and then put in the final assault on the fort, some 300 feet above us, with two platoons, but as I was briefing them, dawn broke and our exposed position became only too apparent both to the enemy and ourselves. We were lying on a bare slope in full view of the fort, and an enemy machine-gun nest was only about 200 yards to our left. I sent off my runner to bring up the 2-inch mortar team while the platoons took cover lower down. Feverish activity was observed in the machine-gun nest and it was a race as to who could start firing first. In the event we won and our second bomb proved a direct hit. Meanwhile our artillery appeared to have lifted to the far side of the fort, so I gave the signal for the assault to begin. The climb so far had been a mere Sunday afternoon picnic compared to those last 300 feet. When we were about half-way up a few scattered shots rang out from the fort and some men in the leading wave slumped in their tracks. A dropped rifle clattered past and we heard the sharp crack of an exploding grenade hurled

114

down from the ramparts. Then we heard a familiar bang in the valley below and the whine of one of our shells overhead; but instead of a thud somewhere beyond us there was a blinding flash and I was picked up bodily and deposited very hard some feet from where I was standing. Then another fell among the reserve platoon. Our 60-pounders were putting down a concentration on the forward slope and evidently our yellow screens* were invisible from the valley. Nevertheless, five minutes later, appearing out of the rubble and dust of our own barrage, we scaled the ramparts and the fort was ours.

The company lost thirty-five men out of little more than a hundred men but they would probably have lost more had not the British guns, short though they fired, kept the enemies' heads down during their last desperate scramble up the scree. As it was, 6.15 am saw them rounding up forty severely shaken Eritreans, an Italian medical officer and a paymaster while the rest of the garrison legged it down the far side pursued by fire and grenades. The rest of the battalion arrived by 7 am.

The taking of Fort Dologorodoc was a magnificent feat of arms, a splendid combination of skill, daring and luck. Holding it was quite another problem. It was flattering to call it a fort. It consisted of a stout but low stone wall circling the summit, the whole barely a hundred feet across, having within it a shelter trench into the sides of which a few cupboard-size excavations had been made for the storage of ammunition. There was only one piece of digging which might be dignified with the name of dug-out. There were two or three embrasures in the walls, each wide enough for a bren gun, but most of the defenders had to put their heads above the wall to fire their rifles. It was, in fact, what it was designed to be, a strongpoint for controlling turbulent tribesmen. To the west Sanchil loomed over it within long machine-gun range and it was scarcely better sited with regard to Falestoh to the east and Zeban to the north-east. Supply was a nightmare as no track led to it from the south and all stores had to be manhandled up the steep slopes by the reserve company. In his orders Messervy had laid down that 'Ammunition must take priority over food and water. No position has ever been lost from lack of rations but lack of ammunition has caused the loss of many a hard-won position.' On his early visits to forward units,

---

*Each man was wearing a yellow patch on his back in the hope that the gunners would be able to see which were on their side.

he noted, such was the thirst that 'many men [had] black and swollen tongues such as I had never seen in war.*' To make matters worse Dologorodoc was almost without shade and the weather was hotter than ever. Things improved slightly after 18 March when the sappers completed a mule track which led half-way up the climb but the sight of their wounded comrades being manhandled down the rocks did nothing to improve the morale of the men who clung to the hard-won position.

The first of many Italian counter-attacks was launched within four hours of the fort's capture with one battalion attacking from Falestoh and one from the gorge. They were repulsed with difficulty and almost entirely by small-arms fire since there were great difficulties in calling for defensive fire from the artillery. The primitive wireless sets which should have linked battalion headquarters with brigade worked badly and spasmodically among the mountains and there was a shortage of cable for field telephones. Even when cables could be laid they were frequently cut by bursting shells and repairing them in daylight was not a healthy activity. In daylight heliographs were used when not obscured by smoke and dust. The enemy, on this first occasion, got to within 300 yards of the fort before crippling casualties drove them back and a company of Mahrattas then joined the Yorkshiremen in the garrison. Eight heavy counter-attacks, each pressed with notable determination and gallantry, were beaten off in the first five days and several others were dispersed before they were properly under way by gunfire and fighter strikes by the R.A.F. and S.A.A.F. The air forces also tried to alleviate the supply situation by using a Wellesley and a Vincent to drop ammunition and food, the first time since 1918 that air supply had been attempted for British troops, but the summit of the hill was too small a target for the primitive means employed and all the precious bundles dropped beyond the reach of the defenders.

Fort Dologorodoc was only the first stage on the road to Keren and Marriott's 29th Brigade, still comparatively fresh, was ordered to move through Messervy's men with 3/2 Punjabis going for Zeban and the Worcesters for Falestoh, an attack scheduled for the night of 16–17 March. Platt decided that yet another attempt, or diversion, should be made to hold the attention of the enemy on dominating

---

* There was a water tank, fortunately full, in the fort itself and it was the men on the surrounding features who suffered from thirst.

Sanchil where remnants of Camerons, Fusiliers, Rajrifs and Mahrattas clung to their toeholds below the crests of both Brig's Peak and Sanchil itself. There could be no question of Fourth Division mounting another attack. 11th Brigade, far understrength on 14 March, had lost more than forty officers and 800 men in the next twenty-four hours and 5th Brigade had suffered only slightly less. The Kaid decided to throw his only reserve, 10th Brigade, into the battle and 3/18 Garhwalis were ordered to storm Sanchil while 4/10 Baluchis completed the capture of Brig's Peak. The H.L.I., recovering from its hammering on the morning of 15 March, was held in reserve for exploitation.

Of all the attacks on Sanchil, 10th Brigade's was the least successful. Timed to go in at 10 pm on 15 March, every sort of a delay occurred, not least when two random mortar bombs landed among the Baluchis as they were forming up, and it was almost dawn before the two battalions went forward. After twenty-four hours, during which they suffered 316 casualties and gained nothing, Platt pulled the brigade back into reserve. Once more Sanchil had proved too strong.

Despite this failure, 29th Brigade's attack was allowed to go forward on the following night. Once again the timing slipped badly. It had been hoped to start forward at 10.30 pm, but the two battalions were not at their forming-up place near the fort until 1 am. The Punjabis actually moved off an hour and a half later and had advanced half a mile before clashing with an Italian force massing for a counter-attack on the fort. Assisted by a company of R.F.F.R., sent down from the fort, they dispersed this threat, capturing forty prisoners and four mountain guns, but the momentum of their advance was lost and, when dawn broke, they were badly exposed to flanking fire from Sanchil. The Worcesters did not manage to start their march until 4 am and their early difficulties stemmed from the ground. No reconnaissance had been possible and their briefing had been done on a sandtable made on the basis of air photographs. This proved misleading since 'ground which appeared to be comparatively easy turned out to be a yawning chasm' and the path on which they advanced soon crumbled into dust. As a result they started to climb Falestoh well behind their artillery preparation and by 4.30 am they were pinned down on the western slope by heavy fire from both Falestoh and Zeban. When they had made no progress after three hours and were out of touch with brigade, their commanding officer took the unusual step of going back to brigade in person to report their position. Marriott called off the attack and at dusk the Worcesters, having lost eighty-five men, pulled back behind Dologorodoc and the Punjabis made a shorter retreat to the re-entrant west of Falestoh.

By 17 March it seemed that the second Battle of Keren had been as unsuccessful as the first. There was scarcely a battalion in the two divisions that had the strength to mount a set-piece attack and, to make matters worse, the weather had turned unusually sultry and was causing a significant number of casualties from heat stroke. It seemed that the gorge could not be forced until Sanchil had been taken and Sanchil was impregnable. The only faint ray of hope was that, under cover of 29th Brigade's attack, a sapper officer had crept down to the road block and made a close examination. All previous calculations had been based on the assumption that it would take ten days to clear. Now it was reported that it could be removed in forty-eight hours. Attempts to make a start on the work by blasting some of the boulders into the gorge were made on the nights of 17–18 and 18–19 March but were frustrated by machine guns firing on fixed lines.

While the British felt that the battle was deadlocked, they could not know the effect that their limited success had had on the enemy commander. It may be an exaggeration to say that Platt was obsessed with the importance of Sanchil but there is no doubt that Carmineo was so concerned with the loss of Fort Dologorodoc that he put the whole defence in jeopardy by his efforts to recover it. The fact was that Dologorodoc was no more vital to the Keren defences than Cameron Ridge. Dominated by Sanchil, Zeban and Falestoh, it could only be a jumping-off point for attacks on those heights which the British had insufficient men to mount in adequate strength. If Carmineo had devoted his energies to strengthening his positions on the routes of advance from the fort he could have prolonged the stalemate until the rains came and made the situation of the British intolerable and untenable, particularly since Frusci was at last convinced of the viability of the Keren position and was sending Carmineo substantial reinforcements. These were thrown into the cauldron in a fierce but doomed determination to recapture Dologorodoc. Again and again counter-attacks were mounted and pressed with the utmost determination and courage. All were ineffective. The nearest approach to success came on the night of 22–23 March when, by astonishing skill, light tanks were driven up on to Falestoh and launched at the rear of the R.F.F.R. who were already fully engaged in holding off a colonial battalion attacking their front. In the event some lucky shots disabled the commanders of the tank detachment and the spirit went out of the attack just as it was succeeding.

These repeated rebuffs started a fatal weakening in the morale of Carmineo's men. The drain of casualties became too great. The two battalions of 61st Colonial Brigade lost half their strength within a week of coming to Keren and other formations suffered as badly. News from the other fronts also disheartened some units. The askaris from Somaliland were depressed to hear that Cunningham's men were overrunning their homeland and the locally recruited Blackshirts of the Africa Division could imagine their women and children being left to the mercies of the British African divisions or, worse still, to vengeful Ethiopians. Even the national troops – Grenadiers, Alpini and Bersaglieri – whose staunchness was beyond praise, were tiring and their situation was not improved by the increased accuracy of the British guns now that they had O.P.s on Centre Bump and Dologorodoc. In the air the British were now supreme. Most of Air Commodore Slatter's six and a half squadrons were flying obsolete aircraft which would not have been safe within sight of the enemy in Europe, but, thanks to the clearing of the skies by the Hurricanes, obsolete biplanes could bomb the Italian positions and communications. Carmineo called repeatedly for air support only to be told that the planes were not available. The Italian pilots did their best with what they had. On 17 July a single CR 42 flew over Dologorodoc only to be shot down by a Gladiator in a dog-fight reminiscent of 1918. Three days later eight CR 42s made an ineffective sortie against the British positions, but, trying to repeat the operations on the following day, they found Hurricanes waiting for them. Four Italian planes were lost, one reputedly being shot down by a Lysander.

It was Major-General Heath of Fifth Indian Division who put forward a way in which the deadlock could be broken and it was a thoroughly unorthodox proposal. In theory it was suicidal to try to break through the gorge itself while the high ground on the whole of one side and most of the other was held by the enemy. Heath pointed out that the east face of Sanchil was so steep that it was impossible for the garrison at the top to fire down on to the railway and that there was a ready-made covered approach with secure assembly areas in the railway tunnel which burrowed its way through the southern spur of Cameron Ridge. He suggested that the attacking force should emerge from the tunnel, advance a mile and take a spur running down from Sanchil and known as Railway Bumps, exploiting beyond to take Railway Ridge, a piece of rising ground which marked a bifurcation in the dry river bed running down the gorge. It would be necessary, at the same time, for a force on the far side of the gorge to capture a ridge of hillocks coming westward from Zeban and named East Gate Spur. If these three objectives could be seized and held, the enemy would find it impossible to bring direct fire to bear on the sappers working to clear the road block, who would then be subject only to mortar fire. Heath believed that an attack on the low ground would be so unexpected by the Italians that the three objectives – Railway Bumps, Railway Ridge and East Gate Spur – could be taken by surprise.

Platt, who could see no other way through, accepted this scheme and sought the approval of Wavell, who was visiting the front. He had taken the opportunity to climb to Dologorodoc, no mean feat at his age, and had come to the same idea independently. He wrote,

> As soon as I had a good look at the position, I said to Platt that it looked to me as if the way through was straight up the main road, neglecting the high peaks. . . . He said that this was his plan.

The principal problem was to find enough troops to carry it out. No more than demonstrations could be called for from Fourth Division and two of Fifth's brigades were needed to hold on to Dologorodoc, although they could find a battalion for the attack on East Gate Spur. This left 10th Brigade which could only field two battalions since the third had been sent to Happy Valley to relieve the Central India Horse which was required for the mobile force Platt formed in expectation of a breakthrough. Even the two available battalions were each short of a rifle company, due to casualties, so that, with one company acting as porters, the fighting strength was only four companies from the whole brigade. Four rifle companies was not a large assault force and 3/2 Punjabis (29th Brigade) was detailed to act as a reserve.

Heath had hoped to attack on the morning of 24 March but it took longer than had been anticipated to clear away the ten trucks loaded with rocks that had been derailed in the tunnel (see p. 78) and Zero hour was finally fixed for 4.30 am on 25 March. During the previous evening two companies of H.L.I. and two of 4/10 Baluchis filed into the tunnel and lay up overnight. Simultaneously, on the other side of the gorge, a patrol of the West Yorkshires found that an intermediate spur was unoccupied and a company was established on it. At 4.30 am 3/5 Mahrattas passed through them and went for East Gate Spur under cover of a barrage. They had heavy fighting since, behind their objective, another counter-attack was being assembled and they became exposed to long-distance fire from Sanchil in their left rear. With considerable loss they gained only a partial hold on the spur but their efforts misled the Italians who believed that another attack on Zeban was intended.

As a result the H.L.I. emerged from the tunnel and got their leading company to Railway Bumps without a shot being fired at them, although their second company drew some fire when someone fell over a tripwire hung with empty tins. Behind them the Baluchis skirmished, with patrols working their way down the eastern slopes of Sanchil, but by 7 am the brigade had a firm hold on Railway Bumps with 500 prisoners and a battery of mountain guns. Among the prisoners was the commanding officer of the Bersaglieri responsible for the sector, who was in a transport of fury but who, when calmer, confessed that it never crossed his mind that anyone would be so foolhardy as to move straight up the gorge. At 9.45 am the Punjabis passed through and took Railway Ridge within three-quarters of an hour, a success which helped the Mahrattas to complete their hold on East Gate Spur. Already the Sappers and Miners were starting to clear the road block, the Italians finding that, though they could bombard the road south of the obstruction, they could not seriously interfere with the clearance work. In thirty-two hours the road was passable, with work going on in five-hour shifts of four companies at a time. During that time Carmineo assembled three counter-attacks, two of which were broken up by artillery before they crossed their start line. By 26 March isolated white flags began to appear on lower Sanchil but these were individual efforts and any attempt to exploit them was met with a shower of grenades and automatic fire.

The end came on 27 March. At dawn 9th Brigade set off towards Mount Zeban and reached the crest with little more trouble than was involved in climbing its steep slopes. To their right Falestoh was found to have been evacuated. In the centre 'Fletcher Force', Platt's mobile column, started up the gorge. As an armoured column it would not have been impressive in most theatres of war – eight Matilda tanks from 4 Royal Tanks, seventeen bren-gun carriers from Central India Horse, thirty-six more from the infantry battalions and the Chevrolet trucks carrying the lorry-borne cavalrymen of C.I.H. bringing up the rear – but it was the nearest thing to a *panzer* spearhead in East Africa. There was a moment of near anti-climax when the leading carrier broke down as it ground its way over the remains of the road block but it was towed clear and the great tanks moved through. By 10 am they were in the streets of Keren, swinging their turrets from side to side. Not a shot was fired. It was then that white flags appeared on the crests of Sanchil and Forcuta. Abandoned by their comrades and with their retreat cut off, the last 3000 defenders surrendered. There was nothing with which they could reproach themselves. They had done their full duty. At about the same time, beyond the mountain barrier, 4/16 Punjabis from Briggs' brigade attacked Mount Engiahat and found it deserted. The Foreign Legion passed through them and joined Fletcher Force in Keren. The British batteries facing the gorge had fired 110,000 shells, but such was the achievement of the improvised line of communications back to Kassala and beyond that there was still a reserve of ammunition at the gun positions.

★   ★   ★

The fifty-three-day battle for Keren cost the Italians, by their own accounts, 3,500 killed and 4,500 injured and, in addition, 3,500 men were taken prisoner. There was also a heavy loss through desertion and, according to some British sources, 6,000 men left the ranks during the battle despite draconian measures being taken to prevent them. On the British side 536 were killed and 3,229 wounded and there there was a handful of prisoners, almost all wounded, who were quickly recaptured. This loss represents about one man in five of all the troops present and almost one in two of those in the front line, the heaviest loss falling on the two brigades of Fourth Indian Division which was engaged throughout. Of the wounds, almost half (46.3%) were to the arms, the result of grenades being thrown against men climbing steep slopes. As might have been expected from the grossly unhygienic conditions on the rocky heights, there was a substantial sick list, 500 men in the second battle alone, of whom 40% suffered from dysentery or diarrhoea and 20% from skin sepsis. It is greatly to the credit of the Indian troops and their medical officers that, although there were roughly twice as many Indian other ranks present as British, only 296 were admitted as sick to hospital compared to 246 British. In the second battle only forty-four men had to be sent to hospital with 'war neurosis'.*

Could this heavy 'butcher's bill' have been reduced by better generalship? After Keren had been taken, Wavell noted in his diary,

> I wonder whether it would have come off if [Platt] had tried it earlier instead of the attempts on the peaks to right and left?

What is certain is that Wavell, on his earlier visits to the front, had never suggested such a solution even after he knew that Sanchil was unlikely to be captured. Orthodox doctrine, reinforced by decades of experience on the North-West Frontier of India, insisted that it was essential to secure the high ground dominating the line of advance. Moreover, the attack from the railway tunnel was not a practicable option until Dologorodoc, covering one flank of the attack, had been captured. Savory had ordered an attack on the fort as early as 3 February but the movement never started since it was rightly judged that a single battalion could not hope to succeed. Thereafter the main effort was devoted to trying to seize Sanchil on the reasonable ground that, if it could be captured, the other defences would crumble and that, if it was not captured, Dologorodoc would probably be untenable. It was not until 15 March, when Sanchil seemed impregnable, that a reinforced brigade was sent against the fort and succeeded at the second attempt, but even then it seemed to be a cul-de-sac, although its possession gave the opportunity of making a close examination of the road block. It is significant that the successful attack on Dologorodoc was made at night, albeit with the assistance of a bright moon. The difficulties of moving over ground as broken as that astride the gorge seem to have impressed every senior officer except Messervy to such an extent that they preferred to continue battering at Sanchil and to make the long exposed approach marches to Acqua Col and Dologorodoc to the hazards of a night attack. The experiences of 10th Brigade against Sanchil and 29th Brigade against Zeban and Falestoh in March show that these fears were far from unjustified.

---

* In Normandy in 1944 war neurosis accounted for fourteen men in every thousand among the British troops.

It has been suggested that the eight-hour delay imposed on Gazelle Force at the Ponte Mussolini on 1 February denied the British the chance to take Keren on the run. General Carmineo, who was in the best position to know, denied this but suggested that Gazelle would have had a clear run into the town if, instead of attempting the gorge, they had gone straight for Acqua Col, since at that time neither Falestoh nor Zeban had a garrison. This may well be true but it can be no criticism of Messervy that he did not do so. Even if he knew of the existence of the col, he would have been wrong to assume that, as was actually the case, Carmineo's superior regarded Keren as no more than a delaying position and had not provided enough troops to hold it properly. Faced with a God-given defensive position that any competent commander would hold to the last, Messervy had to assume that it would be defended and, with his tiny force, he could only make an impression on it by bluff and speed. If, in a flash of inspiration, he had thrown his soft-skinned vehicles over the Acqua Col he would have had to expect that the Italian tanks known to be in Keren would have intercepted him before he reached the town.

If there was ever a fleeting chance of rushing the Italian position, it would have been by using the whole strength available, two battalions, against the west side of the gorge on 3 February. The success of a single company of Camerons in seizing their ridge suggests that a more solid attack, five or six companies, might have overrun the Sanchil defences before they were organized. Since Brigadier Savory was very short of information about both the ground and the enemy's strength, it cannot be held against him that he did not take this chance, if there was a chance. It seems probable that the gorge could not have been forced in any way except the way in which it finally was forced, even if, as hindsight suggests, lives were wasted in the repeated, hopeless attempts to conquer impregnable Sanchil.

In any case there was a limit to what the generals on either side could achieve since it was, in the words of Compton Mackenzie, 'as hard a soldier's battle as was ever fought'. Some idea of the problems faced by the soldiers of both sides is suggested by the recollections of a company commander in the Worcesters.

The situation was one of desperation in locating the Italian defences in the rocky, craggy terrain – being continually shot at but being unable to pinpoint targets for response. One's companies, platoons and sections evaporated on the broken mountain side and it was very difficult to keep contact and organize any concerted attack or arrange covering fire. I got one of my subalterns to manhandle a bren gun forward to take on an Italian post but he was promptly shot in the bum.

When one attempted to find a position from which one could organize a field of fire, it was covered by the Italians. It was similar to jungle fighting – individual enterprise produced some results on a limited scale but a consolidated punch on a wider scale was impractical.

CHAPTER 8 Pursuit

WITH THE LINE of the Juba broken, de Simone was faced with an insoluble problem in attempting to defend the remainder of Italian Somaliland. Whatever plans he may have devised for doing so were superseded by orders from Addis Ababa which directed that his only intact division, 101st, which had just mounted a spirited counter-attack on the Mabungo bridgehead, should be withdrawn from his command and sent to Neghelli, about 300 miles south of the capital. With the rest of his troops, the wreck of 102nd Division, de Simone was told to fall back on the area of Harar and Jijiga where a new stand was planned and where the logistic problems of the British would be exacerbated to the greatest extent. Since radio interception passed these orders to Cunningham as quickly as they reached de Simone, he was reinforced in his decision to advance immediately on Harar.

A few days' pause was inevitable. The port of Mogadishu had been captured almost intact but it had been blocked by British magnetic mines and no sweeping gear was immediately available. Meanwhile seaborne supplies had to be landed at the small and inconvenient port of Merca, seventy miles down the coast, which was operated largely by a party of allied and Yugoslav seamen who had been freed from internment. Even when Mogadishu was operating, it was obvious that only a limited number of troops could be employed on the long, single road that led north from it and he decided to send Eleventh African Division in that direction, reinforcing it with 1st (S.A.) and 22nd (E.A.) Brigades. Twelfth Division, reduced to the Gold Coast Brigade, was to move up the Juba following 101st Division and making it possible to relieve First (S.A.) Division around Mega. This would not only make 2nd and 5th (S.A.) Brigades more easily

available when they were required for Egypt but would give
Cunningham the opportunity of using them in the Ethiopian highlands where he judged they would be more suitable than men reared in
the steamy jungles of West Africa.★ The Gold Coasters reached Dolo
on 5 March and sent one battalion forward to Neghelli two weeks
later. They found more opposition from the local banditti than from
the Italians.

To thrust from Mogadishu to Harar with the three brigades of
Eleventh Division was a formidable undertaking. It was known that
the Italian strength round the objective already consisted of three
colonial brigades apart from whatever could be salvaged from 102nd
Division. This was the least of the difficulties. To reach Jijiga, where
the road reached the east-pointing arm of the Ethiopian highlands,
entailed a journey of 650 miles† on a road that had not been completed
through a scrubby desert with widely spaced wells in trucks that had
already been overdriven by drivers who, while willing and determined, were barely out of training. It was fortunate that, among the
booty of Mogadishu, there was found a store of vehicle springs which
ennabled fifty-seven disabled trucks to be restored to the road. It was
obvious that to move and supply three brigades over this route would
be a very difficult, perhaps impossible, operation and Wavell agreed,
at Cunningham's request, to improvise a force from Aden which
could retake Berbera, from where the road to Jijiga was only 205 miles
long, a reduction by two-thirds of the haul from Mogadishu.

On 1 March, four days after the city had been captured, the advance
guard, some East African armoured cars, two companies of 2
Nigerian Regiment, some machine gunners of 1/3 K.A.R. and a

★ Cunningham wrote, 'I wished for political reasons to give the South African
Division a more prominent part in the campaign.' Anthony Mockler has taken this to
mean that he wished 'to prove his white soldiers' superiority to his blacks'. This
discreditable inference is unjustified. Cunningham's 'political reasons' were the
pressure put on him by Smuts, who, having declared a war which was far from
universally popular, was anxious that his troops should play a distinguished part in it,
thus gaining popularity for his government. Since Cunningham was dependent on
South Africa for most of his supplies, to say nothing of his air force, his wheeled
transport and the greater part of his artillery and engineering services, it is not
surprising that he was anxious to conciliate the South African government.
† Most authorities make this road rather longer, some as long as 744 miles but this
seems to be more or less the correct distance. As the most recent edition of the
Michelin map of North East Africa wisely states, 'In Africa distances can rarely be
given with absolute accuracy.'

detachment of Nigerian sappers, started north from Mogadishu, the rest of 23rd (Nigerian) Brigade following a hundred miles behind. They took two days to cover the first 220 miles through inhospitable desert on the splendid Strada Imperiale, reaching Belet Uen with its airstrip and invaluable wells. Here they paused to let the rest of the brigade, which included a South African field battery and troop of light A.A. guns (Lewis guns and captured Bredas), catch up and every vehicle took on board enough water for three days to reach the next known plentiful supply of water, Daghanur. This place, 530 miles from Mogadishu, was reached on 10 March on a road which was beginning to rise out of the featureless coastal desert. For twenty miles it ceased to exist. At Daghanur they caught up with the Italian rearguard which was as anxious to get clear of the place as the Nigerians were to reach it. There was a brief exchange of fire in which the only casualties were two South Africans who were badly burned when their truck, loaded with petrol, exploded. Almost immediately S.A.A.F. planes started using the air strip so that air cover could be maintained.

On the previous day the Duke of Aosta had flown down to Harar with orders for de Simone. He was to deny Harar to the enemy by making a stand north of Jijiga and he was allocated 5,000 Italian and 26,000 colonial troops. The Italians, apart from two Blackshirt battalions and artillerymen, were a miscellaneous collection including *Carabinieri*, East African police, armed customs officers and a unit composed of drivers who no longer had vehicles to drive. To the east of Harar was another colonial brigade (70th), reputedly a good one, which was occupying British Somaliland. These proved to be a disappointment. At dawn on 16 March four warships, H.M.S. *Glasgow*, *Caledon*, *Kandahar* and *Kingston*, appeared off Berbera and, after a short bombardment, landed two Punjabi battalions who found that 70th Brigade had disbanded itself and that the Italian presence was represented by a lachrymose colonel with sixty men drawn up on parade and anxious to surrender. Next day the Nigerians reached Jijiga and detached 3 Nigerian Regiment and some armoured cars to Hargeisha to intercept the Italian retreat. They found no one to intercept although the Italian commander, General Bertello, managed to evade them on a mule and was to fight again in south-eastern Ethiopia.

The capture of Jijiga was decisive for the rest of Cunningham's campaign. Its well-equipped airfield gave S.A.A.F. the base it needed for supporting the ground advance, an operation which had proved difficult from Mogadishu since the 550 miles to Jijiga was at the extreme range of the Hurricanes (600 miles) and beyond that of the Gladiators (523 miles) and even the Battles which had been bombing Harar and Diredawa had had to refuel at the inadequate airstrip at Belet Uen. Moreover the port of Berbera, unsatisfactory as it was, was brought into use within a week which enabled much of the supplies for Eleventh Division to reach it by the shorter overland route. On 22 March 2nd (S.A.) Brigade was disembarked at Berbera after a six-day voyage from Mombasa.

From Jijiga the direction of advance, hitherto northerly, swung west towards Harar and Addis Ababa and simultaneously the character of the country changed. The open, arid downland gave way to steep, stony hills and, seven miles beyond the town, the road started to climb sharply, winding up to the Marda Pass, the only route by which vehicles could make their way through the line of hills. For the first time since they had left Kenya East Africa Force found themselves facing a position that they could not outflank and, recognizing this, the Italians had fortified the pass and the hills on either side with wire, minefields and entrenched positions hacked out of the rocky soil. By any standards it was a strong position, made more so by its approach which consisted of 9000 yards of completely open ground which could be swept by Italian fire. The garrison was estimated to be four battalions and a group of *bande* but it is probable that even de Simone did not know how many men were there. Reinforcements were arriving but desertion was increasing rapidly and one colonial battalion, thought to be reliable, melted away on the night it reached the battlefield. To the attackers it seemed a daunting prospect. To a South African gunner officer the pass appeared impregnable and a doctor with the Nigerians wrote, 'I could have held it with my stretcher bearers'.

General Wetherall intended a two-brigade attack but this entailed a wait of forty-eight hours since the supply situation dictated that 1st (S.A.) Brigade should be held well to the rear. On 20 March his information, from deserters and radio intercepts, was that the enemy were intending to slip away and he decided on an immediate attack with the two Nigerian battalions which were immediately available, rushing forward two more South African batteries and sending urgent orders to 3 Nigerians to hurry back from Hargeisha. He planned to send one battalion against Camel Saddle Hill, a height three miles to the right of the pass and thought to be unoccupied, from where they would advance southward to the pass across twin hills known as Marda's Breasts. The other battalion would demonstrate against the hills to the left of the pass where the enemy seemed to be in greater strength than on the right. As in the early stages at Keren, a night attack was deemed impracticable, so surprise, in the conventional sense, was impossible and the only alternative was to do the utterly unexpected. It was arranged that the two battalions would drive in trucks to the foot of the rise and de-bus about a mile from the defences. The attack was timed for noon, since it was known that the enemy took their midday meal at that time and during the morning the pass and the flanking hills were pounded by three squadrons of obsolete bombers.

Shortly before noon on 21 March the South African batteries motored forward to within 5,000 yards of the enemy, unlimbered in the open and began to shell the known positions. Two batteries, detailed to support the attack on the right, went into action so close to the slope that they could not be reached by the Italian field guns firing from behind the hills. Similarly the Nigerian Light Battery, whose howitzers would only carry 6,000 yards, had to get so close that they too were safe from the artillery. Only 5th (Natal) Battery, deployed centrally so as to be able to assist either battalion and exposed to guns firing through or from the pass, was in serious danger. It was lucky to escape casualties. As soon as the guns were in action the trucks carrying the infantry raced six abreast to the end of the plain and halted while the two battalions leapt out and deployed into loose formation before starting to advance.

On the left 2 Nigerians found themselves under heavy machine-gun fire both from Observation Hill, the first south of the Pass, which was crowned by a pillbox, and from the next height, known as Saddle Hill and to be distinguished from Camel Saddle Hill on the other flank. Some excellent shooting from the Nigerian howitzers silenced the pillbox and, by setting fire to the dry grass on Saddle Hill, caused a smokescreen which obscured the whole of the left side of the ground and which they thickened with smoke shells. As a result, the battalion, although it could not storm the heavily wired posts at the top of the two hills, secured a foothold on the Ledge, the neck which linked them. They had certainly fulfilled their task of keeping the Italian right from intervening in the main battle and orders were issued for a two-company attack on Saddle Hill during the night.

On the other side of the pass 1 Nigerians also came under machine-gun fire as they de-bussed but it went over their heads and the South African guns silenced most of it within a few minutes. Camel Saddle Hill was unexpectedly found to be strongly held against them and a company which reached its southern end was driven off by a swift and resolute counter-attack by a colonial battalion which itself was shattered by a two-minute concentration from three batteries of 18-pounders. The hill was still in Italian hands at dusk but the left-hand Nigerian company had veered to its left and, after four hours' fighting, had established itself on Marda's Right Breast where they were joined by another company and a platoon of K.A.R. machine guns. They were ordered to storm the Left Breast by moonlight but this proved unnecessary. After dark a patrol of the newly arrived 3 Nigerians reported the pass as still being held and a blue searchlight shining down the approaches, but there were signs of evacuation and at 3.15 am the light was extinguished and another patrol found the whole position abandoned. The 'impregnable' Marda Pass had been forced for the loss of seven killed and thirty-seven wounded, a figure increased when seven Nigerians died of exposure during the bitter mountain night.

It took twenty-four hours to clear the road of mines and demolitions but late on 23 March the brigade was thirty miles further west and probing at the next Italian position. Three roads led towards Harar from Marda but that in the centre, the well-built Italian highway, was believed to be heavily mined. 23rd Brigade therefore took the southern road which had a passable surface while the Natal Carbineers, with a field battery, took a long-disused Ethiopian track which had the advantage that it by-passed the next Italian position at the Babile Gap. Here, just beyond the junction of the central and southern roads, the way leads through a long defile between cliffs. Entering it the East African armoured cars met a road block covered by fire which was soon cleared by 3 Nigerians but a more formidable obstacle two miles further on brought the advance to a halt for the night and the whole of 24 March had to be spent clearing wire on the approaches. Meanwhile the Natal Carbineers, using a road which consisted of 'a series of rocky steps', had a slow journey but no opposition apart from unmanned road blocks. Their mere presence was, however, sufficient to force the Italians holding the Babile Gap to withdraw. By the evening of 25 March the Nigerians came under artillery and automatic fire as they approached the Bisidmo River, the last natural obstacle in front of Harar.

That day Cunningham heard an Italian announcement, relayed by the B.B.C., that Harar had been declared an open town, a statement which seemed inconsistent with the fact that medium and field artillery was firing on his troops from positions on the outskirts of the town. A message was therefore dropped on Harar stating that the place would be regarded as a legitimate target unless all Italian troops were immediately withdrawn from it and its immediate surroundings. Notwithstanding this threat, Italian guns continued to fire on the approaches to the Bisidmo on the following morning and Cunningham ordered all the South African guns, six batteries of field guns and two of mediums, to fire a two-hour concentration on the Italian gun positions and the road to Diredawa, care being taken to avoid Harar itself. This produced a cease-fire and a senior Italian official, 'wearing a good deal of gold braid', on being taken to General Wetherall offered to surrender the town at 7 am on the following morning. The General replied that he wanted the place that day but the Italians claimed that Cunningham's message had implied that time would be allowed to withdraw their men. For answer the emissary was driven back into Harar with an escort of armoured cars and a company of Nigerians. The place was in chaos, and looting, by deserters and the native inhabitants, was in full swing. Two batteries of 105mm field guns and 500 Italians were captured and next morning Wetherall made a formal entry at almost the exact moment that Fletcher Force was driving into Keren.

Brigadier Smallwood's Nigerians had performed a very notable feat. They had advanced 710 miles in twenty-seven days and, with the help of their South African gunners, had overcome in the last sixty-five miles three formidable positions, while operating in a climate that was totally inimicable to them and made worse by the onset of the rains. Credit for this feat must be shared with the drivers from the S.A. Indian and Malay Corps who moved them in their battered trucks which had no time for maintenance but somehow contrived to keep going. It is true that most of the time de Simone's army, always excepting his excellent gunners, had not put up much of a fight. The colonial troops, most of them Somalis and Ethiopians, were now deserting in droves. One battalion mutinied and refused to obey orders to march while several others merely disintegrated, leaving their Italian officers to surrender or make their way to the rear.

Some colonial troops, a minority on this front, stayed loyally with their leaders but the majority either set off for their homes or started looting the stores in the rear. This had its effect on the Italian national troops. The rear areas where deserters were rampant housed large numbers of Italian women and children and stories of murder and rape, which lost nothing in the telling, seeped through to the troops trying to hold the line, sapping their determination. Henceforward they fought looking over their shoulders and their morale was not improved when, during the fighting at the Babile Gap, orders arrived for a phased withdrawal to the line of the Awash River, the last defensive position in front of Addis Ababa where there were 18,000 women and children, many of them the families of the Africa Blackshirt Division. After the strong Marda position was lost within twenty-four hours, Cunningham's advance seemed irresistible.

The safety of the Italian women and children was also exercising the British high command. Wavell was in desperate need of troops. He had 31,000 men in Greece and it was known that the Afrika Korps was going to attack in the Western Desert at any moment – they attacked four days after Harar fell. He had already ordered Fourth Indian Division back to Egypt and he wanted First (S.A.) Division as soon as he could get it. In the circumstances

> It seemed to me that the occupation of Addis Ababa would confront us with an embarrassment of very large numbers of Italian civilians and would have no very great strategical object.

On military grounds that was undoubtedly sound but it was only half the problem. Was it politically possible to abandon the Italian women and children to the vengeance of the Ethiopians, which, it was generally assumed, would be very terrible and, after Graziani's massacre of 1936, could be regarded as a just retribution? Nevertheless, if the Italians were massacred in their turn the effect on neutral opinion, in particular in the United States with its large Italian minority, would be disastrous.* Wavell changed his mind on

---

*In a memorandum of 8 February, 1941, the British Government had come to the conclusion that 'we have an obligation to do what lies in our power . . . to ensure law and order and the safe evacuation of the Italian population and such of their adherents as may wish to go with them; and to arrange for the safeguarding of Italian private and government property.' President Roosevelt had already written to the Prime Minister seeking guarantees for the safety of the Italian civilians, to which Churchill replied (4 April) pointing out the difficulties of being responsible for their health and safety.

Cunningham's assurance that he foresaw no serious opposition to continuing his advance to Addis Ababa, joined to the fact that there was not enough shipping to get the South Africans to Egypt immediately, although their 5th Brigade could start to move there by sea from Mombasa in the first week in April. Rather then leave the rest of them idle, Wavell authorized East Africa Force to press on to the capital.

Meanwhile both sides used the civilians as bargaining counters. On 1 April a message was dropped over Addis Ababa demanding its surrender and calling for an emissary to be flown, at a given time, to Cunningham's headquarters, now at Harar. At the time stated a Savoia duly flew over but only dropped a message saying that it would be back with an emissary on the following day. When negotiation started on 3 April they were confused by a set of instructions from Wavell which were so mangled in transmission that they were incomprehensible. Cunningham therefore proposed that the Italians should be responsible for the security of civilians until the British were in a position to undertake the task. This had to be referred to the Duke of Aosta, who replied that, greatly as he appreciated the British initiative in the matter, he could not agree to his Government having any responsibility for civilians once British troops had entered Addis Ababa. While this message was being passed to Cunningham, a signal from Churchill reached him attempting to link the safety of civilians with the preservation of the docks and shipping at Massawa. At this stage negotiations were broken off but moral responsibility for the civilians remained with the British, a point that no one appreciated more clearly than Aosta.

While this was going on, the advance on Addis Ababa had started. Two roads lead westward from Harar, although they first run together through the Huberta Pass. Thereafter the old road runs along the escarpment of the Chercher Mountains to Asba Littorio (Asbe Tafari) where it turns north to Mieso. The more modern Italian road runs from the Huberta down to Diredawa and then follows the line of the railway up the valley to rejoin the old road at Mieso. Pienaar's South Africans now took the lead and came up the Huberta Pass which had been prepared for a strong defence. The garrison included two companies of machine gunners manned entirely with officers whose colonial troops had left them and a pack battery whose gun-numbers and muleteers were all either officers or Blackshirts. Such units put up a staunch enough front but when their flanks were uncovered by the defection of further colonial battalions they could do nothing but retire, so that demolitions formed their only effective form of defence. Scarcely had Pienaar's engineers made the road passable than he was visited by the panic-stricken Assistant Governor of Diredawa who begged that his town be permitted to surrender without delay as it was being terrorized by a mob of deserters. The reserve battalion, the Transvaal Scottish, was therefore sent into the town with some armoured cars and, after firing a few shots to deter looters, soon restored order. In fact, the terrorization of Diredawa had been exaggerated. No harm came to women and children and the seven Italians who were killed or wounded were all officers or officials who tried to restore order or protect property. Here, as on the northern front, the contribution of the Patriots to the advance of the armies lay not in anything they did but in the fear engendered in the Italians as to what they might do. In the meantime Pienaar's other two battalions raced along the two roads to Mieso, hampered only by demolitions. It is a measure of the confidence felt by Eleventh Division that it was prepared to advance for 110 miles using two isolated battalions each on a separate road and seldom within twenty-five miles of each other.

At Mieso the South African advance came to an abrupt halt for the prosaic reason that they ran out of petrol. There has been no convincing explanation of this mishap though the brigade's records tell of heavy losses from the flimsy four-gallon cans then the standard British issue and of petrol contaminated by seawater when floated ashore at Kismayu. The truth seems to be that the South African quartermasters and supply officers were less enterprising (or ruthless) than those of the rest of the Division, who were still well supplied. At Mogadishu Brigadier Fowkes had told his Transport Officer to 'liberate' enough petrol to enable 22nd Brigade, with its gunners, armoured cars, engineers and field hospital, to cover a thousand miles. This forethought now paid off and the East Africans were told to take the lead.

The three K.A.R. battalions passed through Mieso and came up to the Awash River by noon on 2 April and spent the afternoon searching for possible crossing places. The Awash differs from most Ethiopian rivers in that it has water in it all the year round,* but it is wadeable in most places and little more than thirty yards across. It forms an

---

* Except where the mouth should be. Having got to within a few miles of the Gulf of Jibuti, it loses heart and disappears.

obstacle because, at this stage, it runs between steep banks which have sharp cliffs close to them and the bridges for both road and railway had been blown before the advance guard could get to them. The defending force was adequate in numbers, including 2,000 loyal Eritreans and 4,000 Italians with seventy guns of various calibres and a company of medium tanks, but the national troops, although including a machine-gun company of the Savoia Division, the last of the central reserve, were somewhat diverse in composition, comprising two Blackshirt battalions, a battalion each of engineers and airmen and smaller units of *Carabinieri* and customs officers. Colonel Rolle's group of Shoan *bande*, 1,800 strong, were moving to join them but their trains were halted by the S.A.A.F.

Throughout 3 April there was an inconclusive artillery duel across the river but by the following morning six East African armoured cars had been hauled across the river at a ford a mile downstream from the bridges. Their appearance on the flank of the defenders settled the matter. The Italians knew that orders had already been given to evacuate Addis Ababa and that part of the army was to go north to the Dessie area, while the remainder were to retreat to the lakes of the Great Rift Valley, south of the capital. The defenders saw no reason for not implementing these orders at once. The admirable South African Engineers lost no time in restoring the road bridge with box girders and at 2 am on 4 April the East African Brigade set off in its trucks for the final dash to the capital.

During the advance from Harar there had been occasional harassing attacks on the advancing troops by the *Regia Aeronautica*. There were to be no more. On 5 April six waves of S.A.A.F. Bombers, Glenn Martins, Battles, Ju86s and Hartbeests, each with fighter escort, struck the airfield of Addis Ababa and were followed by a squadron of Blenheims from Aden. All the thirty Italian planes on the field were destroyed.

Brigadier Fowkes was a thrusting commander who had made up his mind that his East Africans would be the first into the enemy capital. With plenty of petrol and no opposition on land or in the air, he set out to cover the last hundred and fifty miles, leading his column in his staff car. At Nazaret, where the road swings north out of the Rift Valley, he was met by an Italian officer, sent by the Military Governor, who urged him to hurry since the Italian army had left Addis Ababa and the civilians were in fear of Ethiopian disorders. Nothing loth, Fowkes pressed on, the only opposition coming from his own superiors.

Pressed by Smuts, who needed a victory to bolster public opinion in the Union, Cunningham had decided that the South Africans must have the honour of being first into Addis now that petrol had been found for them. He told Wetherall to stop Fowkes, and a signal, 'Halt and allow 1 S.A. Bde to pass through' was duly sent. Fowkes blandly replied, 'Your message corrupt and not understood', and motored on, giving orders, since he feared that the General might send a despatch rider forward with a written message, that no one should be allowed to overtake the rear of his column. He was at Acaci, barely ten miles from the city, when Wetherall played his last card. He sent a Hartbeest to drop a message and the pilot, entering into the spirit of the thing, swooped so low that the driver instinctively ducked and the beribboned message bag narrowly missed the staff car's bonnet. Reluctantly Fowkes halted and soon received confirmation of his orders from an Italian motorcyclist who was relaying a message sent to him by wireless through the Military Governor.

Next morning, 6 April, Major-General Wetherall, accompanied by Brigadiers Fowkes, Pienaar and Smallwood and escorted by a solitary armoured car, drove into Addis Ababa and received the formal surrender of the city in the Little Ghebbi Palace which the Duke of Aosta had left three days earlier for the north. The Press Corps preceded the General and he was followed by three companies of K.A.R. and one of Natal Carbineers. The Italian flag was hauled down and replaced by the Union Jack which itself was replaced during the afternoon by the Ethiopian flag. The task of ensuring order in the city was entrusted to 10,000 Italian police and Blackshirts who were still under arms there, and, as it happened, there was very little disturbance.

Eleventh African Division had completed an advance of 1,700 miles from crossing the border of Italian Somaliland in fifty-three days, an average of more than thirty miles a day. The military opposition may not have been very formidable – their action casualties were 135 dead, 310 wounded and fifty-two missing and they took 50,000 prisoners – but the logistic achievement was monumental. To carry out this advance, which must have some claim to being the longest and fastest in military history, they relied on a small number of trucks, worn out before they started, which ferried supplies from a small number of ports which would have been inadequate even before they had been bombed by the S.A.A.F. and shelled by the Royal Navy. The credit for this administrative triumph must largely be given to Colonel Sir

Brian Robertson Bt. (later Field-Marshal Lord Robertson of Oak-ridge) the chief staff officer in the Quartermaster-General's Branch of East Africa Force.

A very heavy burden was carried by the medical services for, even if the action casualties were not heavy – 300 dead and 854 wounded from the outbreak of war to shortly after the taking of Addis Ababa – there was plenty of work for the doctors, almost none of whom were professional soldiers. 249 were killed and 5,607 injured in accidents, largely on the roads, and disease took a heavy toll. In 1st (S.A.) Brigade Group alone, 150 men a day were having to be sent to hospital.

The most astonishing feature of Cunningham's campaign was the way in which the Italians made their own defeat possible. Even supposing that, with conspicuous exceptions, they were reluctant to fight, they could have relied for their defence on the vast stretches of appalling country to be crossed if they took care to deny vital supplies to their enemy. At every stage they left vast stores behind them for the taking. At Kismayu they left 222,000 gallons of petrol, at Mogadishu 350,000, at Addis Ababa 500,000. Without these windfalls East Africa Force would not have got beyond Mogadishu, if they had got that far.

★   ★   ★

While Wetherall was taking formal possession of Harar, Fletcher Force was nosing its way into Keren and, as soon as the Matildas had established that the town was clear of opposition, they paused to let the carriers of C.I.H. take the lead on the winding road to Asmara, fifty-seven miles ahead. They were held up at a road block late that afternoon and it was morning before the arrival of two of Marriott's battalions on their flanks induced the Italians to pull back and it took the rest of that day to get the road clear of two sets of concrete obstacles separated by fifty yards of cratered road. It was therefore not until 29 March that the vanguard approached the line of hills in front of Ad Teclesan, the position that Frusci had designated as the position on which Asmara was to be defended to the last. Once again the indomitable Carmineo was in command, though he had an open wound in his leg, and, as at Keren, he had seen to it that a large section of the cutting through the hills had been blown down on to the road. The garrison was numerically large, including many men who had fought on Falestoh and Zeban and a regiment of the Grenadiers of

Savoy, two battalions and a machine gun-company, which Frusci had not released for the defence of Keren. There were sixty-seven guns and the Italians held all the good sites for artillery observation.

It should have been a major obstacle and a preliminary flanking manoeuvre by the Baluchis failed. General Heath planned a two-brigade attack with Messervy's 9th making a frontal attack while Marriott's 29th turned the flank on the Italians' right. This was ordered for dawn on 31 March and, despite a random shell landing among the West Yorkshires as they were forming up in the darkness, worked so well that it bordered on anti-climax. There was vigorous resistance on the flank but when, in the centre, the West Yorkshires went forward with their bayonets fixed, a battalion of Grenadiers (1/10) 'surged forward and surrendered'. The rest of the defenders fled and all the Italian guns were abandoned. It took the rest of that day and the night that followed to clear the road but when, on 1 April, C.I.H. resumed the advance they met a car flying a white flag and were offered the surrender of Asmara as an open city. Heath accepted the surrender, stipulating only that all stores and installations should be left intact.

Asmara was, to all intents and purposes, a European city perched at a height of 7,800 feet on an Eritrean mountain. There was an Italian population of 50,000, little smaller than the Eritrean population.

> The upper class was Italian, and so also were the mechanics, the craftsmen and the servants. There were Italian shops, Italian restaurants and Italian cinemas showing Italian films. There was even an Italian slum, across the town from the plush quarter where the professional men lived in handsome villas set in carefully drilled gardens well back from the wide tree-lined streets.

All that was lacking was an adequate sanitary system for it seemed that 'the Italian genius for engineering comes to a sudden stop at plumbing'. As one of the first British doctors to reach the city reported,

> Asmara has three public latrines, for Italians only. There are none for the natives, either public or private. Air-raid shelters form a substitue for the modest.

This handsome, if noisome town contained the grossly inflated bureaucracy of a long-established colonial government. The Post Office alone had a European staff of two hundred and sixty and that

139

did not include the personnel responsible for telephones and tele-graphs. As at Addis Ababa, the policing had initially to be left in the hands of the Italians, aided by a dozen Sudanese policemen, and, since there were many disbanded askari at large, the risk of disorder seemed great. Fortunately all the Italians and the vast majority of Eritreans were more than anxious to co-operate and when the electricity supply to the city was cut off, a telephone call to the power station in Massawa restored the current within the hour. There was a little looting but Asmara remained generally orderly and the population accepted without demur a military order that, henceforward, all traffic would drive on the left of the road.

This passivity was welcome since the campaign had to go on and a flankguard, the C.I.H. and two companies of S.D.F. was sent southward to watch the approaches from Adigrat and Adowa. Massawa remained the most important objective though it was now useless to the Italians. The remaining submarines had left for home but, when Keren fell, most of the surface ships were still in harbour as they had been since October, except for one sloop which had slipped through the blockade and taken a shipload of refugees to Japan. On the last day of March three fleet destroyers put to sea but one of them, *Leone*, managed to go ashore as she left the harbour and was scuttled. The others returned to port but left again on the following day with their remaining consorts, the intention being to bombard Port Sudan and then sink themselves. The *Battisti* broke down during the night and was scuttled but the other four were seen at dawn on 3 April by aircraft from Aden. In anticipation of such a sortie, two squadrons of Swordfish torpedo bombers had been moved to Port Sudan and, with help from the Blenheims from Aden, sank *Sauro* and *Manin*. The other two, *Pantera* and *Tigre*, were temporarily lost sight of but were soon found drifting off the coast of Arabia, the crews having gone ashore where they were interned. The abandoned ships were sunk by Wellesleys and by gunfire from H.M.S. *Kingston*. The Italians had one success. An M.T.B. attacked the cruiser *Capetown* and damaged her so badly with a torpedo that she had to be towed to Bombay for repairs.

On 29 March Platt had received Wavell's definitive order to send Fourth Indian Division back to Egypt, one brigade at a time. Briggs's 7th Brigade would be the last to move and would thus be available for a few weeks. There was, however, a chance that Massawa might be secured without fighting and Heath used the telephone, which was still open, to pass a message to Admiral Bonetti, the Port Admiral, from General Platt. On 2 April Bonetti was asked to surrender the town and not only was the hopelessness of his situation pointed out to him but he was informed that, unless the ships in harbour and the port installations were left intact, 'the British forces will consider themselves relieved of all responsibilities either of feeding the Italian population in Eritrea or Abyssinia, or of removing them from those countries'. This threat, originating in Whitehall, probably with Churchill himself, was as ineffective at Massawa as it had been in Addis Ababa. Bonetti was quite prepared to surrender if he could contrive to save his own good name, but he knew very well that the British would not, dare not, wash their hands of the Italian civilians. He asked for time to consider and signalled to Rome, the interchange being monitored by the British. Mussolini's orders were that he was to fight on and to destroy the port before capitulating.

Bonetti had to defend a perimeter of more than ten miles and his garrison – two battalions of marines, two of Blackshirts, one of customs guards and two companies of Grenadiers – was too small, even though he had the support of 127 guns, including heavy coastal pieces which could and did traverse sufficiently to fire inland. Moreover both the R.A.F. and Heath's artillery were hampered by the need not to damage the port and the civilian population. By 5 April the town was encircled with Briggs's brigade and *Bataillon Garby* moving down to the north face and Rees's 10th Indian Brigade, with the Matilda squadron under command, moving down from Asmara to guard the south. That afternoon Bonetti sent out a *parlementaire* to seek better terms but, receiving only Heath's previous offer of unconditional surrender provided that the ships and installations were left undamaged, a truce for twenty-four hours was agreed for further consultations with Rome, a suspension of hostilities acceptable to Heath since he was not ready to attack.

The plan of attack on Massawa was easier to devise since a map had been found in Asmara which marked every Italian gun position, every minefield and every anti-tank obstacle. Heath's plan was for the main attack, Rees and the tanks, to go in centrally while Briggs's two battalions attacked the northern defences and *Bataillon Garby* was detached to press in against the south, the movement to start in darkness on the night of 7/8 April. This movement by night caused a good deal of confusion to both armies but the attack was making progress when, at dawn, the tanks rumbled through and started to attack the defences from the rear. The Italian infantry at once caved in and surrendered in increasingly large batches, although their gunners, as usual, fought on until some air strikes convinced them that all was lost. The last to fight was a group of German merchant seamen. By mid-afternoon Bonetti had surrendered to General Heath and Colonel Monclar of the Free French. He had tried to break his sword over his knee but it refused to snap and he threw it into the harbour, from where it was recovered and sent to General Platt. 9,950 men surrendered with him.

The orders to scuttle the nineteen ships and the floating dock in the harbour had been obeyed but the work had been done without enthusiasm and the port was in operation again before the end of the month. Away from the harbour area a large quantity of rolling stock and other stores was left undamaged and more damage was attributable to the looting of Garby's *tchadiens* than to either the Italians or the Eritreans. The overriding aim of the campaign had been achieved. Even the nominal threat to shipping had been eliminated and, on 11 April, the United States declared that the Red Sea was no longer a war zone and could be used by their merchantmen.* There was no greater prize to be won in East Africa.

---

* A month later the signature of the Lease-Lend Bill enabled the U.S. ships to bring to the Middle East stores which Britain could not earlier have afforded to purchase. It is not clear whether Washington did not know or decided to ignore the fact that the port of Assab was still in Italian hands until June, when it was taken by a small combined force from Aden.

CHAPTER 9 Strongholds

On 3 March East Africa Force completed the conquest of Italian Somaliland. The Nigerians reached Belet Uen and the Gold Coast Brigade took Lugh Ferrandi, moving into Ethiopia at Dolo two days later. That was the day on which Natale, having been frightened out of Burye, blasted his way through 2 Ethiopians near Dembecha. He paused in the fort of Dembecha for two days and then continued his precipitate retreat, abandoning the line of the Tamcha River and Fort Emanuel which commanded the place where the road crossed it. It was only on the Gulit River, on the outlying defence works of Debra Marcos, that he halted and showed a front. Gideon Force had been able to do little against him. There were only three hundred of them and they had outrun their supplies, 'having fed mainly on dry biscuits for three days'. They were delighted to get into Dembecha fort 'where welcome supplies of sugar, tea, salt, macaroni, rice, jam and medical stores were found undestroyed'.

Despite their achievements they were in a parlous state. The temporary destruction of 2 Ethiopians, except for a company guarding the Emperor, had reduced their fighting strength to a tiny level and they were getting little useful help from the Gojjamis. Some local dignitaries were making their submission to the Emperor, who reached Burye on 14 March, but few were prepared to commit their followers to action against the Italians. A number of Patriots duly enrolled themselves and promptly deserted to sell their newly issued rifles. Many were glad to see the return of Haile Selassie but the man who mattered in Gojjam was Ras Hailu. Despite a nine-year absence from the province and an unpleasing reputation as a landlord when he had lived there, his influence was undimmed and, as long as he and his private army were still in the Italian camp, lesser potentates were reluctant openly to support either the Emperor or the British. In particular mules were not forthcoming to sustain Gideon's communications. A vast number was needed – 400 to move Haile Selassie and his entourage alone – but many had already been requisitioned by the Italians and the remainder were jealously guarded by their owners. The price rose from thirty thalers to sixty and the Emperor himself 'found time to chaffer for droves of mules brought into his camp and took a firm hand in keeping prices down.' The hard fact remained that there were not enough mules to keep the supplies flowing. By superhuman efforts four 15cwt Morris trucks were manhandled up the escarpment at Makatal by a small party led by a French-Canadian ex-stunt driver, although a 3cwt Chevrolet had to be abandoned as its wheelbase was too long to cross the steep, narrow watercourses which cut the track. These trucks were useful on the road on the plateau – the Italians had left plenty of petrol – but supplies still had to come up the escarpment on camels and the camels were dying in droves. Among the transport for Boustead's 300 Sudanese thirty camels died on a single day.

So far Gideon Force had had more than its share of luck. Natale had behaved shamefully and given away a series of defensible positions to a force without artillery, trifling air support and a strength less than a tenth of his own. General Nasi, commanding western Ethiopia from Gondar, sacked him and sent him down to Massawa which he reached in time to surrender with Admiral Bonetti. In his place he appointed Colonel Saverio Maraventano, a tough, aggressive commander, who set about planning to recapture the ground that Natale had yielded while Nasi tried to stimulate action from Colonel Torelli who was confined around Bahrdar Giorgis at the southern end of Lake Tana by a cobweb thin screen consisting of a company of the Frontier Battalion and a handful of Patriots. Both Nasi and Maraventano realized what a trifling force had invaded Gojjam but they could not convince their troops, second-line askaris and Blackshirts who were worried for their families, that there was little to fear.

Wingate, furious at the withdrawal of his air support and believing, as always, that everyone was conspiring against him, spent his time snapping at superiors and subordinates alike and planning to capture the garrison of Debra Marcos intact. He appreciated that the enemy must be beginning to realize how small Gideon Force was and saw only two options open to him. He could withdraw before the anticipated attack, a course inimical to him and made more difficult by the Emperor's assertion that he intended to stand and fight to the end at Burye, or he could pile a new bluff on the old and start attacking again. Inevitably he chose the latter and evolved a typically daring scheme. He would circle round Debra Marcos with two Sudanese platoons and block the bridge over the Blue Nile at Safartak, thus cutting Maraventano off from Addis Ababa. He counted on being able to co-operate on the eastern bank with the self-styled 'Lij', Belai Zelleka, who had not submitted to the Italians throughout the occupation and had promised Sandford his help. Meanwhile Boustead, with what was available of the Frontier Battalion, would harass the garrison of Debra Marcos until they retreated into Wingate's arms.

This bold plan was never put to the test. Wingate set out for Safartak and had reached Amba Mariam, twelve miles north of Debra Marcos, with Boustead still in company, when news arrived that Ras Hailu seemed to have got down off the fence. He had sent part of his army to the north to drive away a loyal supporter of Haile Selassie who had been operating in the Chokey Mountains. With the rest of his men he encamped within two miles of Wingate's camp and the latter, quite unruffled, sent under a flag of truce a letter requiring Hailu to return to his obedience to the Emperor. A civil but indefinite reply was returned and Hailu went back into Debra Marcos but, with hostile troops astride his advance, it was judged unwise for Wingate, as commander of the Anglo-Ethiopian force, to risk pushing on for the Nile bridge. The mission, including the liaison with Lij Bellai, was entrusted to Bimbashi Wilfred Thesiger of the S.D.F., who had considerable experience in Ethiopia and who was accompanied by a demolition party.

Nasi ordered both Maraventano and Torelli to drive forward from the two ends of Gojjam on 27 March and, as a preliminary, the former advanced and reoccupied Fort Emanuel on 19 March, killing two of the small Sudanese garrison and taking four prisoners who, for some reason, were shot a fortnight later. This meant that there was nothing between the Italians and Haile Selassie at Burye except his guard company of 2 Ethiopians and a platoon of Sudanese, but Wingate refused to let this inhibit his plans for harassing Debra Marcos. With Boustead, he had reconnoitred the defences of the town and found them to be in two parts. In front were the crossings of the Gulit which were covered by a line of low hills, some of them fortified, while round the place itself, which had a citadel, there was a circle of entrenched heights. It was on one of these, Fort Abima, three miles north of Debra Marcos, that the first attack was launched on the night after Maraventano had retaken Emanuel. Three Sudanese platoons, with the support of two mortars, stormed the fort but immediately evacuated it and did the same at another post on the following night. Having seen his plans for harassment under way, Wingate returned to his headquarters at Burye, where he found Sandford. The two men had a serious quarrel. Nasi's orders to the two commanders in Gojjam had been intercepted in Khartoum and Platt had ordered Wingate to reinforce the exiguous force facing Torelli in the north. Since Wingate was out of touch with Burye and Sandford, his senior, was there, he had despatched an Operational Centre as ordered. Shortly afterwards a message had arrived from Wingate for every possible man to be sent to the siege of Debra Marcos and, when he reached Burye, he was furious that anyone should have been sent to the north. His immoderate language to his superior, both spoken and written, earned him a sharp reprimand from Platt.

Boustead, meanwhile, continued to attack Debra Marcos.

> Each successive night attack was launched between midnight and 3 am. . . . The Sudanese troops were ordered to attack and then when firing was opened to lie down and move on again as firing stopped. This required tremendous discipline and courage; it was so easy to remain like that. The orders were to assault the trenches up to the point of the bayonet and the bomb and then withdraw. It was essential that the withdrawal should be carried out and the troops well clear before daylight, when they could be caught by the enemy machine guns or ridden down on the open hillsides by enemy cavalry.

For five nights this pattern was followed, all the attacks, except one on Fort Addis, commanding the Gulit crossing, coming from the north. Then, after two days' rest, the Frontier Battalion started attacking from the south on 28 March and succeeded in establishing contact with some of the outlying posts where it was very clear that the defenders were more than ready to surrender if they could do so in safety. This sentiment was reinforced when, on 30 March, one of the few active Patriot bands attacked Fort Wonka, the fort nearest to the town, with grenades.

Meanwhile, the date for Nasi's combined offensive had come and gone. The day scheduled for its start had coincided with the fall of

Keren and Harar. There was no point in trying to recapture Gojjam when the Duke of Aosta was planning to concentrate such troops as were left to him in areas where they could do the most good. Torelli, in fact, did make a tentative advance on 29 March. He pushed out of Bahrdar Giorgis with five battalions and several batteries, the whole covered with a screen of *bande*, 3,000 men in all, to find that he was striking at air. His opponents, about 300 strong, did not try to obstruct him but took to the flanking hills and fired into his columns. Within twelve hours Torelli was back where he started, having suffered 175 casualties.

Maraventano started his withdrawal on 31 March by withdrawing from Fort Emanuel, the garrison losing twenty-three men when two of their trucks were mined. That night a feint attack was made by the Sudanese on the Gulit defences, following the established pattern, although Wingate already knew that it was intended to abandon that line the following morning. He planned to intercept the defenders as they withdrew and stationed his only reserve force, the reconstituted 2 Ethiopians, between the river and Debra Marcos in an ambush position. Unfortunately at the last moment the battalion refused to fight and the enemy got away unscathed. Next day 2 April most of the Blackshirts were sent off towards the Nile bridge in a convoy of twenty-eight trucks with two armoured cars since Maraventano had orders to make for Dessie. The convoy fell into a Sudanese ambush and lost twenty-five trucks and, among other casualties, eleven Italian officers. This was satisfactory but it was clear that, in view of the numbers involved, there was nothing more that Gideon Force could do to impede the Italian retreat. If Maraventano was to be stopped, it would have to be done by Bimbashi Thesiger and Belai Zelleka.

Watching from a nearby hill on the morning of 3 April, Boustead saw the Ethiopian flag hoisted over Debra Marcos and heard that Ras Hailu had been left in charge of the town with his own *banda* and some colonial infantry. A summons to surrender to the Emperor was sent in under a flag of truce, but, although the bearer was handsomely entertained, Hailu sent only 'a somewhat vague reply'. Boustead then sent another letter, threatening air and ground attacks on the place, and, getting no answer, went down to the citadel with a few men.

Ras Hailu met me at the gates, dressed in the uniform of an Italian general with several rows of medals. He was a tall commanding figure with a most aristocractic face, jet black hair, despite his age, and a most disarming smile.

147

Hailu had a good deal to smile about since, for the moment, he was in a position to make his own terms with both the British and the Emperor. He knew that Boustead's threats of attack were empty. Gideon Force had had no air support for a month and, as for ground attack, his own force was more than 6,000 strong and Boustead had three platoons. Above all he had discovered that, despite his long exile, he was still the greatest man in Gojjam and especially in his old capital of Debra Marcos. Neither the British nor the Emperor could do without him. He intended to regain his old governorship of Gojjam and to keep his word to the Italians by covering their retreat. Boustead, of course, was in an impossible position, the more so since Wingate had retired to Dembecha, where he could only be contacted by messenger, and had left no instructions to cover such an eventuality. In the circumstances Boustead achieved a remarkable coup by inducing Hailu to evacuate the citadel, although he had to restrain several Patriot leaders, now coming into the open, from bringing their followers into Debra Marcos since a clash between their men and Hailu's would have brought disaster. The situation was not resolved until 6 April when Haile Selassie, accompained by Sandford and Wingate, reached the town. He inspected and congratulated the Sudanese before raising the Ethiopian flag over the citadel.

> He looked a tinier figure than ever. Whilst he was standing below the flagstaff, Ras Hailu, dressed now in a superb white robe and with bared head, walked slowly between the lines of soldiers to the Emperor. Before reaching him, he prostrated himself three times full length on the ground, the third time at the Emperor's feet which he kissed.
>
> The Emperor looked on the ground without a motion of acknowledgement as the old man moved into the background.

At almost the same moment General Cunningham was accepting the surrender of Addis Ababa.

Ras Hailu had not only saved himself from a formal accusation of treachery* but he had kept his word to the Italians. The Nile bridge at Safartak was not blocked and Maraventano and his men crossed without opposition. Belai Zelleka had refused to co-operate with Thesiger, having been heavily bribed by Hailu, the price including the promise of marriage to Hailu's daughter. Competent guerrilla though

---

* He succeeded in retaining an unofficial governorship in Debra Marcos for most of a month before the Emperor felt strong enough to have him escorted to Addis Ababa. He lived there under house arrest until his death, from natural causes, in 1951.

he was, Belai was found in the end to be a bandit rather than a Patriot. He was hanged for another act of disloyalty in 1945.

The liberation of Gojjam was a political triumph but a military irrelevance. It had no effect on either of the main campaigns. It kept occupied a number of second-line troops who would have had to have been stationed in the province as an army of occupation under any circumstances. Its value lay in giving the impression that Haile Selassie was playing some part in the recovery of his own empire. In practice his presence was almost an embarrassment to the operation since his entourage used much of the scarce transport facilities and his contribution in rallying Ethiopian support was, in terms of fighting men, very small. Not a few declared their loyalty, but, when it came to fighting, their contribution was small and erratic. The surge in support for the Emperor came later when Pratt had broken the Italian army at Keren and Cunningham had taken Addis Ababa. The heroes of the campaign were the Sudanese of the Frontier Battalion who, working and marching in a country and climate utterly alien to them, did all the serious fighting with outstanding courage and endurance. Their leaders were lucky to come through successfully. Had some competent Italian officer, someone in the mould of Carmineo, been in charge in place of the despicable Natale, the result could well have been disaster, with the Emperor, alive or dead, in the hands of his enemies. Maraventano might have been able to restore the situation had the operations of Platt and Cunningham given him time.

For the British army the Gojjam campaign had a long-term benefit in the education of Orde Wingate. His drive, imagination, courage and determination kept the campaign going but, despite Natale's incompetence, Gideon Force could never have established itself in the highlands, far less threatened Debra Marcos, had not others supplied the talents that Wingate lacked, the patient diplomacy of Sandford, the tactical skills of Boustead and the organizing ability of Lieutenant-Colonel Donald Nott on whom rested the burden of keeping the tenuous supply lines going. Wingate had constant altercations with each of these men but from them he learned what was practicable. One of his subordinates in Gojjam summed him up, succinctly and accurately, as 'Brilliant, certain and half-right', but he learned all the time and, by the time he got to Burma and more spectacular operations, he had assimilated the techniques which would enable him to succeed. Always a difficult man to command or serve, he remained brilliant and certain but he had learned in Gojjam to be right more than half the time.

There was another group on whom Wingate depended for his success and, though he often cursed them, he never quarrelled with them. Without the 15,000 camels brought from the Sudan the whole rickety enterprise could never have been carried through. Within a month of the occupation of Debra Marcos only fifty-three of them survived and they were soon to die.

★   ★   ★

On 30 March the Duke of Aosta signalled to Rome,

> It only remains for us to resist wherever we can and for as long as we can for the honour of the flag.

Whatever his private thoughts about the disintegration of Mussolini's empire, the Duke was a patriotic Italian and, rather than making a dignified surrender at Addis Ababa, saw it as his duty to tie down as many British troops as possible, for as long as he could. He divided his remaining troops into three portions, instructing General Gazzera, who had seven colonial divisions with 200 guns and thirty tanks, some 38,000 men, to establish himself in the broken country round Jimma, south-west of the capital. In the north-west at Gondar was General Nasi with 41,000 men and seventy guns holding a large and fertile area which could only be approached by large bodies of troops up the 4,000-foot climb of the Wolchefit Pass, as formidable a defensive position as any in the world. With the rest of his army, including whatever could be saved from Eritrea, Aosta took post in the area Dessie – Amba Alagi, rightly judging that stationed astride the Addis Ababa – Massawa road, he would inflict the maximum inconvenience on his enemies.

This choice of position was so clearly an impediment to the British that it is hard to see why both Platt and Cunningham inititially devoted their available troops to operations against Jimma and Gondar, enclaves which interfered with nothing and could have been left until time and resources were available for their reduction. The probable explanation is that both generals had problems other than military ones on their minds. The establishment of civil government in conquered territories was not a question to which the British had ever given much attention. In the war of 1914–18 the problem had only arisen in Iraq and Transjordan, neither of which provided many useful precedents, and the subject was not mentioned in the Staff College curriculum between the wars. G.H.Q. in Cairo had set up a small civil affairs branch but the territory that had been envisaged as requiring military government had been no more than part of western Eritrea, perhaps as far west as Agordat, and Jubaland in Somalia. Then the limited offensive planned for January, 1941, expanded into a campaign of total conquest and, before the summer, the whole of I.E.A., 700,000 square miles with 10 million inhabitants, was in need of government and there were subsidiary problems such as the re-establishment of British rule in Berbera and the need to set up a land blockade of French Somaliland, still obstinately adhering to Vichy and harbouring impassioned fascist refugees from Ethiopia.

Cunningham had the most intractable problems. Much of his supplies still had to come through Italian Somaliland where the tribes were notoriously difficult to contain and had now got their hands on vast quantities of abandoned Italian weapons which enabled them to indulge in their age-old taste for internecine warfare, diversified by general banditry against anything that offered, not excluding British stores and military convoys. To exacerbate the situation the Italian police in the colony was markedly corrupt and had to be disbanded and replaced as early as 15 April by a hastily recruited gendarmerie, built round a detachment of Tanganykan police, imported at short notice. In the first six months of its existence this force succeeded in seizing 14,000 rifles and six million rounds of ammunition from the tribesmen, well knowing that at least as much was still in unauthorized hands.

Some of the same problems applied in liberated Ethiopia but here there was another dimension to the difficulties. Somaliland, like Eritrea, had been for long an Italian colony and could thus be treated as Occupied Enemy Territory. In Ethiopia the Emperor regarded the Italian occupation as no more than an unfortunate incident in his reign so that his territory was that of an ally which he wished to govern himself through his own officials. In practice this was wholly impracticable, if only because Graziani's purge of 1936 had deliberately aimed to eliminate every Ethiopian who had sufficient education to act as a civil servant. Inevitably, in the immediate aftermath of the liberation, government had to be carried on by the British, although acting in the name of the Emperor, a subterfuge which led to successive misunderstandings and embarrassments. To make matters more difficult, the populace, not unreasonably, refused to trust the Italian currency and insisted on all dealings being in Maria Theresa thalers. There was no shortage of these beautiful coins, since the British had bought the dies for them between the wars, but they are large and heavy. Each one was valued at 1s 10½d (c.9p) (its actual value as silver) which meant that £3,000 worth of thalers weighed one ton. On top of all this there were in Addis Ababa 25,000 Italians who had to be protected, fed and, eventually, repatriated. In fact the native citizens had always got on surprisingly well with non-official Italians and continued to do so, but arriving at the capital simultaneously with East Africa Force was the large Patriot group, led by Ras Abebe Aregai, who, having been harried by the Italians throughout the occupation, were unlikely to take a kindly view of their defeated oppressors. Considering that, in the early weeks, the policing of the capital was in the hands of the *Carabinieri* and a company of South African motor-cyclists, there was a gratifying absence of serious incidents.*

Whatever the reasons which induced Platt and Cunningham to direct their advance guards into the dead ends represented by Gondar and Jimma, they were quickly recalled to essentials by Wavell. The victory in East Africa was the only hopeful development in his sprawling command. On the day after Addis Ababa fell, the Germans invaded Greece, reaching Athens by 27 April and inflicting on the Commonwealth forces the loss of 12,000 men, 209 aircraft, 8,000 trucks, the guns for three divisions and the tanks for an armoured brigade. They were now threatening Crete and, in the Western Desert, Rommel had attacked and, by the middle of April, was besieging Tobruk and probing up to the Egyptian frontier. It was becoming clear at the same time that troops would have to be sent eastward to restore a potentially damaging situation in Iraq. Wavell needed troops and his only source of them was East Africa. Fourth Indian Division was already on the move, Fifth would have to follow as soon as possible and the rest of the South Africans must join their 5th Brigade. 2nd Brigade would move from Berbera as soon as shipping was available. 1st (S.A.) Brigade would have to move overland to pick up shipping at Massawa. Their road from Addis Ababa lay over the Duke of Aosta's chosen position at Amba Alagi.

* The only serious problem arose when some *Carabinieri*, believing a crowd to be menacing, opened fire and killed an Ethiopian. The officer in charge was tried by a British court-martial and sentenced to death but the sentence was later quashed.

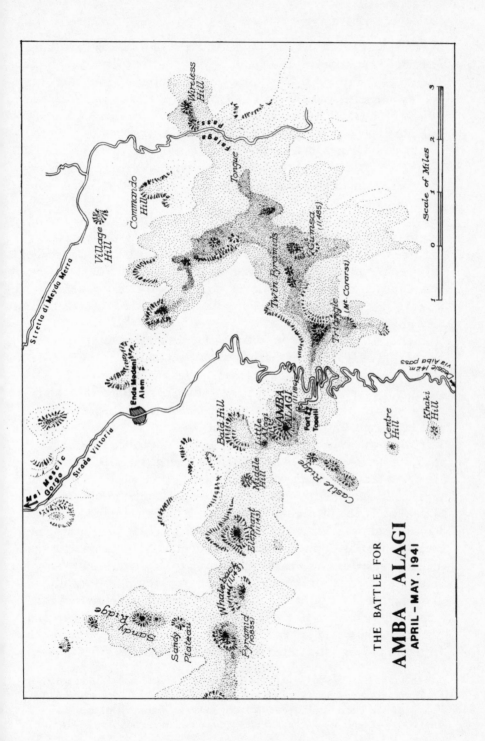

THE BATTLE FOR

AMBA ALAGI
APRIL – MAY, 1941

Scale of Miles

Wireless Hill

Falega Pass

Tongue

Commando Hills

Village Hill

Streta di Meyda Merra

Twin Pyramids

Gumsa (11,485)

Triangle (Mt Corarsi)

Enda Medani Alem

Mai Mescic Gorge

Strada Vittoria

Bald Hill

Little Alagi

AMBA ALAGI (11,860)

Fort Toselli

Dessie (142M) via Alba pass

Centre Hill

Khaki Hill

Castle Ridge

Middle Hill

Elephant

Sandy Plateau

Sandy Ridge

Whaleback (11,743)

Pyramid (10605)

Wavell ordered Platt and Cunningham to clear the long road, working respectively from north and south.

Platt had already sent a small force southward to screen his occupation of Asmara. This consisted of C.I.H, two motor-machine-gun companies, a light battery from S.D.F. and some sappers. Known as Flitforce, it was commanded, like the earlier mobile force, by the resourceful Lieutenant-Colonel Fletcher. On the right he sent a company of S.D.F. towards Gondar but, no sooner had it established that the Wolchefit Pass was held against them than their orders were changed and, on 13 April, they were recalled to the main body. This had moved to Adowa and Adigrat, persuading a colonial battalion and a battery to surrender peacefully. By 5 April C.I.H. had penetrated another seventy miles to Quiha where another battalion was made prisoner. They pressed on to Mai Mescic, 190 miles from Asmara, where they met Italian resistance in the gorge and at that stage C.I.H. was recalled to Massawa for embarkation and its place in Flitforce taken by Skinner's Horse.

Back at Adowa, Ras Seyum Mangasha, the greatest local magnate, had announced to Fletcher that he was changing sides. On the face of it Ras Seyum was as dubious a character as Ras Hailu.* He was the son of the hereditary ruler of Tigre, the grandson of the Emperor John IV and a potential rival to Haile Selassie, who had never trusted him and had appointed him governor only of Western Tigre, an apparent demotion which he resented. In the years before 1935 he had made many contacts with the Italians but they regarded him as 'constantly swinging between treachery and calculation' and when the invasion came he had fought bravely but ineffectively on the Ethiopian side. When the Emperor was defeated, he made his submission to the Italians and was fortunate to be exiled by Graziani during the repression. By 1939 he was back, and frequently appeared with the Viceroy on state occasions, being allowed to return to his governor-ship in West Tigre. In February, in an effort to restore the crumbling position, the Duke of Aosta created him Negus of all Tigre and gave him 7,000 rifles. It was a vain hope. Ras Seyum had the survivor's instinct and, just as he joined the winners in 1936, he swung over to the British in 1941 and soon afterwards, submitted to Haile Selassie, a step

---

* Both Ras Seyum and Ras Hailu had been created Honorary Knights Commander of the British Empire when they had visited England with Haile Selassie (then Ras Tafari) in 1924. The future Emperor had taken them on his visit less for the pleasure of their company than because he was unwilling to trust them out of his sight.

14. A Savoia 79 bomber landing near Diredawa bringing emissaries to negotiate the safety of Italian civilians in Addis Ababa, 3 April, 1941.

15. A Hartbeest dropping a message to Brigadier Fowkes on the approach to Addis Ababa.

16. The entrance to the cave where the Duke of Aosta lived on the side of the mountain at Amba Alagi.

17. Italian troops marching out with the Honours of War below the peak of Amba Alagi.

18. Surrender: the Duke of Aosta with Major-General A. G. O. Mayne of 5th Indian Division, 20 May, 1941.

19. The road over the Wolchefit Pass.

which earned him the governorship of all Tigre until his violent death in 1960. His private army, with their new Italian rifles, was the first large accession of Ethiopian strength to the British since the campaign began. He was given a liaison officer, Major Rankin of the S.D.F. and sent to turn the west flank of the Amba Alagi position by going through the mountains, impassable to regular forces, to Socota, forty miles south-west of Amba Alagi. The existence of this large Patriot band had a considerable psychological effect on the beleagured Italians.

These beleagured Italians had a very powerful position. The great *Strada Vittoria*, one of the supreme monuments to Italian road-building, at this point reaches its greatest height at the pass just below the 11,300 foot peak of Amba Alagi. It was here that the brave, if misguided, Major Toselli with his 2,150 men made his epic stand to the death in December, 1895, (see p 9), an act of gallantry which is commemorated by a chapel and a monument. More than 350 miles from Addis Ababa and more than 200 from Asmara, any attack on it must stretch the British resources even further than they had already been stretched. It is interesting that Marshal de Bono had remarked in November, 1935, that the Toselli Pass 'has no strategic importance and is tactically useless since it can be turned on all sides'. Hardly had he made this pronouncement that he was removed from his command, showing that not all Mussolini's military judgements were wrong.

Since Cunningham had committed 1st (S.A.) Brigade to the south of Addis Ababa, they could not start north from the capital until 13 April so that the initial attacks could only come from the north and the forces available to Major-General Mayne, now commanding Fifth Indian Division, were wholly inadequate. After the essential needs of security in Eritrea had been met, he had available, apart from Flitforce, five battalions (29th Brigade and one each from the other two brigades of his division), 51 Commando, two field regiments and a battery of medium guns. Air support was puny, consisting of a flight of Wellesleys and a composite squadron of Gladiators, Hardys and Lysanders. Even transport animals were short and the force was largely dependent on 800 donkeys requisitioned from the countryside.

The Duke of Aosta's position was in many ways more formidable than that at Keren. The climb from the valley floor to the main defences was a thousand feet greater in vertical terms than that to Brig's Peak and, once reached, the height produced oxygen deficiency, shortage of breath, among unacclimatized troops. As at Keren there was no way in which the position could be turned by troops dependent on road transport, but at Amba Alagi the Italians were occupying a ten-mile stretch of a razor-backed ridge punctuated by steep rocky cones and two roads crossed it. In the centre was the fine *Stada Vittoria*, passable in all weather, which zig-zagged its way up to the Toselli Pass (9,750 feet above sea level), where it was dominated by a permanent fort. Five miles to the east, a subsidiary road, *Stretta di Meyda Merra*, motorable on the north face but only a track to the south, crossed the watershed by the Falaga Pass at a little over 10,000 feet. Since the decision to turn Amba Alagi into a redoubt had been taken early, according to some accounts before the end of 1940, the Italians had had plenty of time to prepare their positions with pits for weapons of all sizes and shelters blasted from the rock and strengthened with concrete. There were stores of ammunition and rations sufficient for several months and an adequate supply of fresh water and the only thing not plentiful was the number of troops which at about 7,000 was rather too small for the position to be held.

Although appreciating the need for speed in opening the main road, Mayne was quite unable to make a major attack on Amba Alagi before the beginning of May, since, with an inadequate number of deteriorating trucks, some weeks were needed to ferry forward the supplies, in particular the huge tonnage of artillery ammunition that would be needed for an attack and it soon became clear that, small as it was, any increase in the attacking force would cause a breakdown on the lines of supply. In his planning of the attack Mayne was helped by a present from Platt in the form of a copy of Marshal Badoglio's book published in 1936, *The War in Abyssinia*. The Marshal had recognized that there was no better position in which the Ethiopian army could have made a stand against the Italian invaders and had given much thought about how to overcome it. In practice this contemplation had been wasted, for while Haile Selassie, who admitted to being no soldier, had agreed with Badoglio that Amba Alagi was the best defensive position in the north of his empire and had given orders to concentrate his army there, his generals had disobeyed him, fighting and losing the decisive battle at Amba Aradem, a less formidable position fifty miles to the north. As distilled by Mayne in 1941, Badoglio's plan had been to seize the Falaga Pass and then drive west along the ridge.* Believing that his

---

*It is not clear how Mayne came to this reading of Badoglio's intentions. In the English edition (p99–100) he intended to advance a regular division on each flank, while demonstrating with Blackshirt groups in the centre. 'The flank columns were to proceed along the ridge where they would . . . open the way for the centre column.'

opponent would also have read the book and would accordingly expect an attack on his right so that he would keep it strong and be prepared to reinforce it to the detriment of the rest of his line, he decided to feint at Falaga and launch his main attack at the other end of the line.

Since the Duke of Aosta had neither the experience nor the inclination to command in person, his Chief-of-Staff, General Valetti-Borgnini, was in charge of the defence and did see the Falaga Pass as his most vulnerable point. He stationed there his only complete formation, Colonel Postiglione's 43rd Colonial Brigade, two battalions which had started the campaign at Um Hagar and had seen no more fighting than the retreat to Aressa, harried by some S.D.F. and followed by a dispiriting march to Adowa. They had a battery of pack guns under command.

The main bastion of the defence, the Toselli Pass and its flanking mountains – the group round Amba Alagi to the west and Triangle (Mount Corarsi) to the east – absorbed most of the Italian strength – two Blackshirt battalions, the bulk of a machine-gun battalion from the Savoia Division, four field and two A.A. batteries with some pack guns, together with some miscellaneous units such as a battalion of airmen, some sailors and a large group of transport drivers whose abandoned vehicles cluttered both the pass itself and the road leading to it. Few men were left to garrison the western end of the line which had to be entrusted to some companies of customs officers and a machine-gun company.

The information available to Mayne about the Italian position was incomplete and inaccurate. He heard from deserters that their strength was only 4,000 National and 1,000 Colonial soldiers but he could gather nothing about their dispositions and it was the merest luck that he chose the most weakly held part of their line for his heaviest attack. The approach to the western end had the advantage that from the ridge there ran down a very poor track along a spur known as Sandy Ridge. This stretched for about three miles, almost reaching the point where the *Strada Vittoria* emerges from the long Mai Mescic gorge. The mouth of the gorge was under observation and long-range fire from Amba Alagi, but the track up Sandy Ridge was in dead ground until it emerged on to a higher feature, Sandy Plateau. Mayne decided to commit his only complete brigade, the 29th, to a night attack up this track. 3/13 R.F.F.R. were to lead and seize the steep rocky height, known from its shape as Pyramid (10,855 feet), which stood at the junction of Sandy Plateau and the main ridge. 3/2 Punjabis would then pass through them, heading east, and capture in succession the lower height named Whaleback, the formidable Elephant (11,143 feet) and the smaller, rounded Middle Hill. The final assault on Amba Alagi and its outlying features, Little Alagi and Bald Hill, would be made by the Worcesters. This was an optimistic plan for three understrength battalions, even given that estimates of Italian numbers and morale were too low, and matters were made no easier by inaccurate maps and air photographs which showed nothing south of the crestline. In particular no one realized how narrow that crestline was and how difficult it would be to manoeuvre on either side of it.

For the feint attack on the Falaga Pass, Flitforce was renamed Fletcher Force★ and strengthened by the addition of 51 Commando, a company of 3/12 R.F.F.R, a battery of field guns and a troop of 60-pounders. At Platt's suggestion a further feint was mounted in the centre. No less attractive military operation could be imagined than a frontal attack on the Toselli Pass but Platt argued that the British had won at Keren by making a wholly unexpected frontal attack up the Dongolaas Gorge. The Italians would not therefore be able to ignore the possibility of their attempting something equally unlikely in this case. 3/18 Royal Garhwal Rifles were therefore detailed to make a demonstration up the main road.

It was late April before the tedious business of stockpiling in the forward area was complete and the attacking force could be brought up. On 26 April the Garhwalis occupied the northern tip of Sandy Ridge without a fight and on the following day Fletcher Force drove up the *Stretta di Meyda Merra* and established their forward posts on Village Hill, a low, free-standing rise beyond the end of the complicated spur which ran down from Falaga Pass to the west of the road. It was a dangerous approach as the last part of their advance was along a gorge which was defiladed by Italian guns but they escaped with few casualties. On the same day Major Rankin led Seyum's irregulars into Socota.

The next advance was on the night of 30 April, when, after a daylong bombardment, 51 Commando moved up the long spur towards Falaga. It was a difficult move since the rocky slope was so

★ To add to the confusion of this retitling, Fletcher was promoted to command 9th Brigade and, during the Alagi fighting, his brigade headquarters was sent up to join him. In the later stages of the battle his command was known indiscriminately as Fletcher Force and 9th Brigade.

precipitous that each man had to be helped up by his comrades and it was fortunate that their objective, known thereafter as Commando Hill, was found to be unoccupied by the Italians who used it only in daylight as an O.P. It was found impossible to occupy Commando Hill by day since it was dominated by the next step in the spur, known as Tongue, so that the Commandos spent the day just below the northern rim of the plateau, their supplies being hauled up to them on a rope belayed round one of the rare stunted trees at the top. On the following night they moved east across the road and took possession of Wireless Hill thus taking the last place from which the enemy could see the mouth of the Meyda Merra gorge and making it possible for trucks to be brought to the foot of the pass.

Fletcher had been ordered to maintain pressure on Falaga until the night of 2/3 May when 29th Brigade's attack was to go in, but, when that had to be postponed for twenty-four hours, he decided to try an attack on the pass itself, having heard from deserters that it was only lightly held. At dark on 3 May he attacked with the Commando on the right of the road and Skinner's Horse, a unit not trained for this type of fighting, on the left. The assault did not succeed. A foothold was seized on Tongue but it could not be held and the troops fell back to Wireless and Commando Hills where a determined counter-attack was beaten off by the company of R.F.F.R. It was, however, enough to induce Valetti-Borgnini to send reinforcements to the pass. Simultaneously the Garhwalis were making their demonstration in the centre. They took the village of Enda Medani Alem before darkness fell, thus deliberately drawing attention to themselves, and under cover of night moved up the steep slopes of Bald Hill. In fact they only went far enough to find themselves faced with a thick and continuous belt of barbed wire but a lot of ammunition was fired on both sides before they fell back to a position in front of the village. They had served their purpose and convinced the Italians that something serious was intended in their centre. They reinforced their garrison on Bald Hill.

The main attack at the west of the line started in dashing style. R.F.F.R. took Pyramid on the run and the Punjabis raced through them and swept the customs officers off Whaleback and Elephant but by that time dawn was breaking and it was decided to postpone the attack on Middle Hill until the following evening. Then it was found to be a formidable operation with the machine gunners of the Savoia Division clinging tenaciously to their prepared position and having to be winkled out with bayonets and grenades. Once more dawn was breaking before the Worcesters could get through for the final attack on Little Alagi. It was not a success. Tied to the narrow, curving crest of ridge they were fired on not only from their front but from Bald Hill on their left. They were brought to a halt by a thick wire entanglement and, although one platoon found a gap, they could not get forward and the battalion had to spend the day taking what cover was available from the scattered boulders. They fell back to Middle Hill, thankful that they had suffered only thirty-six casualties although one of the dead was a company commander, the fourth to be lost since February. Their attack was repeated before dawn on 6 May by R.F.F.R. who advanced without artillery preparation and were through the gap in the wire without being detected. The Italian reaction was quick and violent but the Indians held their ground until a large counter-attack force was seen to be massing against them. At that moment cloud and mist descended on the heights so that the British artillery could not be used to disperse them and there was a period of confused hand-to-hand fighting before R.F.F.R. were pushed back on to Middle Hill. Two nights later an attempt was made to turn the Alagi heights by seizing Castle Ridge, the long, lofty spur that runs southward from them. It failed but that night Fletcher Force succeeded in getting possession of Tongue. It was, however, clear that Mayne did not have enough men to reduce the remaining defences and help would have to come from the south.

*   *   *

Brigadier Pienaar's 1st (S.A.) Brigade was on the Omo River at Abalti, 100 miles south of Addis Ababa, when they received Wavell's order to turn in their tracks and make for Dessie and Amba Alagi. It was not until 13 April that their vanguard passed through the capital and even then the Transvaal Scottish were twenty-four hours in the rear and a company from another battalion was detained in Addis on security duties. They were, however, accompanied by an armoured car company, a field regiment, two troops of A.A. guns, a composite troop of mediums*, a field company of engineers, a field hospital and a mobile workshop.

---

* These 60-pounders and 6″ howitzers, veterans of 1918, had been adapted with pneumatic tyres for moving but had to revert to their original steel-shod wheels for firing, the conversion taking a well-drilled crew eight minutes. It was widely believed in the S.A. Artillery that two of the howitzers had been taken from the 1914–18 war memorial in Johannesburg.

On the excellent metalled road which ran along the watershed between the Blue Nile and the Awash, they covered more than a hundred miles on their first day north of the capital, the only obstruction being an incompletely manned road block near Debra Berhan. Their main trouble was the cold at night since they were still wearing the shorts and bush-shirts which had been appropriate to the torrid heat of Somalia. On 14 April they were relieved to capture intact the Mussolini tunnels where the road bores through a mountain barrier. Even the magnificent South African engineers might have found restoring them to be beyond their capabilities. Just beyond them, however, a large section of cliff had been blown across the road on a hairpin bend so the Duke of Edinburgh's Own Rifles dismounted from their trucks, skirted the block and descended on the town of Debra Sin where they found what was left of the garrison very willing to surrender and to purchase their freedom by helping the sappers clear the road block. Nevertheless, it was not until 16 April that the brigade, with which the Transvaal Scottish had now caught up, was able to pass through Debra Sin. The following day the Dukes, again in the lead, crossed a causeway improvised to replace a blown bridge on the approaches to the Cambolcia Gorge and came under concentrated artillery fire, some from pieces of heavy calibre. Almost immediately a flash flood carried away the causeway, isolating the battalion.

In an attempt to retain Dessie, which commanded the transverse road to Gondar, the Duke of Aosta had detached General Frusci, anxious to restore his reputation after the Eritrean calamity, with 10,000 men to block the South African advance. He hoped to be reinforced by Maraventano's men from Debra Marcos; these failed to arrive but he could spare 4,500, more than half of them national troops, to block the gorge which led to the Cambolcia Pass. These comprised four Blackshirt and two colonial battalions with some sailors and engineers acting as infantry. In support were forty guns, including eight mediums and twelve naval guns which were British-made and dated 1916. Against them Pienaar could bring three battalions, none of them more than 400 strong, twenty-four 18-pounders, one 6-inch howitzer, one 60-pounder and four 4.5-inch howitzers. Since the Italians had had plenty of time to prepare their position – the naval guns were in concrete emplacements – they should have been immovable.

Four days of manoeuvring and probing attacks rewarded the South Africans with nothing but a single hill on the right of the road and outside the main Italian position, but, while trying to find a way round the gorge, a patrol met a party of about 250 Patriots being led by a subaltern of the Black Watch who told Pienaar of a way in which the rear of the defences might be taken from a flank. The brigadier decided that he would attempt a *coup de main* with a single battalion, the Natal Carbineers, on the night of 21/22 April. It was a bold gamble. To send off one third of his infantry, a battalion with only 321 fit men which had had little training for this type of operation, on a curving compass march on a dark night could well result in their disorganization or destruction. In the event everything went well. The Blackshirt sentries, believing that they were four miles from their nearest enemies, were so inattentive that the Carbineers were within ten yards of them before they were detected. The Blackshirts fled and the forward defences, hearing that their rear had been overrun, crumbled when the rest of Peinaar's brigade attacked them. Four hundred Italians were killed, 1,200 taken prisoner, against South African casualties of thirty-eight. There could be no pursuit since a road block stopped the armoured cars and the infantry was exhausted by their six-day battle. It was not until 25 April that Cambolcia village was occupied and from its airstrip the last of the *Regia Aeronautica* in the north, two bombers and two fighters, took off for temporary safety at Gondar. Dessie surrendered on 26 April. Frusci tried to defend the place but his colonial troops were deserting fast and his Italians getting increasingly nervous, one result being that they blew a road bridge with their last six medium guns on the wrong side. The South African engineers replaced the bridge by a causeway made of 2,752 barrels from a conveniently sited dump and, before they had finished their task, the commandant of Dessie offered to surrender the place. There were 1,500 Italian women and children there and, around it, bandits masquerading as Patriots were looting and murdering Italian stragglers. Pienaar accepted the town's surrender and allowed the prisoners to keep their small arms for self-defence. There were 8,000 of them, roughly twice the number of the whole of the South African brigade group. Between Cambolcia and Dessie fifty-two guns, 236 machine guns and more than 40,000 rifles had been taken. In and around Dessie were found 310,000 gallons of petrol and 75,000 of oil. Pienaar's men had suffered less than fifty casualties since leaving Addis Ababa.

On 11 May the South Africans reached the Aiba Pass and were in sight of Amba Alagi, their advance having been delayed by frequent demolitions. Their arrival coincided with that of a swarm of Ras

Seyum's Patriots, coming up from Socota. Some of them were susceptible to discipline but the majority were more addicted to looting Italian or South African property than to fighting. They were especially addicted to stealing lengths of copper and wire, a practice which made the operation of field telephones almost impossible since every day the signallers would lay the cables and every night the Patriots would steal them.

The brigade was now under command of Fifth Division and, as soon as they reached Mai Ceu, Mayne flew over to see Pienaar. On the northern front there had been little further progress since the attacks on Little Alagi had failed. On the east the Garhwalis, having replaced Skinner's Horse in Fletcher Force, had taken Mount Gumsa, but, on the debit side, the weather had broken and the road to the north of the Falaga Pass was impassible to trucks so that all Fletcher's supplies had to be carried forward on donkeys or manhandled. The garrison of Gumsa (11,485 feet) had had to be supplied with greatcoats and blankets if they were not to be disabled by exposure, another strain on the supply line. It had been hoped that an attack could be made from the east on the Twin Pyramids and Triangle features but Fletcher had reported that the line of advance was a saw-edged ridge, 'each serration of the saw being held by little posts built up with stones and manned by machine guns. There seems to be no possibility of advancing this way.' Since this was the kind of terrain that had stopped 29th Brigade's advance, Mayne had been forced to agree with Fletcher and asked Pienaar to assault Triangle, the mountain immediately east of the Toselli Pass, by way of Khaki Hill near which the South African guns could be deployed. Pienaar immediately agreed, stipulating only that the attack should be carried out in daylight since 'he considered that every foot put wrong would betray the exact position of the men at night before they could close for the attack.' In view of his highly successful night attack at Cambolcia a few weeks earlier, this was a somewhat strange contention since it must be easier to pinpoint 'the exact position of the men' if you can see them than if they merely kick an occasional stone in the dark, but Mayne, who had feared that Pienaar might 'object to tasks I gave them to do and, maybe, appeal against them to their own South African headquarters in Addis Ababa', gladly accepted Pienaar's timing and the attack was fixed for 15 May.

The first problem encountered lay in getting the brigade down the north face of the Aiba Pass since the road was reduced to single track by a continuous line of parked Italian lorries and covered by anti-aircraft guns firing horizontally from Amba Alagi with the aid of a powerful searchlight. There were torrential rains and gale-force winds on the night of 12/13 May which, while blinding the searchlight, made driving down the winding road almost impossible, but by the evening of 14 May Khaki Hill had been taken, the South African artillery deployed around it and a telephone link established with 29th Brigade at Pyramid. The guns from both sides pounded the Italian positions as did the available aircraft and Ras Seyum appeared at Pienaar's command post and offered to co-operate. It was arranged that some of his men would provide carrying parties and the remainder would operate on their right to establish a link with Fletcher Force. During 14 May the Duke of Edinburgh's and the Transvaal Scottish moved to their start lines and prepared to attack.

At this stage there was an impromptu addition to the programme. Only about 500 of Ras Hailu's men were under control and even they were affronted by being asked to act as porters. The remainder, who were not devoid of courage, launched themselves at Twin Pyramids, the heights which link Gumsa to Triangle. They took the more easterly of the peaks by surprise and, after a hard struggle in which they fought with equal bravery and brutality, captured the second. Then they rushed for Triangle but their onslaught was checked by a double apron of barbed wire covered by machine guns. Suffering terribly, they fell back on Twin Pyramids only to be shelled off it, although the Garhwalis were able to move forward and retain them. On the following night the Garhwalis launched their own attack on Triangle, using Bangalore torpedos to breach the wire. Simultaneously the South Africans, led by the Transvaal Scottish, were scaling the south face of the same mountain and had got to within 200 feet of the summit when the garrison fell back across the Toselli Pass. They could hear the Indians coming from the east, the South Africans from the south and they had seen the fate of their wounded comrades on Twin Pyramids whom the Patriots had hurled over cliffs and they had had enough. The Garhwalis and Transvaalers raced for the summit, the former winning by a short head. They were delighted to discover that the commanding officer of the Scottish spoke their language.

The Italians were now penned into their innermost perimeter, an area of three square miles and including Fort Toselli, Amba Alagi, Little Alagi and Bald Hill. They had no hope of victory but, merely by clinging to what they held, they could impose unacceptable delay on the British. With Rommel besieging Tobruk and beating off a relief expedition (Operation Brevity), Wavell, who was trying to reinforce Crete and had had to send troops to extricate the beleagured R.A.F. station at Habbaniya in Iraq, now needed Fifth Indian and First South African Divisions more than ever and the only way to get them to Egypt quickly was to take Amba Alagi by assault. Few people had any illusions about the difficulties of doing so. If the Italians fought as their comrades had done at Keren the attack could resemble one of the less successful operations of the First World War.

The final attack was never made. A lucky shell, probably from the South Africans' 6-inch howitzer, struck an Italian fuel dump and the petrol, flowing downhill, contaminated the spring on which the garrison mainly depended for water. The Duke of Aosta was not sorry to be able to surrender with an honourable excuse. The morale of his miscellaneous units had been sinking rapidly and it was essential to make a capitulation to a civilized enemy rather than be left to the mercies of the Patriots. All he could do was to make the best terms he could.

CHAPTER 10 Mopping Up

AT DAWN ON 16 May two Italian officers with a white flag walked down the *Strada Vittoria* from the Toselli Pass to the north and reached the outposts of C Squadron, Skinner's Horse. By an ironical chance the junior of the two Italians, the interpreter, had already met the Indian squadron leader, Captain Shaukat Hyat Khan, who had been taken prisoner on the Sudanese frontier in November, 1940, and whom he had interrogated before he was released at the fall of Asmara. Blindfolded, the two envoys were escorted further down the hill to see General Mayne. They proposed an armistice so that their many wounded could be handed over to the British and they could obtain water. Mayne refused but agreed to receive a plenipotentiary from Aosta. He also consented to a ceasefire until seven o'clock that evening.

At three o'clock that afternoon, the appointed time, Colonel Dudley Russell, Mayne's chief staff officer, arrived at the rendezvous but found no Italians. He could hear an almost continuous fusillade where the Italians were fighting off Ras Seyum's less reliable followers, who, it was later learned, had murdered the plenipotentiary and his three companions on their way to the rendezvous. Eventually Mayne received a wireless message explaining the delay, requesting an extension of the ceasefire until the following noon and proposing that British delegates should come to the Italian positions on the following morning. The fusillade continued all night but, soon after dawn, Russell, with a strong escort of gunners, toiled up the steep face of Bald Hill to be admitted to the inner defences and revived with a large glass of brandy. Thus fortified, he was taken to meet General Claudio Trezzani, Aosta's representative, to whom he presented Mayne's

166

terms. The garrison should surrender as prisoners of war, handing over all their weapons and equipment intact and indicating the positions of all minefields and, in time, clearing them.

The negotiations went on for so long that the ceasefire had again to be extended. Trezzani, who explained that his chief concern was to spare the Duke the humiliation of surrender, proposed that the garrison should stay where it was, retaining its arms and ammunition but handing over their wounded and such men as wished to be prisoners to the British. In return they would give an undertaking not to interfere with British use of the *Strada Vittoria*. This was unacceptable to the British. To leave an island of armed Italians in the middle of Ethiopia would cause immense problems with Haile Selassie who already harboured suspicions that Britain was plotting with Ras Seyum to split Tigre from the empire. In addition, as Russell point out,

> There are still a number of Abyssinians sitting on the fence which delays the furtherance of the country's welfare. This would be further delayed by such a compromise.

For a time the talks were deadlocked, Trezzani maintaining that,

> If we had sufficient accommodation for our wounded we would be all right. Generally in a siege it is a case of shortage of water. We are not troubled by that, but we did not have time to make caves for our hospitals.

Unfortunately Russell had not appreciated that it was the water shortage that had brought the Italians to consider surrender. All he could do was to reiterate Mayne's terms and threaten further bombardment and a culminating assault. While the British delegation were given a midday dinner, Terrazzi consulted the Duke and returned with a new proposal. This was to resurrect the eighteenth century conception of 'Surrender with Honour', of permitting the vanquished to march out of their fortress with their arms which they would deposit as soon as they were clear of the fortifications, with an exchange of salutes as befitted worthy adversaries. It was a custom which had fallen into disuse after the Napoleonic wars though it had been employed when the Turkish garrison of Plevna surrendered to the Russians in 1877, but Mayne was happy to agree to it. His concern was to obtain a quick surrender, as much undamaged equipment as possible and a battlefield clear of mines. By putting Aosta on his honour, he could be sure of gaining a 'clean' battlefield and this was well worth 'the price of allowing the Italian troops to march out in military formation – handing over their arms a couple of miles away instead of on the battlefield itself'. On the evening of 17 May these terms were agreed and, allowing the Italians twenty-four hours to bury their dead and pack their baggage, the formal surrender was fixed for 19 May. For some detachments of the British army 18 May was improbably spent in cleaning their uniforms and rehearsing their ceremonial drill.

At 11.15 am on 19 May the garrison started to march down the main road to the village of Enda Medani Alem. The road was lined by detachments, an officer and twenty-five other ranks, from every unit, British, Indian, Sudanese and South African, which had taken part in the battle, who presented arms as each Italian unit passed. Mayne took the salute, wearing service dress, and beside him the pipes of the Transvaal Scottish played *The Flowers of the Forest*. Although these antiquated honours were provided to gratify the Italians, it was they who reduced the occasion to bathos. By tradition when the Honours of War were rendered,

> The Governor with the officers and soldiers, both horse and foot, march out armed soldierlike, viz: the foot with flying colours, drums beating, bullets in mouth, matches lighted at both ends, their pouches full of powder and shot. The horse with their trumpets sounding, standards displayed, armed in such sort as when they march towards the enemy.

Twentieth-century reality was very different. The Italian officers did their best to maintain the dignity of the occasion, the regulars saluting in military style, the Blackshirts in the fascist. Their troops paid no attention to such niceties. They were too busy coping with their luggage, which varied from bulging suitcases to cabin trunks, which all too often caused them to stumble on the steep descent. As one of Mayne's brigadiers remarked, 'A memorable and historic occasion. What a rabble they look.' Headed by Valetti-Borgnini, Frusci and the head of the *Regia Aeronautica*, Pietro Pinna, 185 officers and 4,592 other ranks, of whom only 412 were colonials, marched down to Enda Medani Salem and piled their arms. Most were then despatched by truck to a temporary prison camp at Quiha. 1,200 were retained to clear the battlefield and assist in the evacuation of the wounded.

Next morning the Duke of Aosta, having paid his respects at the Italian cemetery, walked down to the Toselli Pass with two members of his personal staff and Brigadier Marriott. There he was met by

General Mayne and inspected a guard of honour from the Worcesters, the senior regiment present. He died from tuberculosis in Kenya in the following year, having enchanted those who guarded him both there and in Asmara and Khartoum.*

1st (S.A.) Brigade Group had covered 2,500 miles in a hundred days from the Juba to Massawa and, with the rest of the First South African Division was in Egypt before the end of July. Most of Fifth Indian Division reached the Middle East by the same time.

★   ★   ★

Two days after the Duke of Aosta made his personal surrender to Mayne, Orde Wingate scored his greatest Ethiopian triumph. He had had an unsatisfactory time since he had captured Debra Marcos and failed to cut off Maraventano's column. Haile Selassie was anxious to re-enter his capital and Cunningham, who had many worries, was understandably reluctant for him to do so while there were still 10,000 armed Italians in the city. Wingate naturally sided with the Emperor and urged him to get London to put pressure on the General for an early return. Eventually Cunningham, against his better judgment, agreed to the Emperor arriving on 9 May, signalling to Wingate that he 'will be delayed from starting [from Debra Marcos] by persuasion and every means short of force. . . . If the Emperor starts in spite of your efforts you will . . . provide adequate protection.' Haile Selassie, who was becoming prone to the delusion that the British were planning to colonize or partition his empire, was not to be dissuaded and set out on 27 April escorted by what remained of 2 Ethiopians and part of the Frontier Battalion. Even these latter were provided only with difficulty since Wingate had sent the three companies which he had in hand to reduce the fort at Mota, fifty miles north of Debra Marcos, the last Italian stronghold in Gojjam apart from the garrison of Bahrdar Giorgis who evacuated themselves across Lake Tana on 28 April. To reach Mota the Frontier Battalion had to cross the Chokey Mountains by the 14,000 foot high Chaigul Pass, a march which they carried out in a blizzard with the Sudanese wearing tropical uniforms and sandals and with only one blanket each. They reached Mota on

---

* When he was transferred from Khartoum to Nairobi, his aircraft was flown by two South African pilots suffering from severe hangovers. His escorting officer awoke from a short doze and saw to his horror that both pilots were sleeping on the floor while the princely prisoner piloted the aircraft.

23 April and unsuccessfully summoned the colonial battalion holding it to surrender. At this stage Wingate's order arrived for the whole force, less one platoon, to return to Debra Marcos immediately. Fortunately the garrison failed to notice this diminution of the besieging force and meekly held their ground while Hugh Boustead with sixty men and two mortars surrounded them, harassing them at intervals during the night by bursts of bren fire and flights of mortar bombs. They surrendered within forty-eight hours.

On 5 May, five years to the day after Marshal Badoglio had entered the city, Haile Selassie returned to Addis Ababa in triumph. Before him, passing a guard of honour from the King's African Rifles, marched 2 Ethiopians led by Wingate, while the Frontier Battalion brought up the rear.

Colonel Maraventano with the garrison of Debra Marcos was still at large. With 8,000 men he was marching north, aiming, in accordance with Aosta's orders, for Dessie, but his progress was slow since his column was encumbered with 2,000 Ethiopian women and 600 children, the families of his colonial troops, apart from 800 sick and 700 dispossessed civil servants, the bureaucracy of Gojjam. Shepherding them on their way were 140 Sudanese under Bimbashi Henry Johnson who had the intermittent assistance of a small number of Patriots. By mid-May the Italians had reached the fort at Addis Derra, about half-way on their 200-mile march, and there they seemed disposed to make a stand, launching a counter-attack on their pursuers which was held off with difficulty since the Frontier Battalion men were short of both ammunition and food while the rainy season, now well under way, had brought them outbreaks of malaria and pleurisy. Johnson could only wait until they moved on but soon Wingate arrived, bringing with him a substantial force of Patriots led by Ras Kassa, the Emperor's cousin, who had spent the years of exile in Jerusalem. The column also brought supplies of ammunition but the food they carried was only bully beef which was unacceptable to the Muslim Sudanese. The news of Wingate's arrival, the ferocious reputation of Ras Kassa's men and, most of all, the fall of Dessie to the South Africans, which meant that the only way to safety now led to Gondar, decided the Italians to move on and they marched nearly forty miles to a cluster of forts around Agibar. Wingate, who could inspire the Sudanese if he could not adequately feed them, followed, but found himself faced by an intractable problem – how to attack a naturally strong and fortified position defended by a force which, even counting the Patriots, was four time his own strength and was supported by artillery while he had no more than half a dozen mortars. To complicate the problem further, he received orders from Cunningham to ignore Maraventano and to send all his troops to assist at Amba Alagi. These instructions he evaded first by asking them to be repeated, then by disputing them and finally by closing down his wireless set.

His problem, however, remained and an attempt to send a small force round the flank while the main body made a frontal attack made only small gains, soon lost to a counter-attack, and was expensive in casualties. He therefore decided that he must gain by diplomacy what he could not obtain by force and, on 19 May, he wrote to the Italian commander, drawing attention to the surrender at Amba Alagi, telling him of large (and imaginary) Patriot forces which were coming towards him and adding that he had been ordered:

> To withdraw all British personnel from your neighbourhood during the rainy season, leaving the conduct of operations against you to the very considerable guerrilla forces under Ras Kassa.

The Patriots, he pointed out, would have air support now that the main Italian army had capitulated. Maraventano replied that he must fight to the last round unless his surrender was sanctioned by General Nasi at Gondar so Wingate recommended him to contact him by radio and repeated the threat of leaving the Italians to the mercies of the Patriots.

> Your continued resistance will merely make you a prey to these forces without in the least assisting the resistance of your fellow countrymen in other parts of Ethiopia or elsewhere.

Agibar surrendered on 23 May, the garrison marching out and laying down their arms under the watchful eyes of thirty-six Sudanese with the only three bren guns in Wingate's force. Maraventano made his personal surrender to Wingate and Ras Kassa and a guard of honour of ten men, all that could be spared. Wingate had given a textbook demonstration of the use of a small force against a large. Within two weeks he was back in Cairo where, convinced that his services had been underrated, he tried to cut his throat.

A month after the fall of Agibar, Jimma was taken by a concentric operation on a grand scale. From Addis Ababa Eleventh African Division pushed south, consisting now of only two brigades although temporarily reinforced by two battalions from 2nd (S.A.) brigade at Berbera. Twelfth African Division moved up from the south with the Gold Coast Brigade advancing from Neghelli and 21st (E.A.) Brigade from Yavello. To the west a newly raised brigade of K.A.R. moved north from Lake Rudolf to Maji where they met the Equatorial Corps of S.D.F. operating from Boma. To the north of them a Belgian contingent, eventually expanded to three battalions from the Congo, invaded the Baro Salient. It was ideal defensive country and the Italians, in superior numbers, should have been able to hold out as long as their plentiful ammunition lasted. They were, in practice, half-hearted and were usually content, having made gestures of resistance, to surrender to formed troops rather than risk falling into the hands of the irregulars who, in this part of the country, could hardly be described as Ethiopian Patriots since they felt no allegiance to Addis Ababa and were apt to attack and plunder their liberators as much as the Italians. Only once did the latter make a serious show of resistance. Between 8 April and 10 May two largely Eritrean brigades with a battalion of Blackshirts held off the Gold Coast Brigade near Wadera. The eventual breakthrough was a triumph of skill and determination and cost the West Africans 118 casualties, the longest list of losses for any single action suffered by East Africa Force in the entire campaign.

That the force was able to operate at all was a logistic miracle. The rains having set in with depressing soddenness, the campaign was a struggle against ground and mud. Wheeled transport was almost useless, with road convoys taking two weeks to cover 300 miles and petrol consumption of three miles to the gallon and the troops frequently on short rations. It was not only the local difficulties that held up supplies. The supply line for Eleventh Division ran back from Addis Ababa for 560 miles to the inadequate port of Berbera, although it was possible to use the railway between Diredawa and Awash, where the rail bridge could not be restored until 11 July. For Twelfth Division the situation was even worse. Their base port was Mombasa and from there supplies could go by rail to Nairobi and thence by road to Dolo where all trace of a recognizable road petered out. The troops at the front endured hardships and did all the fighting that could be asked of them but the real heroes were the truck drivers, mostly coloured South Africans, and the engineers, mostly white South Africans. In the event all the links in this rickety chain just contrived to hold. 12,000 Italian and 3,000 colonial troops surrendered to Brigadier

Fowkes at Jimma on 21 June and, on 6 July, General Gazzera with the last of his army, 6,500 men including 2,000 loyal members of *bande*, gave themselves up to the Belgians at Dembidollo.

The Italian empire in East Africa was now reduced to an enclave north of Lake Tana where General Nasi, with his headquarters at Gondar, commanded more than 40,000 men and seventy guns. This is the most fertile region of Ethiopia and is difficult to approach from any direction. The only all-weather road to it, that from Asmara, was perhaps the greatest of all the Italian engineering achievements, ascending the escarpment through the Wolchefit Pass where it climbs 4,000 feet 'winding round ninety-nine hairpin bends from the valley up the cliff face and could be blocked with the greatest ease at a score of different places'. In General Platt's opinion Wolchefit had a natural strength five times that of Keren and it was held by a garrison of 5,000 men well supplied with artillery. The only other ways on to the Gondar plateau were a wretched track round the western coast of Lake Tana, two equally bad paths leading down to the Sudan at Gallabat and Um Hagar and a rather better road, passable for vehicles in good weather, which linked Gondar with Dessie. This, however, was blocked by substantial Italian posts, notably at Debra Tabor and Kulkaber.

Little could be done about this unapproachable stronghold in the immediate aftermath of the surrender at Amba Alagi. The South Africans and almost all the Indians were shipped away to the Middle East while Eleventh and Twelfth Divisions were fully engaged to the south of Addis Ababa until late June when the two West African brigades returned to their homelands. Apart from the Sudan Defence Force, the K.A.R. were now the only infantry left in Ethiopia, although they had the support of South African engineers, A.A. gunners and transport companies with two British Indian mountain batteries and a light battery from the Gold Coast which was being re-equipped with 60-pounders. Until the East Africans could be brought north, little could be done except to harass the Italian outposts. A composite S.D.F. battalion and part of 3 Ethiopians made a spirited but unsuccessful attack on Chilga, on the Gondar – Gallabat road (17 May) and a company of 3 Ethiopians, led by a major of the Notts Yeomanry, and a Patriot force under Dejaz Ayulu Birru, whom Nasi had appointed governor of Gondar, infiltrated behind the Wolchefit garrison and succeeded in largely isolating them although, in the ensuing counter-attacks, Dejaz Ayulu was captured with a dispiriting effect on his followers. The only lasting gain was on the Dessie road where Debra Tabor had been under loose Patriot siege since the end of April. There was a large garrison, about 6,000 men, in the town, which was sited on a commanding hill, encircled by wire entanglements and had an excellent field of fire. In June command of the siege was taken by Major Douglas, H.L.I, of No.2 Operational Centre, who brought with him reinforcements in the shape of a squadron of Skinner's Horse and a company of 3/2 Punjab with a platoon composed of four captured Italian mortars.

The Indian squadron commander found the situation unusual.

> War, as carried on by the Patriots, was somewhat different from the methods used by European Powers. For instance, before the plan of attack could be discussed, an agreement had to be made between the Patriot forces and ourselves as to the distribution of loot. Until a satisfactory arrangement had been made, they would not co-operate. The conclusion of this agreement was of far more importance than the capture of the town. Agreement having been finally reached, discussion could then begin about how the town could be taken. . . . Recces were carried out and as dusk was falling [the Indian contingent] took up its position, though nothing was seen of the Patriot forces who were to co-operate. Just before zero hour a breathless and angry liaison officer came up to say that the attack was off. The Patriot leader was having his hair dressed and would not be ready in time. The attack was therefore postponed to the following night. Once again we took up our position. Shortly after, it began to rain, it was a pitch black night and, though uncomfortably wet, the conditions were ideal. The Patriot commander thought otherwise. Having had his hair done the previous night, he had no intention of getting it spoilt by going out in the rain.

In all, five attacks were arranged, only to be cancelled for similar reasons, but the R.A.F. continued to bomb the town and, on 6 July, the garrison surrendered. 79 Colonial Battalion, less its Italian officers, volunteered to join the British and was incorporated into Douglas's command under the name of Seventy-Ninth Foot*. With his reinforcement he pressed forward and laid siege to Kulkaber. An attempt made to induce the garrison at Wolchefit to surrender on 10 July failed.

By this time the rains were in full spate, not only making all movement difficult but inducing most of the Patriots to make for their homes. Even those who remained in the field became restless since the

---

* Presumably so named because Major Douglas's forebear, Lieutenant-Colonel Neil Douglas, had commanded the 79th (Cameron Highlanders) Regiment of Foot at Waterloo.

supplies of money, provided by the British, threatened to dry up. This danger was averted when 100,000 thalers were dropped to Douglas by air. Such was the weight of coin that this amount, equivalent to £9,675, required six Wellesley bombers for transport. It was decided that further operations would have to be postponed until the weather improved towards the end of October and by that time Twelfth African Division, now composed of two East African brigades with supporting units and commanded by Major-General Fowkes, had moved to the north.

Meanwhile the conditions of war in East Africa had changed. There was no longer pressure to remove formations and units out of the theatre to the Middle East. Apart from some specialist troops, the burden of the British campaign was being borne by the K.A.R. who, although later greatly to distinguish themselves in Burma, were not considered suitable for war in the Western Desert. Even Sudanese units were being taken from Ethiopia and sent to garrison the Kufra Oasis and other outlying parts of the Egyptian front. The air support available consisted of a squadron of Wellesleys and a composite squadron of obsolete S.A.A.F. planes which would have had no chance against the *Luftwaffe* but were good enough to harass Nasi's command where only two C.R.42 fighters remained airworthy until one of them was shot down by a Gladiator in September. After the fall of Addis Ababa the Italian plan had been to tie down as many British forces which could be used elsewhere but they were no longer engaging anything that could be of service on other fronts. Their stand had no further purpose.

The first crack in the defences came unexpectedly on 27 September when the garrison of Wolchefit, much shrunk by desertion, surrendered. This stroke of good fortune, and a prolongation of the rains, allowed Fowkes to change his plan. Faced with the impregnability of Wolchefit, he had planned to attack with two brigades from Debra Tabor, an operation for which the logistics would have been a nightmare even by previous standards in Ethiopia. Now he was able to reduce this advance to a single battalion with supporting arms, largely pioneers, while 25th and 26th (E.A.) Brigades came up the Wolchefit Pass and attacked from the south and diversionary attacks by Sudanese and Patriot forces (including the Seventy-Ninth Foot) came in on the other approaches. The available air force, temporarily reinforced by a S.A.A.F squadron newly equipped with American Mohawks, rained bombs to their utmost capacity, contriving on a single day to drop 12,000lbs. Kulkaber, which put up a strong defence, surrendered on 21 November and six days later Nasi capitulated with 10,000 Italian and 12,000 colonial soldiers. His two remaining strongholds, Celga and Gorgora, followed suit when his orders, dropped to them by the faithful Hartbeests, reached them on the following day. Italian East Africa no longer existed.

One military operation in the area remained. French Somaliland obstinately refused to follow the example of Equatorial Africa and declare for General de Gaulle. Endless negotiations proved abortive and, although supplies of milk for women and children were allowed in, the colony was blockaded, a K.A.R. brigade being needed to enforce the land blockade. The entry of Japan into the war meant that ships could no longer be spared to watch the port so that dhows from all round the Red Sea and even from British-occupied Assab ran cargoes of grain and livestock into Jibuti while a French submarine from Madagascar brought in tinned food, coffee, tobacco and other supplies. On the land side the blockade was a tedious farce enlivened by skirmishes with the local tribesmen from outside the colony in one of which the K.A.R. lost eleven killed.

Matters dragged on until November, 1942, when Madagascar finally surrendered to the British and an Anglo-American army invaded French North Africa wringing from Admiral Darlan a promise of co-operation from all French forces against the axis. Still the Governor at Jibuti, General Dupont, who was stiffened by the presence of an Italian Armistice Commission in the colony, refused to make concessions. His officers thought otherwise and on 28 November Colonel Raynal of 1 Senegalese crossed the border with about a third of the garrison to join the allies. Dupont continued obdurate even after a personal visit by Major-General Fowkes and it was decided to act. After Christmas French Somaliland was invaded by a column headed by Raynal's Senegalese and some East African armoured cars. There was no fighting; the garrison was very ready to surrender. Dupont capitulated on 28 December and, with the Armistice Commission, became a prisoner of war.

*   *   *

The Italians lost their East African empire through faulty command decisions. They never recovered from Mussolini's original illusion that, merely by declaring war and letting the Germans win it for him, he could gain all he wanted. He forbade his commanders in East Africa to take the offensive in June and July, 1940, when glittering prizes were open to them. It was fully within the capability of Aosta's army, using the Savoia Division and the best of the Eritrean brigades, to advance from Kassala and there was little but their own fears to stop them from seizing Khartoum and Port Sudan. Such a conquest would have set Wavell an insoluble problem and would have made it possible for the Libyan army successfully to invade Egypt. It is almost beyond belief that no plans for such an advance were even considered and, to the astonished delight of the British, the Italians contented themselves with filching a few Sudanese frontier posts and, after Mussolini decided that Britain would not surrender without a fight, with a safe and useless grab at British Somaliland. The chance of invading the Sudan had gone by the middle of September when most of Fifth Indian Division had been added to Platt's command.

Given that the Duke of Aosta's forces were tied to a strict defensive, the high command in Addis Ababa made some correct decisions but not enough. They recognized that Britain's prime objective must be Massawa and gave priority in troops and aircraft to retaining it. To effect this they under-estimated the difficulties of an attack from Kenya. They assumed that since their own troops could not operate in strength across the *cordon sanitaire* of desert their enemy would be equally incapable. Their defence on the Somaliland border had too few and inferior troops and, since only raids were expected, only a hard thin crust of defence was established. This was the responsibility of General Presenti who lost his nerve when Cunningham's raid on El Wak showed him he was wrong. His successor, de Simone, had no time to reorganize a defence in depth for which, thanks to Presenti's earlier complacency, he had insufficient troops. Thus once Cunningham had pierced the crust there was nothing to stop him until, more than a thousand miles later, he reached the Marda Pass, by which time the opposition was wholly demoralized.

The extraordinary incompetence of the Italian intelligence services confounded all the calculations of their generals. Their inflated estimates of British strength distorted every appreciation made by the high command. With more than 700 Italians at liberty in the Sudan until the declaration of war it passes belief that they were able to calculate three British battalions and the S.D.F. as 31,000 men. The fact was that Italian intelligence would accept any inflated report at its face value, and more. Thus the occasional sight of a bren-gun carrier was represented as at least one tank, if not a squadron. The presence of Fourth Australian Division (see p 100) was accepted as gospel on the basis of a few slouch hats and some amateur radio deception. It is said that, finding, or hearing on the air, a reference to 'Five Indian Division', the usual military way of referring to Fifth Indian Division, the Italians jumped to the conclusion that five such divisions were attacking them.

Having rightly divined that the British would make their main effort against Eritrea, it was unfortunate that the chief command there was entrusted to Luigi Frusci. He had had a good record as a colonel in the 1935 invasion but as a commander-in-chief he was a disaster. He clung obstinately to the idea that the main British thrust would come from the north and, although ready to prepare defensive positions at Agordat-Barentu and Ad Teclesan, neglected Keren which, it might be supposed, any acting corporal would have recognized as a God-given position to halt an advance on Massawa. Only the inspiration and energy of Carmineo ensured that the mountain barrier was defended, but without the benefit of prepared positions, except the far-from-impregnable Fort Dologorodoc, which dated from many years earlier. Had Frusci fortified the Dongolaas Gorge in advance, it is more than problematical whether the Indian divisions would have been able to force their way through before the rains or the demands of other fronts forced them to give up the attempt.

Despite all the miscalculations and occasional lapses of their enemy, the campaign was a triumph for the British who used only five divisions, including some very green troops, to overcome an army of a quarter of a million men, many of them highly trained, apart from the by no means despicable *bande*. From the Ethiopians they received negligible help in the crucial stages of the campaign. Platt took Asmara and Massawa while Cunningham took Harar and Addis Ababa without an Ethiopian hand being raised to help them. It is true that, simultaneously, Haile Selassie, Sandford and Wingate held the attention of the troops in Gojjam, which could scarcely have been withdrawn in any case, but even there it was Boustead's Sudanese who did the work. Even after the campaign was decided at Amba Alagi and the Patriots started to show up in quantity, they were always unreliable. They could be outstandingly brave for short periods, showing a fatalistic disregard for death, their own or other people's, but, as the Official History remarks, their activities 'fluctuated with the weather, the supplies of money and food, and their own feuds and rivalries'. The fear they inspired in the Italians, afraid for their families, far outweighed any fighting they actually did. While there was much desertion from some colonial units, very large numbers, mainly Eritreans, but including Shoans, Gojjamis and Tigreans, stayed loyal to the Italians to the very end. Even discounting the ambiguous activities of Ras Hailu and Ras Seyum, the Italians got as much help from the Ethiopians as did the British.

The stars of the campaign were the Indian battalions, including many men who had learned the skills of mountain warfare in the hard school of the North-West Frontier. Of the six British battalions who fought with them, only the Cameron Highlanders showed themselves as being first-class infantry although the West Yorkshires pulled off the most spectacular feat of arms. On the same front and all along their eastern frontier, the Sudanese soldiers also made an outstanding contribution, from the earliest skirmishes around Kassala, through Keren, Gojjam, Amba Alagi and on to Gondar. On the southern front the Nigerians were pre-eminent, though they would not have achieved what they did without the support of the South African gunners, mostly amateurs, engineers, transport drivers and airmen. The King's African Rifles and 1st (S.A.) Brigade also did all that could be expected of them.

In estimating British generalship in East Africa, it must first be acknowedged that the campaign was a striking and spectacular victory and by noting that the only officer present who ended the war as a field-marshal sustained on the Sudanese border a unique but definite defeat. Before Gondar had fallen Alan Cunningham was promoted to Command the newly christened Eighth Army, a command to which he was to show himself unequal, but this should not obscure the boldness and vision with which he conducted a truly remarkable advance from Kenya through Mogadishu and Harar to Addis Ababa, which, despite the excellence of his Q staff and the incompetence of some of his enemies, was a feat of which any general could be proud. In September, 1941, Sir William Platt was transferred to East Africa command (which excluded the Sudan) at Nairobi and was left there until he retired. This does not suggest that his talents were highly appreciated in the higher reaches of the army and it must be remembered that the way to his great victory was suggested by two subordinate officers – Brigadier Messervy, who planned the seizure of Dologordoc, and Major-General Heath, who devised the final breakthrough up the gorge. It was a tragedy that Heath's talents were lost when, commanding a corps, he was made prisoner at Singapore. Nevertheless Platt cannot be denied credit for his active and ingenious defence of the Sudan in the desperate summer of 1940 and for his domination of the eastern frontier for the rest of that year. It need hardly be mentioned that Wingate loathed and vilified both Cunningham and Platt for failing to give him what they did not have.

The presiding genius of the campaign was Wavell. He was the man who saw the need for the operations, realized the possibility of overwhelming success and fed in just enough resources to enable it to succeed. He did this in the teeth of the opposition of Churchill who, most of the time, opposed undertaking it, hoping that Italian East Africa would waste away if ignored and blockaded. This raises the question of whether the East African campaign was worth fighting at all. The idea of economic collapse – an echo of the belief in both 1914 and 1939 that the German economy could survive only a short war – is clearly fallacious. If an example is needed, it was believed in London that I.E.A. had stocks of petrol that would only last for five months, and yet, long after that period had elapsed, vast stocks of petrol were found all over their empire, to say nothing of the amounts that the air forces and the retreating Italians had destroyed. Any economic wasting away would have been a most protracted business. Nor, as was also widely believed, could Ethiopia have been conquered by internal revolt. Many of Haile Selassie's former subjects had become reconciled to Italian rule and many more were acquiescent. Internal disturbances would doubtless have rumbled on, as they did under Haile Selassie, but it needed major victories by both Platt and Cunningham to stir up anything like a nation-wide rebellion. Gideon Force would have been useless if the central Italian reserve had not been committed at Keren.

Nor would the troops which Wavell put into Eritrea, Fourth Indian Division with a squadron of Matildas for five months, and the six Indian battalions of Fifth Division for nine months, have made an appreciable difference to the situation in the Western Desert in their absence. As for the rest, the East and West African Brigades were widely acknowledged to be unsuitable for employment in Egypt and, in 1940 and early 1941, the South Africans were insufficiently trained to be used there.

On the credit side the campaign succeeded, with remarkably little loss, in achieving a most valuable objective. Wavell never lost sight of the overriding importance of clearing the Red Sea coast. The liberation of Ethiopia was a useful political adjunct, reparation for a blemish on the British conscience, but what mattered was the removal of the Italian military and naval presence from Massawa so that American merchantships could carry their invaluable cargo up to the Suez Canal. It may be that Wavell had in mind the use of Massawa as a base should the worst come to the worst and the *Afrika Korps* capture Alexandria. Above all the campaign gave Britain and her sympathizers the first enduring victory of the war, a boost for morale which would have been all the greater had it not been for a simultaneous propaganda campaign which sought to show the Italians as contemptible adversaries. That was a sentiment which would not be shared by anyone who fought against them at Keren.

APPENDIX Orders of Battle

1. BRITISH TROOPS AT KEREN.

Lt. Gen. William Platt, Cmdg.

Force Troops. B. Sqn. 4th Royal Tank Regiment.
P Bty (A/T) Royal Horse Artillery.
68 Medium Regiment, Royal Artillery (2 batteries).
41 Light Anti-aircraft Battery, Royal Artillery.
Jammu and Kashmir Mountain Battery, Indian Army.
Battery, Sudan Horse, Sudan Defence Force.
Two Motor Machine Gun Companies, Sudan Defence
Force.
51 (Middle East) Commando.

Fourth Indian Division. (Maj. Gen. N. M. de la P. Beresford-Peirse).

Divisional Cavalry Regiment.
Central India Horse (21st King George's Own Horse).
Royal Artillery (Brig. W. H. B. Mirrlees).
1st and 31st Field Regiments, Royal Artillery.
25th Field Regiment, Royal Artillery (less one battery).
Royal Engineers (Lt. Col. R. V. Cutler).
4 Field Company, King George's Own Bengal Sappers &
Miners.
12 Field Coy, Queen Victoria's Own Madras Sappers & Miners.
18 & 21 Field Coys, Royal Bombay Sappers & Miners.
11th Field Park Coy, Queen Victoria's Own Madras Sappers &
Miners.

5th Indian Infantry Brigade (Brig. W. L. Lloyd).
    1st Bn. The Royal Fusiliers (City of London Regiment).
    3rd Bn. 1st Punjab Regiment.
    4th Bn. (Outram's) 6th Rajputana Rifles.
    4th Bn. 11th Sikhs. (Joined from 7th Brigade, via Gazelle Force.)
11th Indian Infantry Brigade (Brig. R. A. Savory).
    2nd Bn. The Queen's Own Cameron Highlanders.
    2nd Bn. 5th Mahratta Light Infantry.
    1st Bn. (Wellesley's) 6th Rajputana Rifles.
    3rd Bn. 14th Punjab Regiment.

Fifth Indian Division. (Maj. Gen. L. M. Heath).

Divisional Cavalry Regiment.
    Skinner's Horse (1st Duke of York's Own Cavalry).
Royal Artillery (Brig. A. B. van Straubenzee).
    4th, 28th and 144th (Sussex and Surrey) Field Regiments, Royal
        Artillery.
Royal Engineers (Lt. Col. A. H. G. Napier).
    2 Field Coy, King George's Own Bengal Sappers & Miners.
    20 & 21 Field Coys, Royal Bombay Sappers & Miners.
    44 Field Park Coy, Queen Victoria's Own Madras Sappers &
        Miners.
9th Indian Infantry Brigade (Brig. A. G. O. Mayne (until late
February)), (Brig. F. W. Messervy (from late February)).
    2nd Bn. The West Yorkshire Regiment (The Prince of Wales's
        Own).
    3rd Bn. 5th Mahratta Light Infantry.
    3rd Bn. 12th Royal Frontier Force Regiment (less one coy).
10th Indian Infantry Brigade (Lt. Col. B. C. Fletcher, H.L.I. (acting
vice Brig. J. W. Slim, wounded)), (Brig. T. W. Rees, from 21
March).
    2nd Bn. The Highland Light Infantry (City of Glasgow Regi-
        ment).
    4th Bn. (Duke of Connaught's Own) 10th Baluch Regiment.
    3rd Bn. 18th Royal Garhwal Rifles.
29th Indian Infantry Brigade (Brig. J. C. O. Marriott).
    1st Bn. The Worcestershire Regiment.
    3rd Bn. 2nd Punjab Regiment.
    3rd Bn. 13th Royal Frontier Force Rifles.

Detached Force operating from the north. Brig. H. R. Briggs (comdg).

> Bty. 25th Field Regiment, Royal Artillery.
> 7th Field Coy, Sappers & Miners.
> 7th Indian Infantry Brigade (Brig. H. R. Briggs).
>> 1st Bn. The Royal Sussex Regiment.
>> 4th Bn. 16th Punjab Regiment.
> *Brigade d'Orient* (Col. Monclar).
>> 14me Bn. *Légion Étrangère.*
>> 3me Bn. *de Marche (Tchad).*

2. EAST AFRICA FORCE, 1 JANUARY, 1941.

Lt. Gen. A. G. Cunningham, Comdg.

Force Troops 1 East African Armoured Car Regiment (less 2 squadrons).
> 1 Light Tank Company, S.A.T.C.
> 1 Medium Brigade, S.A.A. (2 batteries).
> 1/3rd Bn. King's African Rifles (machine guns).

First South African Division (Maj. Gen. G. L. Brink).

Divisional Troops.
> 3 Field Brigade, S.A.A. (T.H.A.)
> 3 A/T Battery, S.A.A.
> Section, 6 A.A. Battery, S.A.A.
> 21 Field Park Company, S.A.E.C.

2nd South African Infantry Brigade Group (Brig. F. L. A. Buchanan).
> 1st Bn. Natal Mounted Rifles.
> 1st and 2nd Field Force Bns.
> 2 Armoured Car Company, S.A.T.C.
> 12 Field Coy, S.A.E.C.

5th South African Infantry Brigade Group (Brig. B. F. A. Armstrong).
> 1st Bn. South African Irish Regiment.
> 2nd Bn. Botha Regiment.
> 3rd Bn. Transvaal Scottish.
> 1 Armoured Car Company, S.A.T.C.
> 5 Field Company, S.A.E.C.

25th East African Infantry Brigade Group (Brig. W. Owen).
    3/2 Bn. and 2/4 Bn. King's African Rifles.
    27 Mountain Battery, Royal Artillery.
    Det. Somali Camel Corps Armoured Cars.
    3 Field Company, S.A.E.C.

Eleventh African Division (Maj. Gen. H. C. de R. Wetherall).

Divisional Troops.
    Sqn. 1 East African Armoured Car Regiment.
    7 Field Brigade, S.A.A. (3 batteries).
    1 A/T Battery, S.A.A.
    Section 6 A.A. Battery, S.A.A.
    16 Field Company, S.A.E.C.
21st East African Infantry Brigade Group
(Brig. A. McD. Ritchie).   } To 12th
    1/2 & 1/4 Bns, King's African Rifles.   African
    1st Bn. Northern Rhodesian Regiment.   Division
    53 Gold Coast Field Company.   11 Mar 41
23rd Nigerian Infantry Brigade Group (Brig. G. R. Smallwood).
    1st, 2nd and 3rd Battalions, The Nigeria Regiment.
    52 Nigerian Light Battery.
    53 Nigerian Field Company.

Twelfth African Division (Maj. Gen. A. R. Godwin-Austen).

Divisional Troops.
    Sqn. 1st East African Armoured Car Regiment.
    1 Field Battery, S.A.A.
    2 A/T Battery, S.A.A.
    19 Field Park Company, S.A.E.C.
1st South African Infantry Brigade Group
(Brig. D. H. Pienaar).   }
    1st Bn. Royal Natal Carbineers.
    Duke of Edinburgh's Own Rifles.   To 11th
    1st Bn. Transvaal Scottish.   African
    3 Armoured Car Company, S.A.T.C.   Division
    4 Field Brigade, S.A.A. (3 batteries).   11 Mar 41
    1 Field Company, S.A.E.C.

22nd East African Infantry Brigade Group
(Brig. C. C. Fowkes). } To 11th African Division 11 Mar 41
    1/1, 1/5 and 1/6 Bns, King's African Rifles.
    22 Mountain Battery, Royal Artillery.
    54 East African Field Company.
24th Gold Coast Infantry Brigade Group (Brig. C. E. M. Richards).
    1st, 2nd and 3rd Bns, The Gold Coast Regiment.
    51 Gold Coast Light Battery.
    52 Gold Coast Field Company.

BIBLIOGRAPHY

Allen, W. E. D., *Guerrilla War in Abyssinia*, Penguin, 1943
     Manuscript letters of Dr Robert Alexander
Aron, Robert, *The Vichy Regime 1940–44*, (Tr. H. Hare), Putnam, 1958
Avon, Anthony Eden, Earl of, *The Eden Memoirs*, Vol. iii, Cassell, 1962
Badoglio, Pietro, *The War in Abyssinia* (English Edn), Methuen, 1937
Barker, A. J., *The Civilizing Mission; The Italo-Ethiopian War 1935–36*,
     Cassell, 1968
     Eritrea 1941, Faber and Faber, 1966
Birdwood, Lord, *The Worcestershire Regiment 1922–1940*, Gale and Polden,
 1952
Boustead, Hugh, *The Wind of Morning*, Chatto & Windus, 1971
Brett-James, Anthony, *Ball of Fire: 5th Indian Division in World War II*, Gale
 and Polden, 1951
Buxton, David, *Travels in Ethiopia*, Lindsay Drummond, 1949
Historical Records of the Queen's Own Cameron Highlanders, Vol V, William
 Blackwood, Edinburgh, 1952
Churchill, Winston S., *The Second World War, Vols II & III*, Cassell, 1949 &
 1950
Ciano, Galeazzo (Ed. M. Muggeridge), *The Ciano Diaries*, Heinemann, 1947
     Diplomatic Papers, Odhams, 1948
Cochrane, Peter, *Charlie Company*, Chatto & Windus, 1977
Connell, John, *Wavell: Scholar and Soldier, Vol I*, William Collins, 1966
Crew, F. A. E., *Army Medical Services: Campaigns. Vol I*, H.M.S.O., 1956
Crosskill, W. E., *The Two-Thousand Mile War*, Robert Hale, 1980
Del Boca, Angelo, *The Ethiopian War 1935–41* (Tr. P. D. Cummins,
 University of Chicago Press, 1969
Dower, K. Gandar, *Abyssinian Patchwork*, Frederick Muller, 1949
Evans, Geoffrey, *The Desert and the Jungle*, William Kimber, 1959
Evans, T. E. (Ed.), *The Killearn Diaries 1934–46*, Sidgwick & Jackson, 1972

Fergusson, Bernard, *The Black Watch and the King's Enemies*, Collins, 1950

Filose, A. A., *King George's Own Central Indian Horse, Vol II*, William Blackwood, Edinburgh, 1950

Gilbert, Martin, *Finest Hour*, Heinemann, 1983

Graham, C. A. L., *History of the Indian Mountain Artillery*, Gale and Polden, 1959

Guedella, Philip, *Middle East 1940–42, A Study in Air Power*, Hodder & Stoughton, 1944

Haywood, A. & Clarke, F. A. S., *The History of the Royal West African Frontier Force*, Gale & Polden, 1964

Henderson, K. D. D., *The Making of Modern Sudan: The Life and Letters of Sir Douglas Newbold*, Faber & Faber, 1953

Jackson, H. C., *The Fighting Sudanese*, Macmillan, 1954

Jackson, W. G. F., *The North African Campaigns 1940–43*, B. T. Batsford, 1975

Jouin, Yves, *La Cote Francaise des Somalis de 1936 à Juin 1940*
 La Participation Francaise à la Résistance Éthiopienne 1936–40.
 Révue Historique de l'Armée xix 4. November, 1954, Paris

Kennedy, John, *The Business of War*, (Ed. B. Fergusson), Hutchinson, 1957

Klein, H., *Springboks in Armour*, Purnell, Cape Town, 1965

Knott, A. J., *The Sudan Defence Force Goes to War*, R. E. Journal, lviii, 1944

Lawford, J. P. & Catto, W. E. (Eds), *Solah Punjab; History of the 16th Punjab Regiment*, Gale and Polden, 1967

Lewin, Ronald, *The Chief*, Hutchinson, 1980

Longmore, Arthur, *From Sea to Sky, 1910–45*, Geoffrey Bless, 1946

Luther, Ernest, J., *Ethiopia Today*, Stanford University Press, 1958

Mackenzie, Compton, *Eastern Epic, Vol I*, Chatto & Windus, 1951

Marcus, H. R., *The Life and Times of Menelik II*, Clarendon Press, Oxford, 1975

Markaris, John, *Ethiopia: Anatomy of a Traditional Policy*, Clarendon Press, Oxford, 1974

Marshall-Cornwall, James, *Wars and Rumours of Wars*, Leo Cooper, 1984

Martin, T. A., *The Essex Regiment 1929–50*, Essex Regimental Association, 1952

Martineau, G. D., *The History of the Royal Sussex Regiment*, Moore & Tillyer, Chichester, 1955

Maule, Henry, *Spearhead General*, Odhams Press, 1961

Ministry of Information, *The Abyssinian Campaigns*, H.M.S.O., 1942
 The First to be Freed, H.M.S.O., 1944

Mockler, Anthony, *Haile Selassie's War*, O.U.P., 1984

Mosley, Leonard, *Gideon Goes to War*, Arthur Barker, 1955
 Haile Selassie; The Conquering Lion, Wiedenfeld & Nicolson, 1964

Moyse-Bartlett, H., *The King's African Rifles*, Gale & Polden, 1956

Oatts, L. B., *Proud Heritage, The Story of the Highland Light Infantry, Vol IV*, House of Grant, Glasgow, 1963

Orlebar, John, *Tales of the Sudan Defence Force*, privately printed, 1981

Orpen, Neil, *South African Forces in World War II, Vol II, East Africa and Abyssinia*, Purnell, Cape Town, 1968

Pakenham-Walsh, R. P., *History of the Corps of Royal Engineers, Vol VIII*, Institute of Royal Engineers, 1958

Pankhurst, Richard, *The Secret History of the Italian Fascist Occupation of Ethiopia, 1935–41*, Africa Quarterly, XVI, iv, April, 1977

Parkinson, C. Northcote, *Always a Fusilier*, Sampson Low, 1949

Paxton, Robert O., *Vichy France: Old Guard and New Order 1940–44*, Barrie & Jenkins, 1972

Pitt, Barrie, *The Crucible: Western Desert 1941*, Jonathan Cape, 1980

Playfair, I. S. O., *The Mediterranean and Middle East, Vols I and II*, H.M.S.O., 1954 & 1956

Prasad, Bisheshwar, *Official History of the Indian Forces in World War II, Vol II, East African Campaign*, Orient Longmans, 1963

Fourteenth Punjab Regiment, A Short History, Lund Humphries, n.d.

Qureshi, Mohamed Ibrahim. *The First Punjabis*, Gale & Polden, 1958

Rennell of Rodd, Lord, *British Military Administration in Occupied Territories in Africa, 1941–47*, H.M.S.O., 1948

Roskill, S. W., *The War at Sea 1939–45, Vol I*, H.M.S.O., 1954

Sandes, E. W. C., *From Pyramid to Pagoda, The Story of the West Yorks, 1939–45*, F. J. Parsons, London, 1952

Sandford, Christine, *The Lion of Judah hath prevailed*, J. M. Dent, 1955

Skinner, M. A. R., *Sworn to Die*, Lancer International, New Delhi, 1948

Stewart, Adrian, *Hurricane: The Story of the Fighter Aircraft*, William Kimber

Slim, William, *Unofficial History*, Cassell, 1959

Steer, George, *Sealed and Delivered*, Hodder & Stoughton, 1942

Stevens, G. R., *Fourth Indian Division*, McLaren & Sons, Toronto, 1949

Surtees, G., *A 'Q' War*. Journal of the Royal United Service Institute, August, 1963

Sykes Christopher, *Orde Wingate*, Collins, 1959

Terraine, John, *The Right of the Line*, Hodder & Stoughton, 1985

Waugh, Evelyn, *Waugh in Abyssinia*, Longmans Green, 1936

INDEX

The ranks and titles shown are those held during the campaign.

Abalti, 160
Abebe Aregai, Ras, 152
Abima, Fort, 146
Abu Gamal, 65
Acaci, 137
Academy, Royal Military, Woolwich, 45
Acland, Bimbashi Peter, 90, 91, 93, 94
Acqua Col, 80, 81, 82, 100, 107, 123, 124
Active Citizen Force (S.A.), 56, 57
Addis Ababa, 3, 10, 12, 14, 24, 33, 41, 42,
  50, 60, 63, 65, 73, 76, 83, 95, 96,
  126, 129, 133, 134, 136, 137,
  138, 139, 140, 141, 145, 148,
  149, 150, 152, 155, 160, 162, 165,
  170, 171, 172, 173, 175, 177, 178,
  179
Addis, Fort, 146
Addis Derra, Fort, 170
Aden, 5, 23, 25, 26, 30, 31, 32, 33, 38, 39, 127,
  136, 140, 142fn
Adigrat, 8, 140, 154
Adowa, 4, 8, 9, 10, 13, 90, 140, 154, 157
Ad Teclesan, 76, 83, 138–9, 178
Afmadu, 101, 102, 103
Afrika Korps, 106, 133, 181
Agibar, 170, 171
Agordat, 8, 140, 154
Aiba Pass, 162, 163
Aicota, 64, 65, 66, 67
Aircraft,
  R.A.F. & S.A.A.F.,
    Albacore, 110
    Battle, 101, 102, 129, 136
    Blenheim, 19, 21, 25, 26, 31, 87, 111, 136,
      140

Bombay, 19
Fury, 19
Gauntlet, 52
Gladiator, 19, 21, 31, 33, 52, 87, 119, 129,
  155, 175
Glenn Martin (Maryland), 136
Hardy, 52, 111, 155
Hart, 28
Hartbeest, 24, 104, 136, 137, 176
Hurricane, 24, 87, 101, 110, 119, 129
JU 86, 15, 102, 136
Lysander, 19, 119, 155
Mohawk, 175
Swordfish, 140
Vincent, 19, 48, 50, 52, 116
Wellesley, 19, 21, 25, 48, 52, 110, 111,
  116, 140, 155, 175
Italian,
  Caproni C111, 98
  Fiat CR 42, 53, 119, 175
  Savoia Marchetti *79*, 21, 29, 34, 87,
    134
  Savoia Marchetti *81*, 102
Alexandria, 1, 4, 42, 61, 107, 181
Ali Sabieh, 29
Amba, Mount (Keren), 81, 84, 109
Amba Alagi, 8, 9, 150, 152, 155–65, 171, 173,
  178, 179
Amba Aradem, 156
Amba Mariam, 145
Anderson, Lt.-Col. A., 78
Andrews, Maj. Æ. Chapman, 97fn
Anseba, River, 64
Anti-Slavery Society, 2
Antonelli, Count Pietro, 8

Aosta, Amadeo, Duke of, 15, 16, 22, 23, 41, 59, 63, 65, 95, 101, 128, 134, 137, 147, 150, 152, 154, 155, 157, 161, 165, 166, 167, 168, 169, 170, 177
Arabia, 3, 140, 141
Aressa, 71, 157
Army Council, 46
Artillery,
  British, 19, 38, 45, 79, 122, 173
    Units,
      1 Field Regt. R.A., 79fn
      4 Field Regt. R.A., 79fn
      25 Field Regt. R.A., 66fn, 86
      31 Field Regt. R.A., 69, 79
      68 Medium Regt. R.A., 79
      1 Jammu & Kashmir Mountain Bty., 31fn
      1 East Africa Light Bty., 30
      Gold Coast Light Bty., 173
      Nigerian Lt. Bty., 30, 130
      Sudan Horse, 23, 79
  South African, 24, 56, 102, 129, 130–1, 132, 160, 161, 164, 165
    Unit,
      5 Natal Bty., 130
  Italian, 21, 79, 83
Arussi, 10
Asbe Tafari (Asba Littorio), 12, 134
Asmara, 7, 25, 63, 68, 70, 73, 76, 83, 87, 110, 138, 139, 140, 141, 154, 155, 166, 169, 173, 178
Assa Hills, 31
Assab, 5, 25, 142fn, 176
Athens, 107, 152
Awash River, 133, 135, 136, 161, 172
Axum, 4
Ayulu Birru, Dejaz, 173

Babile, 131, 133
Baccari, Gen., 68
Badoglio, Marshal Pietro, 156, 170
Baghdad, 19
Bahrdar Giorgius, 94, 96, 97, 147, 169
Bald Hill (Amba Alagi), 158, 159, 160, 164, 166
Bande, 20, 25, 27, 32, 33, 50, 59, 63, 64, 85, 94, 97, 99, 100, 101, 103, 136, 147, 173, 178
Bangalore Torpedo, 102, 164
Baratieri, Gen. Oreste, 8, 9
Baraka River, 67, 74
Bardera, 74, 100, 101, 102

Bardia, 62
Barentu, 64, 65, 68, 69, 70, 76, 81, 87, 113fn, 178
Barkasan, 34
Baro, 172
Basra, 19, 39
Bath, 43
B.B.C., 132
Beda Fomm, 83
Beghember, 4, 5, 6, 7, 11, 25, 41, 62
Belai Zekkeka, 'Lij', 145, 147, 148–9
Belaya, Mount, 44, 90, 91, 93, 94, 96, 100
Beles Gugnari, 102
Belet Uen, 128, 129, 143
Belgian Congo, 49, 172
Belgium, 2, 25
Bengal Sappers and Miners, Royal, 70, 71
Berbera, 23, 30, 31, 32, 34, 35, 39, 127, 128, 129, 151, 152, 172
Beresford-Peirse, Maj.-Gen. N. M. de la P., 68, 69, 70, 76, 80, 81, 84, 112
Bertello, Gen., 32, 33, 128
Bhagat, 2nd Lieut. Preminda Singh, V.C., 71
Birmingham, 50
Biscia, 66, 67, 109, 110
Bisidmo River, 132
Blackshirts (Militzia Voluntaria di Securezza Nazionale), 14, 16, 20, 32, 52, 63, 68, 70, 94, 119, 128, 133, 134, 136, 137, 141, 144, 147, 156fn, 157, 161, 162, 168, 172
Blue Nile River, 4, 21, 94, 97, 145, 161
Bofors L.A.A. gun, 34, 68
Boma, 172
Bombay, 5, 140
Bonetti, Admiral, 140, 141, 142, 144
Borema, 10
Bosworth, Battle of (1485), 95
Boustead, Miralei Hugh, 92, 93, 94, 96, 99, 100, 144, 145, 146, 147, 148, 149, 170, 178
Boyes A/T rifle, 23, 33, 38, 51, 52, 68, 100, 114
Boyle, Maj., 99
Brava, 101, 102, 104
Breda A/T gun, 34, 128
Brevity, Operation, 165
Brigades,
  British etc.,
    1st (South African), 56, 59, 103, 126, 129, 134, 135, 137, 138, 152, 155, 160, 161, 162, 168, 169, 178

2nd (South African), 56fn, 72, 73, 126, 129, 152, 162, 172

5th (Indian), 64, 65, 69, 80, 81, 109, 112, 120, 132

5th (South African), 56fn, 72, 73, 109, 126, 134, 152

7th (Indian), 64, 65, 66, 84, 122, 140, 141

9th (Indian), 71, 109, 121, 139, 158fn

10th (Indian), 52, 64, 69, 109, 117, 120, 123, 141

11th (Indian), 64, 65, 66, 69, 77, 81, 84, 117

21st (East African), 172

22nd (East African), 102, 103, 104, 126, 135, 136

23rd (Nigerian), 102, 104, 128, 129, 130, 131, 143, 173, 179

24th (Gold Coast), 59, 103, 104, 126, 127, 143, 172, 173

25th (East African), 59, 72, 136, 175

26th (East African), 175

29th (Indian), 64, 66, 81, 109, 116, 117, 118, 120, 123, 139, 155, 157, 163, 164

French,
De L'Orient, 85

Italian,
15th (Amhara), 101
41st Colonial, 66, 67
43rd Colonial, 64, 157
61st Colonial, 119
70th Colonial, 128

Briggs, Brig. H. R., 84, 85, 86, 112, 122, 140, 141

Brig's Peak (Keren), 77, 79, 81, 107, 108, 109, 111, 112, 117, 155

Brink, Maj.-Gen., 72, 73

British Columbia, 106

Broken Hill, 57

Bulu Erillo, 101, 103

Bura, 102, 103

Burao, 31

Burgi River, 94

Burma, 102, 149, 175

Burye, 97, 98, 99, 143, 144, 145, 146

Butana Bridge, 50

Cairo, 5, 17, 20, 32, 35, 64, 91, 110, 151, 171

Cambolcia Gorge, 161–2, 163

Camels, 48, 91, 97, 98, 144, 150

Camel Saddle Hill (Marda), 129, 130, 131

Cameron Ridge (Pt. 1616), 77, 78, 79, 80, 81, 82, 107–8, 118, 120, 124

Cameroons, 49

Caporetto, Battle of (1917), 15, 83

Caproni Factory, 110

Carabinieri, 14, 20, 128, 136, 152

Carmineo, Gen. Nicolangelo, 83, 84, 85, 86, 118, 119, 121, 124, 138, 149, 178

Castle Ridge (Amba Alagi), 160

Celga, 176

Centre Bump (Keren), 78, 112, 119

Chad, 19, 87

Chaigul Pass, 169

Chamberlain, Neville, 24

Channel Islands, 35

Charterhouse, 45

Chater, Brig. Reginald, 30, 31, 32, 33

Chequers, 38

Chercher Mountains, 134

Chilga, 173

Chokey (Ciocche) Mountains, 94, 145, 169

Churchill, Winston S., 2, 18, 35, 37, 38, 39, 40, 42, 43, 48, 55, 61, 62, 63, 72, 106, 107, 133fn, 134, 141, 180

Ciano, Count Galeazzo, xxi, 16, 23

Cochen, Mount, 68–70

Cochrane, 2nd Lieut. Peter, 77fn, 78

Colonial Office, 30

Commando Hill (Amba Alagi), 159

Compass, Operation, 62

Congo River, 49

Coptic Church, 4

Corsica, 22

Corarsi, Mount. See Triangle (Amba Alagi)

Crete, xxi, 152, 165

Crispi, Francesco, 8, 9

Cub Cub, 85, 86

Cunningham, Admiral A. B., 58

Cunningham, Lt.-Gen. Alan, 47, 58, 61, 62, 72, 100, 101, 105, 107, 119, 126, 127, 128, 132, 134, 137, 138, 148, 149, 150, 151, 152, 154, 155, 169, 171, 177, 178, 179, 180

Dadatte, 29

Daghanur, 128

Danakil (Donakil), 5

Dangila, 91, 96

Dar-es-Salaam, 106

Darlan, Admiral L. X. F., 49, 176

De Bono, Marshal Emilio, 155

Debra Berhan, 161

Debra Libanos, 14

Debra Marcos, 4, 94, 95, 96, 97, 99, 100, 143, 144, 145, 146, 147, 148, 149, 150, 161, 169, 170

Debra Sin, 161

Debra Tabor, 173, 174, 175

Defence Rifle Associations (South Africa), 56

De Gaulle, Gen. Charles, 29, 49, 176

De Lesseps, Ferdinand, 5

Dembecho, 99, 143, 148

Dembidolla, 173

Deniken, Gen. Anton Ivanovich, 92

Derby, Thomas Stanley, 1st Earl of, 95

De Simone, Gen. Carlo, 32, 33, 60, 63, 100, 101, 126, 128, 129, 132, 177

Dessie, 12, 136, 147, 150, 160, 161, 162, 170, 173, 174

Deverell, Field-Marshal Sir Cyril, 47

Dickinson, Maj.-Gen. D. P., 55, 58

Dingaan's Day, 59

Dinsor, 101

Diredawa, 10, 25, 33, 95, 129, 132, 134, 135, 172

Divisions,
  British etc.,
    1st South African, 56, 76, 100, 126, 127fn, 133, 165, 169
    4th Indian, 32, 51fn, 62, 63, 64, 65, 66, 68, 79, 82, 83, 89, 100, 107, 109, 110, 117, 120, 122, 133, 140, 152, 180
    '4th Australian', 100, 178
    5th Indian, 39, 40, 41, 50, 51, 52, 64, 66, 67, 70, 79, 81, 82, 107, 109, 110, 111, 119, 120, 152, 155, 163, 165, 169, 177, 178, 180
    7th Armoured, 62
    11th African, 58, 101, 102, 103, 126, 127, 129, 135, 137, 171, 172, 173
    12th African, 58, 101, 102, 126, 172, 173, 175
  Italian,
    Savoia, 21, 63, 136, 157, 159, 177
    Africa, 20, 21, 63, 119, 133
    1st Colonial, 63
    2nd Colonial, 64
    4th Colonial, 63, 64, 68
    101st Colonial, 101, 126
    102nd Colonial, 101, 126, 127

Dolo, 100, 101, 127, 143, 172

Dologorodoc, Mount and Fort, 76, 77, 78–9, 82, 107, 109, 112–16, 118, 119, 120, 123, 178, 179

Dongali, 7

Dongolaas Gorge, 74, 76, 77, 80, 111, 119, 158, 178

Douglas, Maj., 174, 175

Driver, Capt. K., 87

Dubats, 20, 101

Dukana, 72

Duncan, Maj. Colin, 70

Dunkirk, 18

Dupont, Gen., 176

Durban, 24

East Gate Spur, 120, 121

East India Company, Honourable, 5

Edelston, Capt. John, R.N., 102fn

Eden, Anthony, 47, 61

Egypt, 1, 4, 19, 22, 23, 24, 28, 38, 39, 40, 41, 61, 62, 63, 81, 86, 92, 107, 111, 127, 133, 134, 140, 165, 169, 177, 180

Eighth Army, 179

Elephant Hill (Amba Alagi), 158, 159

El Gogni, 66

El Gumu, 72

El Sod, 73

El Wak (El Uach), 28, 58, 59, 177

Emanuel, Fort, 143, 145, 146, 147

Enda Medani Alen, 159, 168

Engiahat, Mount, 86, 112, 122

Engineer Corps, South African, 57–8, 136, 161, 162

Enjibara, 94, 96, 97

Eritrea, xxi, 3, 4, 7, 8, 9, 11, 20, 38, 40, 41, 62, 63, 67, 68, 73, 76, 77, 83, 84, 85, 86, 87, 89, 106, 141, 150, 151, 155, 178, 180

Everest, Mount, 92

Eyadera, 103

Faguta, 48, 79

Falaga Pass, 156, 157, 158, 159, 163

Falestoh, Mount (Keren), 76, 80, 107, 109, 115, 116, 117, 118, 119, 121, 123, 124, 138

Falvy, Gen., 49

Flat Top (Keren), 108, 112

Fletcher, Brig. B. C., 67, 154, 158fn, 159, 163

Fletcher Force, 121–2, 132, 138, 158, 160, 164

Flitforce, 154, 155, 158

Fongoli, Gen., 66, 67

Force T, 102fn

Forcuta Peak (Keren), 78, 79, 81, 122

Foreign Office, 3, 8, 30, 42, 43, 47

Fowkes, Maj.-Gen. C. C., 28, 102, 103, 135, 136, 137, 173, 175, 176

France, 1, 8, 9, 10, 13, 15, 16, 18, 22, 24, 28, 38, 43, 46, 49, 87, 95, 101

Freetown, 107

French Equatorial Africa, 48, 49, 87, 176

French North Africa, 176

Frusci, Gen. Luigi, 63, 64, 65, 68, 76, 78, 83, 84, 86, 118, 138, 139, 161, 162, 168, 178

Galla, 4, 6, 20, 89fn

Galla Sidamo, 16, 58, 62

Gallabat, 23, 27, 41, 43, 51, 52-4, 62, 63, 64, 71, 173

Galmagalla, 72

Guarda Finanza (armed customs officers), 20, 128, 136, 141

Garby, Col., 85, 142

Garissa, 72, 101, 104

Gazelle Force, 51, 64, 65, 66, 67, 68, 70, 74, 76, 77, 80fn, 84, 124

Gazzera, Gen. Pietro, 150, 173

Gedaref, 25, 44, 48, 50

Geneina, 86

Gentilhomme, Gen. Paul le, 28-9, 30

Germany, 1, 2, 16, 45, 56

Gibraltar Spur (Agordat), 68-70

Gideon Force, 97, 98, 99, 143, 144, 147, 148, 149, 180

Gobwen, 101, 103, 104

Godwin-Austen, Maj.-Gen. A. R., 31, 33, 34, 35, 59, 101

Gojjam, 4, 10, 20, 25, 41, 43, 62, 90, 91, 93, 94, 95, 97, 106, 143, 144, 145, 146, 147, 148, 149, 150, 169, 170, 178, 179

Gold Coast, 19fn, 59, 86, 87, 127

Gondar, 4, 6, 7, 10, 31fn, 71, 94, 113fn, 144, 150, 152, 154, 161, 162, 170, 171, 173, 179

Good Hope, Cape of, 19

Gorai, 72

Gorgora, 176

Graziani, Marshal Rodolfo, 14, 15, 20, 95, 133, 151, 154

Great Rift Valley, 136

Greece, xxi, 61, 107, 133, 152

Grenades, 82

Gubba, 41, 94

Gugsa Wule, Ras, 11

Gulit River, 143, 145, 146, 147

Gumuz, 90

Gumsa, Mount (Amba Alagi), 163, 164

Guru, 25, 87, 110

Habbaniya, 165

Habta Georgius, 11

Hagadera, 71, 72, 100

Haifa, 19fn, 46

Haile Selassie, Emperor, 2, 6, 11, 12, 13, 14, 41, 42-4, 47, 48, 54, 61, 89-90, 91, 93, 94, 95, 96, 97, 143, 144, 145, 147, 148, 149, 151, 154, 156, 167, 169, 170, 178, 180

Haile Selassie Gugsa, Ras, 95

Hailu, Ras of Gojjam, 12, 94-6, 97, 143, 145, 147-8, 154, 164, 179

Halifax, Edward Wood, 3rd Viscount, 43

Happy Valley (Keren), 80, 81, 82, 120

Harar and the Hararje, 5, 6, 10, 11, 16, 24, 31, 105, 126, 127, 128, 129, 131, 132, 133, 134, 136, 138, 147, 178, 179

Hargeisha, 31, 32, 33, 128, 129

Heath, Maj.-Gen. L. M., 52, 67, 70, 71, 112, 119, 120, 139, 140, 141, 142, 167, 179

Hitler, Adolf, 20, 22, 28, 45

Hobok, 72

Hogarth, William, 95

Hog's Back (Keren), 108, 112

Home Guard, 89

Hotchkiss light machine gun, 43

Howitzers, 19, 21, 23, 24, 27, 30, 31, 33, 35, 79, 102, 130, 160fn, 161, 165

Huberta Pass, 134

Hunzinger, Gen. Charles Leon, 49

India, xxii, 5, 6, 19, 24, 32, 39

Iraq, xxi, 19, 151, 152, 165

Ironside, Field-Marshal Sir Edmund, 47

Isayu, Lij, 10, 11, 12, 95

Ismay, Maj-Gen. Hastings, 38

Italy, 1, 2, 5, 7, 8, 9, 10, 13, 15, 18, 19, 21, 22, 23, 24, 43, 89

Italy, Bank of, 8

Japan, 1, 2, 106, 140, 176

Jelib, 101, 103, 104

Jerato Pass, 31, 33

Jibuti, 3, 5, 8, 10, 12, 14, 22, 23, 24, 28, 29, 30, 135fn, 176

Jijiga, 24, 126,' 127, 128, 129

Jimma, 10, 150, 152, 171, 173

Jirreh, 29

John IV, Emperor, 6, 7, 154

Juba (Sudan), 20
Juba River (Somaliland), 58, 59, 63, 73, 100, 101, 103, 104, 126, 169
Jubaland, 151
Jumbo, 101, 104

Kafa, 10
Kano, 86
Karora, 27, 85
Kassa Hailu, Ras, 170, 171
Kassa Sabarges. See John IV
Kassala, 8, 9, 23, 25, 26, 27, 39, 43, 50, 51, 62, 63, 64, 65, 66, 68, 69, 71, 83, 84, 86, 109, 110, 111, 122, 177, 179
Kenya, 16, 21, 24, 25, 27, 28, 31, 35, 39, 40, 41, 42, 43, 44, 54, 55, 56, 57, 58, 59, 61, 62, 71, 72, 99, 100, 107, 116, 129, 169, 177, 179
Keren, xxi, 17, 31fn, 68, 73, 74–84, 85, 86, 88, 107–25, 130, 132, 138, 140, 147, 149, 155, 158, 165, 173, 178, 179, 180, 181
Keru, 64, 65, 66, 67, 69, 84
Khaki Hill (Amba Alagi), 163, 164
Khartoum, 7, 17, 23, 25, 27, 39, 41, 42, 43, 44, 47, 48, 49, 61, 64, 65, 86, 87, 89, 93, 96, 97, 146, 177
Khalifa, The, 7
Khan, Capt. Shaukat Hyat, 166
Khedive of Egypt, 5, 7
King's African Rifles (see also under Regiments), 24, 34, 170, 173, 175, 176, 179
Kirkham, John, 6
Kismayu, 22, 58, 62, 63, 72, 101, 103, 106, 107, 135, 138
Kufra, 118, 175
Kulkaber, 173, 174, 176
Kurmuk, 25, 27

Lacquetat, Mount (Agordat), 68–70
Lagos, 86
Lampson, Sir Miles Locker, 42
Laval, Pierre, 1, 49
League of Nations, 2, 11
Lease Lend Act, 142fn
Lebanon, The, 45
Lewis guns, 24, 56, 128
Liberia, 3
Liboi, 72
Libya, 1, 13, 15, 17, 19, 21, 48, 63
Little Alagi, 158, 160, 163, 164
Lloyd, Brig. W. L., 70, 80, 81
London, 5, 22, 32, 50, 87, 106, 169

Longmore, Air Chief Marshal Sir Arthur, 19
Lovat, Simon Fraser, 12th Baron, 95
Luftwaffe, 106, 175
Lugh Ferrandi, 100, 101, 143

Mabungo, 104, 126
Mackenzie, Compton, 124
Madagascar, 176
Mafeking, Relief of, 103
Mai Ceu, 163
Maiduguri, 86
Mai Edega, 110
Mai Mescic, 154, 157
Maji, 172
Makalle, 9, 110
Makatal Pass, 96, 97, 144
Makonnen Haile, Ras, 6, 11
Malta, 1
Mandel, Georges, 25
Mandera, 100
Mankusa, 97, 99
Maraventano, Col. Severio, 144, 145, 146, 147, 148, 149, 161, 169, 170, 171
Marda, 129–31, 133, 177
Mareb River, 7, 9
Margherita, 103
Maria Theresa thalers, 90, 152, 175
Marriott, Brig. J. C. O., 66, 116, 118, 138, 139, 168
Marsabit, 54, 55, 57, 72
Marshall-Cornwall, Lt.-Gen. Sir James, 38
Martinique, 49
Massawa, 5, 7, 21, 25, 26, 38, 40, 63, 67, 68, 76, 83, 84, 88, 106, 110, 111, 134, 140–2, 144, 150, 152, 154, 169, 177, 178, 181
Matteos, Abuna, 11
Mayne, Maj.-Gen. A. G. O., 71, 109fn, 155, 156, 157, 160, 163, 166, 167, 168, 169
Meadowforce, 85
Mediterranean Sea, 5, 18, 110
Mediterranean Fleet, 1, 21
Mega, 72, 73, 100, 126
Menelik I, 3
Menelik II, Emperor, 6, 7, 8, 9, 10, 11, 90
Merca, 126
Mersa Matruh, 61
Mersa Taklai, 85–6
Mers-el-Kebir, 49
Mescelit Pass, 86
Messervy, Brig. Frank, 51, 52, 66, 67, 70, 74, 77, 109, 113, 115, 116, 123, 124, 139, 179

Metemma, 7, 41, 52, 53, 54, 62
Meuse River, 22
Meyda Merra Gorge, 159
Middle Hill (Amba Alagi), 158, 159, 160
Mieso, 134, 135
Mission 101, 44, 47, 93, 96, 97
Mogadishu, 101, 102, 104, 106, 107, 126, 127, 128, 129, 135, 138, 179
Mohammed Ahmed, the Mahdi, 7
Mole Hill (Keren), 112
Mombasa, 20, 24, 43, 55, 56, 100, 129, 134, 172
Monclar, Col., 85, 142
Monnier, Col. Paul, 25
Mortars, 37, 43, 51, 79, 98, 146, 174
Mota, 169–70
Moyale (Moiale), 25, 27–8, 54, 72, 73
Mussolini, Benito, 1, 13, 14, 15, 16, 17, 20, 21, 22, 23, 24, 29, 42fn, 65, 141, 150, 155, 176, 177
Mussolini Tunnels, 161

Nairobi, 25, 55, 57, 72, 169fn, 172, 179
Napier, Lt.-Gen. Sir Robert, 3, 5, 6
Napoleon Bonaparte, 83
Nasi, Gen. Gugliemo, 144, 145, 146, 159, 171, 173, 175, 176
Natale, Col., 97, 98, 99, 100, 143, 144, 149
Nazaret, 136
Neghelli, 126, 127, 172
Nigeria, 86
Nile, River (see also Blue Nile), 49
Normandy, 123
Northern Frontier District, Kenya, 24, 57
Northern Rhodesia, 57
North-West Frontier of India, 123, 179
Norway, 85
Nott, Col. Donald, 149
Nyasa, Lake, 4

Obok, 5
Observation Hill (Marda), 130
Observation Hill (Tug Argan), 34
O'Connor, Lt.-Gen. Richard, 62
Odweina, 31, 32, 33
Ogaden, 13
Olympic Games, 92
Omdurman, 4
Omo River, 160
Operational Centres, 44, 48, 89fn, 97, 146, 174

Osborn, Capt. Michael, 114–15
Oxford University, 92

Palestine, 19, 20, 31, 43, 44, 45–6, 109
Pearl Harbor, 106
Persian (Arabian) Gulf, 26
Pesenti, Gen. Gustavo, 59, 60, 177
Pétain, Marshal Henri Philippe, 29
Pienaar, Brig. D. H., 103, 104, 134, 135, 137, 160, 161, 162, 163, 164
Pimple (Keren), 113
Pinna, Gen. Pietro, 168
Pinnacle (Keren), 113, 114
Platt, Lt.-Gen. Sir William, 39, 41, 43, 47, 48, 49, 50, 51, 52, 61, 62, 63, 64, 65, 73, 81, 82, 87, 88, 89, 96, 111, 112, 116, 117, 118, 120, 121, 140, 142, 146, 149, 150, 152, 154, 156, 158, 173, 177, 178, 179, 180
Plevna, 167
Ponte Mussolini, 74, 124
Port Sudan, 23, 25, 26, 39, 49, 64, 65, 76, 84, 85, 86, 140, 177
Portugal, 15
Postiglione, Col., 157
Pyramid (Amba Alagi), 157, 159, 164

Quiha, 154, 168
Q Services Corps, South African, 154, 168

Railway Bumps and Ridge (Keren), 120–1
Ram, Subedar Richpal, V.C., 80, 82
Rankin, Maj., 155, 158
Raynal, Col., 176
Red Sea, 3, 4, 7, 19, 22, 23, 26, 30, 38, 40, 62, 67, 106, 110, 142, 176, 180
Regia Aeronautica, 21, 25, 34, 50, 52, 67, 97, 101, 109, 110, 136, 162, 168
Rees, Brig. T. W., 141
Regiments,
    United Kingdom,
        Royal Tank Regiment, 52, 65, 122
        Nottinghamshire Yeomanry, 173
        Royal Fusiliers, 70, 81, 108, 112, 117
        West Yorkshires, 50, 113, 114, 115, 116, 121, 139, 179
        Worcestershires, 50, 67, 116, 117, 118, 124, 158, 160, 169
        East Surreys, 34
        Royal Sussex, 85, 86
        Black Watch, 30, 31, 32, 33, 34, 162
        Essex, 50, 52–4

Regiments, United Kingdom—*contd*
   Royal Marines, 30
   Yorkshire and Lancashire, 50
   Durham Light Infantry, 50
   Highland Light Infantry, 65, 67, 109, 113, 117, 121, 176
   Gordon Highlanders, 92
   Cameron Highlanders, 69, 70, 77, 78, 108, 111, 112, 117, 124, 174, 175, 179
   51 (Middle East) Commando, 109, 155, 158, 159
Indian,
   Skinner's Horse, 51, 66, 67, 69, 74, 77, 154, 159, 163, 166, 174
   Central India Horse, 51fn, 80, 82, 120, 122, 138, 139, 140, 154
   1st Punjab Regiment,
      3rd bn., 70, 80fn, 81, 82, 108
   2nd Punjab Regiment,
      1st bn., 30, 32
      3rd bn., 66, 67, 116, 117, 118, 120, 121, 158, 159, 174
   5th Mahratta Light Infantry,
      2nd bn., 39, 108, 112, 117
      3rd bn., 113, 114, 116, 121
   6th Rajputana Rifles,
      1st bn. (Wellesley's), 67, 69, 70, 77, 78, 80, 81, 108, 112, 117
      4th bn. (Outram's), 80, 81, 108, 112, 117
   10th Baluch Regiment,
      4th bn., 52, 117, 121, 139
   11th Sikh Regiment,
      4th bn., xxii, 66, 67, 68, 69, 80fn, 81
   12th Royal Frontier Force Regiment,
      3rd bn., 113, 114, 117, 119, 158, 159
   13th Royal Frontier Force Rifles,
      3rd bn., 117, 119, 157, 159, 160
   14th Punjab Regiment,
      3rd bn., 69, 70, 80, 108
   15th Punjab Regiment,
      3rd bn., 30, 32, 33
   16th Punjab Regiment,
      4th bn., 85, 86, 122
   18th Royal Garhwal Rifles,
      3rd bn., 52–3, 117, 158, 159, 163, 164
Central African,
   Gold Coast Regiment,
      2nd bn., 59
   King's African Rifles,
      1/1st bn., 17, 28, 32
      1/2nd bn., 30, 35, 100

      3/2nd bn., 27
      1/3rd bn., 27, 127
      1/4th bn., 100
      1/5th bn., 28
      1/6th bn., 59
   Nigeria Regiment,
      1st bn., 131
      2nd bn., 127, 130
      3rd bn., 128, 129, 131
   Northern Rhodesia Regiment, 23, 30, 32, 102
   Somali Camel Corps., 23, 29, 30, 32, 33, 34, 35
   Sudan Camel Corps, 92
   Sudan Defence Force,
      Frontier bn., 42, 90, 92, 93, 96, 97, 99, 144, 145, 146, 169, 170
South African,
   S.A. Tank Corps, 24, 56
   Royal Natal Carbineers, 104, 131, 137, 162
   Duke of Edinburgh's Own Rifles, 161, 164
   Transvaal Scottish, 92, 104, 135, 160, 161, 164, 168
French,
   Foreign Legion,
      14me bn., 85, 122
   Bataillon de Marche,
      3me (*Tchad*), (*Bataillon Garby*), 85, 86, 141, 142
   Senegalese, 1er bn., 176
Italian,
   Alpini, 21, 77, 81, 83, 84, 110
   Bersaglieri, 19, 21, 81, 83, 119, 121, 128
   Grenadiers of Savoy, 21, 76, 77, 78, 79, 83, 114, 119, 138, 139, 141
   Colonial Infantry,
      79th bn., 174
      94th bn., 102
      97th bn., 81
      112th bn., 85
Ethiopian,
   1st Ethiopian bn., 48, 89fn
   2nd Ethiopian bn., 48, 89, 92, 93, 97, 99, 100, 143, 145, 147, 169, 170
   3rd Ethiopian bn., 89fn, 173
   4th Ethiopian bn., 98fn
Rhodes, 106
Rhodesian Air Force, 28, 52
Richards, Brig. C. E. M., 103
Richardson, Lt. A. G., 72
Robertson, Col. Sir Brian, Bt., 138

Rolle, Col., 50, 136
Rome, 4, 15, 16, 33, 59, 101, 141, 150
Rommel, Gen. Erwin, xxi, 88, 152, 165
Roosevelt, President F. D., 133fn
Rosieres, 50, 90, 91, 93
Royal Air Force, 18, 19, 25, 42, 52, 53, 54, 85, 87, 93, 99, 107, 116, 141, 165, 174
Royal Navy, 18, 19, 34, 102, 137
Rudolf, Lake, 9, 55, 172
Russell, Col. Dudley, 166, 167

Sabderat, 64, 82
Saddle Hill (Marda), 130
Safartak, 94, 97, 145, 148
Sagalle, 6
Sahle Maryam. See Menelek II
Sakkala, 93, 94, 96
Samana, Mount (Keren), 108, 109
Sanchil, Mount (Keren), 76, 77, 78, 79, 81, 82, 107, 108, 109, 111, 112, 113, 114, 115, 117, 118, 119, 120, 121, 122, 123, 124
Sandford, Brig. D. A., 41, 43, 44, 47, 48, 62, 63, 90, 94, 96, 97, 146, 147, 148, 149, 178
Sandy Ridge and Plateau (Amba Alagi), 157, 158
Sappers and Miners, 121, 128
Savory, Brig. Reginald, 66, 69, 70, 77, 79, 86, 108, 112, 123, 124
Senegal, 16
Setit (Takkase) River, 63, 64
Seyum Mangasha, Ras, 154, 155, 158, 163, 166, 167, 179
Sheba, Queen of, 3
Sheikh Pass, 31, 32, 33
Shepheard, Thomas, 5
Ships,
    Royal Navy,
        Caledon, 128; Capetown, 102fn, 140; Carlisle, 26; Ceres, 102fn; Formidable, 110; Glasgow, 128; Hawkins, 102fn; Hermes, 102fn; Kandahar, 102fn, 128; Kimberley, 26; Kingston, 128, 140; Moonstone, 26; Shropshire, 102fn.
    Royal Australian Navy,
        Hobart, 33, 35
    Royal Italian Navy,
        Battisti, 140; Francesco Nulli, 26; Galileo Galilei, 26; Leone, 140; Manin, Pantere, Sauro, Tigre, all on 140
    Imperial German Navy,
        Königsberg, 92

Shoa, 4, 5, 6, 10, 20
Sidamo, 6, 10
Sidi Barrani, 39, 61, 62, 64
Singapore, 180
Slatter, Air Commodore Leonard H., 87, 119
Slim, Brig. William J., xxii, 52, 53, 54, 65, 67
Smallwood, Brig. G. R., 104, 132, 137
Smuts, Gen. Jan Christian, 47, 55, 56, 58, 61, 62, 127fn, 137
Socota, 155, 158, 163
Solomon, King of Israel, 3
Somaliland, British, 5, 10, 21, 23, 28, 29, 30–6, 43, 52, 60, 128, 177
Somaliland, French, 5, 10, 21, 23, 28, 29, 30, 31, 151, 176
Somaliland, Italian, 6, 11, 13, 20, 21, 28, 40, 58, 59, 72, 73, 100–5, 106, 119, 126, 137, 143, 151, 161, 177
South Africa, Union of, xxii, 24, 55–8, 62, 137
South African Air Force, 24, 25, 52, 87, 101, 102, 116, 128, 136, 137, 175
South African Indian and Malay Corps, 132
Spahis, 71
Spanish Civil War, 25, 84
Spartivento, Cape, 19
Special Night Squads, 46
Sphinx (Mount Zelale) (Keren), 80, 81, 84
Springfield rifles, 89
Staff College, Camberley, 45, 82, 151
Strada Imperiale, 128
Strada Vittoria, 155, 156, 157, 166, 167
Stretta di Meyda Merra, 156, 158
Suakin, 84, 85
Sudan, xxii, 4, 10fn, 20, 21, 23, 15, 26, 27, 38, 39, 40, 41, 42, 43, 44, 47, 48, 49, 50, 51fn, 61, 62, 63, 64, 65, 71, 82, 86, 87, 89, 90, 92, 108, 110, 173, 177, 179, 180
Sudan Defence Corps (see also under Regiments), 23, 27, 39, 42, 45, 49, 51, 65, 66, 69, 71, 89, 90, 92, 93, 96, 140, 145, 154, 155, 157, 172, 173, 177
Sudan Civil Service, 92
Sudan Cotton Syndicate, 92
Sudan Labour Corps, 86
Sudan Veterinary Service, 91
Suez Canal, 5, 18, 61, 65, 106, 181
Suez, Gulf of, 5
Sugarloaf (Keren), 78, 108
Syria, 45, 46, 71

Tadjoura, Gulf of, 5
Taffare Zellenke, Fitauri, 90, 91

INDEX

Tafari, Makkonen. See Haile Selassie
Taitu, Empress, 10
Takkasi River. See Setit
Takoradi, 19fn, 86, 87
Tamcha River, 143
Tana, Lake, 4, 48, 94, 97fn, 144, 149, 173
Tana River, 40, 55, 58, 72, 101
Tanga, 106
Tanganyika Police, 151
Tanks,
  Cruiser (A13). 52, 53
  Light Mk V, 24
  Light Mk IV, 52, 53
  Matilda (Infantry Mk II), 62, 64, 65, 69, 70, 77, 84, 122, 138, 141, 180
Tekla Georgius, 'Emperor', 6
Tessenei, 64, 65
Theodore II, Emperor, 3, 5, 6
Thesiger, Bimbashi Wilfred, 145, 147
Tigre, 4, 5, 6, 7, 8, 9, 10, 16, 20, 95, 154, 155, 167
Tobruk, xxi, 152, 165
Tongue Spur (Amba Alagi), 159, 160
Torelli, Col., 94, 96, 144, 145, 146, 147
Toselli, Maj. Pietro, 9, 155
Toselli Pass and Fort, 155, 156, 157, 158, 163, 164, 166, 168
Transjordan, 45, 151
Trezzani, Gen. Claudio, 166, 167
Triangle (Mount Corarsi) (Amba Alagi), 157, 163, 164
Tripoli, 88
Tripolitania, 106
Tug Argan, 31, 32–3, 36
Tuma, 96
Tunisia, 22
Turkey, 3, 5, 11, 107
Twin Pyramids (Amba Alagi), 163, 164

Uahni, 71
Uganda, 55
Um Hagar, 71, 157, 173
Um Iddla, 89
United States of America, 2, 25, 26, 47, 89, 106, 133, 142

Valetti-Borgnini, Gen., 157, 159, 168
Vickers medium machine gun, 23, 37

Vichy, 30, 49, 71, 87, 151
Victoria, Queen, 3
Village Hill (Amba Alagi), 158

Wadera, 172
Wadi Halfa, 42, 43
Wagsum Gobaze of Beghember. See Tekla Georgius
Wajir, 55, 59, 100, 101, 103
Wal Wal, 13
War Office, 30, 37, 46
Washington D.C., 142fn
Wavell, Gen. Sir Archibald, 19, 23, 24, 25, 26, 30, 31, 32, 33, 34, 35, 38, 39, 40, 41, 44, 46, 47, 52, 58, 61, 62, 63, 72, 73, 74, 88, 90, 91, 105, 106, 107, 111, 120, 123, 127, 133, 134, 140, 152, 154, 160, 165, 177, 180, 181
'Water Diviners' (42nd Geological Section, S.A.E.C.), 57–8, 71
Western Desert, 18, 40, 58, 62, 65, 83, 133, 152, 175, 180
Western Desert Force, 106
Wetherall, Maj.-Gen. H. E. de R., 101, 129, 132, 137, 138
Whaleback (Amba Alagi), 158, 159
Wilson, Capt. E. C. T., V.C., 34
Wilson, Lt.-Gen. Sir H. Maitland, 34, 62
Wingate, Lt.-Col. Orde, 44–8, 89, 90, 91, 92, 93, 96, 97, 98, 99, 144, 145, 146, 147, 148, 149, 150, 169, 170, 171, 178, 180
Wireless Hill (Amba Alagi), 159
Wolchefit Pass, 150, 154, 173, 174, 175
Wollo, 6, 10
Wonka, Fort, 146

Yavallo, 172
Yonte, 104
Yei, 49

Zanzibar, 6, 106
Zaudita, Empress, 10, 11
Zeban, Mount (Keren), 76, 80, 107, 109, 114, 115, 116, 117, 118, 120, 121, 123, 124, 138
Zeila, 31, 32
Zelale, Mount. See Sphinx
Zionism, 45, 46, 97